Advances in Aromatization/Aromachology in Different Environments

Advances in Aromatization/Aromachology in Different Environments

Editors

Jakub Bercik
Davide Giacalone
Marek Dolezal

MDPI • Basel • Beijing • Wuhan • Barcelona • Belgrade • Manchester • Tokyo • Cluj • Tianjin

Editors
Jakub Bercik
Slovak University of Agriculture in Nitra
Slovak Republic

Davide Giacalone
University of Southern Denmark
Denmark

Marek Dolezal
University of Chemistry and Technology
Czech Republic

Editorial Office
MDPI
St. Alban-Anlage 66
4052 Basel, Switzerland

This is a reprint of articles from the Special Issue published online in the open access journal *Applied Sciences* (ISSN 2076-3417) (available at: https://www.mdpi.com/journal/applsci/special_issues/aromatization_aromachology_food).

For citation purposes, cite each article independently as indicated on the article page online and as indicated below:

LastName, A.A.; LastName, B.B.; LastName, C.C. Article Title. *Journal Name* **Year**, *Volume Number*, Page Range.

ISBN 978-3-0365-2297-5 (Hbk)
ISBN 978-3-0365-2298-2 (PDF)

© 2021 by the authors. Articles in this book are Open Access and distributed under the Creative Commons Attribution (CC BY) license, which allows users to download, copy and build upon published articles, as long as the author and publisher are properly credited, which ensures maximum dissemination and a wider impact of our publications.

The book as a whole is distributed by MDPI under the terms and conditions of the Creative Commons license CC BY-NC-ND.

Contents

About the Editors vii

Preface to "Advances in Aromatization/Aromachology in Different Environments" ix

Jakub Berčík, Katarína Neomániová, Jana Gálová and Anna Mravcová
Consumer Neuroscience as a Tool to Monitor the Impact of Aromas on Consumer Emotions When Buying Food
Reprinted from: *Appl. Sci.* **2021**, *11*, 6692, doi:10.3390/app11156692 1

Dámaris Girona-Ruíz, Marina Cano-Lamadrid, Ángel Antonio Carbonell-Barrachina, David López-Lluch and Sendra Esther
Aromachology Related to Foods, Scientific Lines of Evidence: A Review
Reprinted from: *Appl. Sci.* **2021**, *11*, 6095, doi:10.3390/app11136095 19

Davide Giacalone, Bartłomiej Pierański and Barbara Borusiak
Aromachology and Customer Behavior in Retail Stores: A Systematic Review
Reprinted from: *Appl. Sci.* **2021**, *11*, 6195, doi:10.3390/app11136195 39

Jakub Berčík, Katarína Neomániová, Anna Mravcová and Jana Gálová
Review of the Potential of Consumer Neuroscience for Aroma Marketing and Its Importance in Various Segments of Services
Reprinted from: *Appl. Sci.* **2021**, *11*, 7636, doi:10.3390/app11167636 55

Karol Čarnogurský, Anna Diačiková and Peter Madzík
The Impact of the Aromatization of Production Environment on Workers: A Systematic Literature Review
Reprinted from: *Appl. Sci.* **2021**, *11*, 5600, doi:10.3390/app11125600 75

Zdeňka Panovská, Vojtech Ilko and Marek Doležal
Air Quality as a Key Factor in the Aromatisation of Stores: A Systematic Literature Review
Reprinted from: *Appl. Sci.* **2021**, *11*, 7697, doi:10.3390/app11167697 89

Jana Štefániková, Patrícia Martišová, Marek Šnirc, Peter Šedík and Vladimír Vietoris
Screening of the Honey Aroma as a Potential Essence for the Aromachology
Reprinted from: *Appl. Sci.* **2021**, *11*, 8177, doi:10.3390/app11178177 101

Melina Korčok, Nikola Vietorisová, Patrícia Martišová, Jana Štefániková, Anna Mravcová and Vladimír Vietoris
Aromatic Profile of Hydroponically and Conventionally Grown Tomatoes
Reprinted from: *Appl. Sci.* **2021**, *11*, 8012, doi:10.3390/app11178012 111

About the Editors

Jakub Bercik is Assistant Professor at the Department of Marketing and Trade and the Director of the Laboratory of Consumer Studies at the Faculty of Economics and Management of the Slovak University of Agriculture in Nitra, Slovak Republic. His scientific research activity is mainly focused on neuroscience, represented by neuromarketing and neuroeconomics and their application in the sphere of marketing and business. He is also the CEO of an innovative startup, SAMO Europe, which develops own technologies and devices for examining comprehensive consumer behavior.

Davide Giacalone is Associate Professor in Consumer Product Testing and Optimization at the Faculty of Engineering, University of Southern Denmark. He holds a PhD in sensory science from the University of Copenhagen; his research centers on consumers' perceptions and behavior towards everyday products, primarily within fast-moving consumer goods. His special areas of proficiency include methodological research on perceptual product tests with consumers, and the application of sensory methods to product development in research and industry. He is also very interested in sensometrics (i.e., statistical modeling of sensory and consumer data), particularly multivariate methods to relate instrumental, perceptual and affective product evaluations.

Marek Dolezal is Associate Professor of Food Chemistry and Analysis and Science Leader of the Sensory Analysis Team at the Department of Food Analysis and Nutrition, University of Chemistry and Technology, Prague in Czech Republic. He has a Ph.D. in Food Chemistry and Analysis from the University of Chemistry and Technology, Prague. He has 30 years' experience in the chemical analysis of food and feed, analysis of biological materials and environmental samples, development and validation of analytical methods, control of food contaminants and nutritional and sensory evaluation of food. He and his team are also actively involved in the transfer of scientific knowledge to the technological practice of the food industry, from global to small producers.

Preface to "Advances in Aromatization/Aromachology in Different Environments"

The scientific monograph *Advanced Tools of Collecting Feedback in Aromachology* provides insight into innovative practices and implementations of consumer neuroscience and smart research solutions in aromachology, which form the basis for a systematic review of the synergistic linking of brain, physiological and psychological processes with aromachology, as well as an assessment of their economic efficiency and effectiveness in selected sectors of the national economy, namely manufacturing, commerce and services. Innovative research solutions and consumer neuroscience, represented by biometric, neurobiological and behavioral studies in both real-world and laboratory conditions, enable businesses to make more effective strategic decisions. We are interested in examining the targeted impact of aroma deployment in spaces on the behavior of visitors, customers, and employees, as a growing number of companies are implementing aroma technologies (i.e., aromatizing their spaces or creating branded olfactory footprints) in various fields.

The publication is important for future studies and research, and in the development of scientific and theoretical skills and key competencies by using all available opportunities for consumer neuroscience research and engaging in intensive activities using smart research solutions to develop a reference database of aroma preferences for business in the field of production, trade and services, as well as the dissemination of existing and newly acquired knowledge in aroma science and aroma marketing. Last but not least, it also provides scope for the effective use of digital smart technologies, services, and knowledge transfer with a high degree of potential economic benefit in the field of education and training.

This scientific monograph was supported by the Erasmus+ KA2 Strategic Partnerships Project *"Implementation of Consumer Neuroscience and Smart Research Solutions in Aromachology"* (NEUROSMARTOLOGY), no. 2018-1-SK01-KA203-046324.

The publication is designed for researchers, professionals in the field and commercial practice, as well as for the general public interested in the research topic.

Jakub Bercik, Davide Giacalone, Marek Dolezal
Editors

Article

Consumer Neuroscience as a Tool to Monitor the Impact of Aromas on Consumer Emotions When Buying Food

Jakub Berčík [1], Katarína Neomániová [1,*], Jana Gálová [2] and Anna Mravcová [3]

[1] Department of Marketing and Trade, Faculty of Economics and Management, Slovak University of Agriculture, 949 76 Nitra, Slovakia; jakub.bercik@uniag.sk

[2] Center for Research and Educational Projects, Faculty of Economics and Management, Slovak University of Agriculture, 949 76 Nitra, Slovakia; jana.galova@uniag.sk

[3] Department of Social Science, Faculty of Economics and Management, Slovak University of Agriculture, 949 76 Nitra, Slovakia; anna.mravcova@uniag.sk

* Correspondence: katarina.neomaniova@uniag.sk

Abstract: Building a unique USP sales argument (unique selling proposition) through various forms of in-store communication comes to the fore in a challenging competitive environment. Scent as a means to influence the purchase of goods or services has a long history, however, aromachology as field of in-store communication is a matter of the present. This new trend, the importance and use of which has grown in recent years, is the subject of a wide range of research. In order to increase the efficiency of these elements, it is necessary to familiarise ourselves with the factors that affect the customer, whether that be consciously or unconsciously. Consumer neuroscience is addressed in this area. This paper deals with the comprehensive interdisciplinary investigation of the impact of selected aromatic compounds on consumer cognitive and affective processes as well as assessing the effectiveness of their implementation in food retail operations. At the end of the paper, we recommend options for the effective selection and implementation of aromatisation of different premises, by which the retailer can achieve not only a successful form of in-store communication, but also an increase the retail turnover of the store.

Keywords: consumer neuroscience; aromachology; emotions; retail

1. Introduction

The retail sector has undergone massive changes over the last few years, mainly due to the development of new technologies; this is not the case for the two primary objectives of retail strategy, which are to provide a shopping experience and bring value to the customer regardless of which trading channel they use. The building and creation of a unique USP sales argument (unique selling proposition) ensures differentiation from competition in the form of added value so that the customer ultimately decides to visit the store or purchase the product. There are several ways to achieve higher product sales or services by involving human senses. One option is to provide a pleasant shopping environment atmosphere. In addition to interior and exterior equipment, design, staff, the arrangement of goods, lighting, sounding (noise) and, last but not least, the smell and/or air quality, which appears to be the most important environmental factor at the point of sale on the basis of the research that has been conducted so far, while the aroma is also of particular importance to people's memory. A pleasant atmosphere due to a well-selected aroma, whether it be in a shop or in the workplace or a public space, can fundamentally influence the overall perception of people, which will ultimately also affect economic results. Thanks to an innovative interdisciplinary approach using consumer neuroscience tools, it is possible to get a detailed view of the real emotions of a person through the influence of individual aromas. In this way, it is possible to choose an aroma that will positively contribute to improving the perception of the environment of not only customers but also of employees as well.

1.1. Unique Selling Proposition

In a challenging competitive environment, in addition to effective communication at the point of sale, it is necessary to emphasise the benefits of a USP (unique selling proposition). AUSP can be defined as dramatically improving product placement and sales. The USP identification process helps to focus on the key benefits that help sell products or services and contribute to profits [1]. We can say that the USP (sometimes also called the unique selling point) is an important marketing concept that can be understood as the one element that differentiates a particular product or brand from others in the market, and it is understood as the reason why the product shall be bought or why it is better than other products are. It belongs to a company's overall marketing strategy, and it needs to be strong enough that it has the power to reach masses and also gain new customers [2]. According to [3], when applied correctly, the USP can greatly support positive brand perception and can increase product name value. Of course, nowadays, in an environment that is overcrowded by competition in different markets, it is much more difficult to procure such a strategy and underline such a special benefit for products or brands.

1.2. Aromachology

Aromachology is a young scientific discipline that examines the effects of fragrances across a range of human feelings [4]. Specific obtained results confirm that inhaling aromas may elicit relaxation, sensuality, happiness, or exhilaration [5–7]. We can agree with [7] that aromachology is increasingly used for monitoring employee performance and consumer behaviour in various places, and it is based on scientific research that examines the psychological effects of natural and synthetic scents on humans. As a science, aromachology is strongly interconnected with the marketing field. Aroma marketing (also known as scent marketing or olfactory marketing) is still a relatively weakly researched field, however, it can play an enormous role in supporting shopping processes and human behaviour, as smell has an advantage over other senses because it can immediately stimulate human emotions. Using aromas, marketers can create a connection with customers at a deeper emotional level and provide them with an unforgettable experience [8]. The main goal of aroma marketing is the creation of the pleasant atmosphere in order to encourage customers to stay in stores longer to buy more products and raise consumption [9]. It relies on the neuropsychological processing of olfactory stimuli in the human brain [10]. Mell perception varies, and it involves many factors, including individual preferences. Therefore, the most important thing is to find those aromas that will attract as many potential people as possible [11]. As Ref. [12] claims, through this, aroma marketing becomes an essential part of marketing communication. We can also agree that the positive results resulting from the use of aroma in a business environment suggest that customer satisfaction can be increased through the thoughtful manipulation of ambient stimuli [13].

1.3. Consumer Neuroscience

Consumer neuroscience is an interdisciplinary area that combines the knowledge of several disciplines, trying to study how the human brain responds to external marketing impulses/stimuli [14]. It combines knowledge from neurology, psychology, economics, and information technologies with the help of modern tools, examining emotions that affect consumer behaviour [15,16]. Neuromarketing examines the mind and brain of the consumer and is able to bring his/her needs and views closer to a particular company, advertisement, or product. Advanced methods related to neuromarketing will reveal which parts of the brain are active in the reaction to stimuli and determine what emotions they produce in the consumer [17]. We can state that consumer neuroscience has an important place in the marketing field. We agree with Plassmann et al. [18] that consumer neuroscience research has made huge developments in identifying the basic neural processes underlying human judgment and decision making. Concretely, consumer neuroscience research applies tools and theories from neuroscience to better understand decision making and entire network of related processes. Therefore, it has created extensive interest in marketing and its associated disciplines [19–23]. Within the focus on research and the understanding of the mind and behaviour of the consumer, the main purpose of neuromarketing is to transfer insights from neurology to research on consumer behaviour by applying neuroscientific methods to marketing relevant problems [24]. Therefore, neuromarketing is understood as a marketing strategy that is connected to the subconscious, emotional aspect of the customer, and it then aims to create an unbreakable bond with the customer and the product [25]. Consumer neuroscience can therefore help and support research in the field of consumer behaviour in a significant way, especially in marketing efforts to better understand human behaviour in decision-making processes. As Ref. [26] claim, although consumer neuroscience is a fledgling discipline, it constitutes a complementary advancement toward more comprehensive testing and expansion of the theory. As such, through this and many other benefits, this discipline can move marketing research to a completely new level. For these reasons, the structure of this paper consists of three research stages. The first stage is aimed at gaining an overview of the scent preferences associated with the confectionery department. In this experiment, in addition to declarative statements, control mechanisms using facial biometrics are used as well. Based on the results of the first experiment, testing is performed under laboratory conditions in order to reveal the influence of selected aromas on the emotional responses of participants. Findings from the laboratory experiment are then used in the implementation of aromatization in real conditions in Experiment 3.

2. Materials and Methods

The object of the submitted contribution is the impact of selected aromatising compounds on people's emotions and consumer behaviour in the food market through consumer neuroscience tools for the purpose of creating a USP (unique selling proposition) and the effective use of in-store communication in commercial operations. Aromas suitable for the confectionery department in food retail outlets are subject to testing. The research process is divided into three separate stages/experiments:

- Biometric implicit test;
- Research on the impact of selected aromas on human emotions using electroencephalography (EEG) and monitoring facial expressions (FA) in laboratory conditions;
- Research on the impact of selected aromas and air quality on implicit and explicit linkages in real conditions of commercial operation.

2.1. Stage 1—Biometric Implicit Test

On the basis of available studies [8,27–29] and interviews with managers from companies dealing with aromatising, five aromas have been profiled to be suitable for use in the confectionery department. Subsequently, a survey was conducted to identify the views of respondents and associations that are associated with different types of aromas. The purpose of the test was to establish the suitability of the selected aromas for the confectionary department on the target segment (the economically active population responsible for food purchases). In the case of Experiments 1 and 2, the probability sampling principle was applied, which involves random selection, allowing the creation of strong statistical inferences about a whole group. There were 147 respondents in Experiment 1 from the external panel of the research agency MNFORCE Ltd. (Bratislava, Slovakia), who were selected according to predetermined criteria (gender, age, being a customer of the selected retail company). FaceReader 7 software was used as a tool to analyze the visible demonstration of mimic muscles. Maison and Pawłowska [30] used it on a sample of 100 respondents when testing images, and, using the same software, Yu and Ko [31] conducted graphic style testing on a sample of 120 respondents. The relevance of the respondents' responses was controlled through facial biometrics and response time. The tests were conducted using a special platform called samolab.online. Samolab.online is a platform that allows a range of specialised tasks (e.g., association tests, A/B testing). It can be adapted for several forms of use (in the laboratory and through remote mailing to respondents). It is also available in several languages. Respondents can carry out such testing via home computers, tablets, or even through mobile devices outside og the laboratory. Visible manifestations of mimic muscles are recorded through video recordings and are then processed through analytical tools. The survey was conducted during the period from 4 May 2020 to 15 May 2020.

2.2. Stage 2—Testing in Laboratory Conditions Using EEG and Face Reading (FA)

Aromatic compounds that have been profiled on the basis of the biometric preferential tests have been subject to further testing under laboratory conditions. The added value of qualitative testing was realistic sample testing of the aromas in question (sampling interaction) as well as the recording of direct implicit and explicit feedback. A total of 48 participants took part in Experiment 2, and the precondition was that they had to be customers of the selected retail company (they buy food most often in that particular store). The sample size was determined based on similar studies. Krbot Skorić et al. [32] examined the effect of aromas using electroencephalography (EEG) on a sample of 16 respondents in Croatia. The commercial research agency 2muse Ltd. (Bratislava, Slovakia). monitored the effect of Christmas scents on consumer emotions using a sample of 20 respondents [33]. The European Society for Opinion and Marketing Research (ESOMAR) argues that most consumer neuroscience research agencies use much smaller respondent samples than those used in traditional market research, with 15–30 respondents being sufficient to achieve quality results [34].The research process under laboratory conditions consisted of five parts:

- Introduction of the instructions to the respondents, completion of consent to biometric and neuroimaging testing, and the processing of personal data in accordance with GDPR regulation and ethical code of sociological surveys;
- Olfactory sensitivity threshold test;
- Input controlled interview in the form of CAPI;
- Tests of selected aromas using consumer neuroscience tools and an aromatising box;
- Final interview in the form of CAPI.

The olfactory sensitivity test was conducted in order to create consumer segments with different sensitivity thresholds as part of the experiment. A certified test from the German company Burghart contains three sets of samples (one N-butanol; two phenylethanol), marked red, blue, and green, and are arranged in descending order from 1 to 10.

The Emotiv EPOC headset wireless device was used to measure brain activity, consisting of 14 data and 2 reference electrodes distributed in accordance with the international 10–20 electrode distribution system based on both international standards [35] and Nuwer et al. [36] and was distributed in the following positions: AF3, F7, F3, FC5, T7, P7, O1, O2, P8, T8, FC6, F4, F8, and AF4, as illustrated by Figure 1. The validity of data obtained via mobile electroencephalograph (EEG) using the Emotiv EPOC has been verified by several researchers, such as [37–39], who used this device to examine the emotional state of respondents and who have demonstrated that the device provides the same results as traditional stationary electroencephalographs (EEGs). The Emotiv EPOC wireless kit is capable of detecting the most important functions of brain activity that are commonly used in medical computer processing/brain simulations of a brain—computer interface (BCI).

We were monitoring three basic emotional states: excitement, frustration, and emotional involvement. Individual emotions were calculated on the basis of electrical activity recorded through a group of electrodes necessary to calculate the emotion. The EEG channels that were needed to calculate emotional involvement were allocated in positions O1, O2, F3, F4, F7, F8, FC5, and FC6. With gradual regression, the variables for this model were profiled from similar studies [40–42]. Excitement was calculated using (BetaF3 + BetaF4)/(AlphaF3 + AlphaF4) based on Giraldo and Ramirez [43], which was also used in another study [44]. There are no specific studies focussing frustration and how to deal with its calculation directly on the basis of recorded brain activity through electroencephalography (EEG), but there are several studies [45–47] that have clarified the role of the prefrontal cortex and the crown lobe in recognising frustration, which gives some form of credibility to our experiment. The data in question were obtained using the software tool Affective Suite, which records changes in emotions in real time. Each test subject had a unique profile within which the data was recalculated according to certain personality characteristics. The sum of these differences was then used to standardise the data. The software recorded three main types of emotions: excitement, emotional engagement, and frustration.

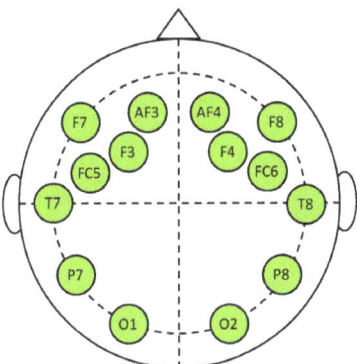

Figure 1. Image X Emotiv EPOC headset—10–20 system.

At the same time, emotional feedback was monitored through the somatic biometric method FaceReader 7 by the Dutch company Noldus, which identifies the emotional feedback (valence, excitement) of respondents with maximum accuracy based on observable changes in mimic muscles and recognises basic micro-emotions (happy, sad, angry, disgusted, surprised, neutral) [48]. In particular, the validity of the recorded data is influenced by the scanning angle, the luminosity of the environment, and the resolution of the recording equipment [49]. The data obtained from individual measurements were synchronised and correlated with each other in the Noldus Observer XT 10 program environment. This program allows the synchronization of structured and unstructured data from individual instruments and the creation of custom variables during the implementation of the experiments [50]. The survey was conducted during the period from 1 July 2020 to 10 July 2020.

2.3. Stage 3—Experiment on the Influence of Aromas in Real Conditions

Based on the results of Experiment 2, aromatisation with fragrance was deployed in the confectionery department of the retail sector, which affected the highest level of emotional involvement. Aromatising units as well as their initial settings were gradually implemented. All aromas used were safe in accordance with international standards and manufactured under the supervision of the Research Institute for Fragrance Materials (RIFM) [51]. The use of fragrances in research was governed by the ESOMAR Code of Ethics for sociological surveys. The deployment of aromas in real conditions was governed by rules developed by the International Fragrance Association (IFRA) [52], which sets out precise procedures and recommendations while respecting consumer rights. Last but not least, aromatisation was also governed by the internal code of ethics of the participating institutions—in this case, the company Kaufland and the Slovak University of Agriculture in Nitra.

A total of two aromatising units from Reima AirConcept AS650 (see Figure 2) were located in operation (one separately and one as part of the feedback kiosk). Aromatisation units were placed in operation so that they were away from the air conditioning intake(ventilation air outlets). The monitoring of conscious and unconscious customer feedback was conducted through a special 42-inch smart aromatising kiosk, which can be seen in Figure 3. Observation of unconscious feedback in real conditions through facial biometrics was significantly affected by the situation related to the COVID-19 pandemic, which has taken place since March 2020. The obligation to cover upper airways in the interiors of buildings was introduced, which made it impossible to obtain data based on the visible manifestations of mimic muscles. In this context, the feedback collection methodology has been modified several times. The originally planned collection of conscious and unconscious feedback was limited to conscious feedback, as the system was not able recognize emotional responses if the person was wearing a face mask and if only the eyes were visible.

Figure 2. Installation of aromatising units in retail outlet.

Figure 3. Special technology—smart aromatising kiosk.

The obtained processing of the data was processed through descriptive and inductive statistics in programme environments:

- MATLAB R2020a;
- RapidMiner 9.3;
- Mathematical statistical program R version 3.6.3, CCA version 1.2.1 package;
- Microsoft Excel 2010.

3. Results

In the first stage, 6 aromas (vanilla, chocolate, nougat, coffee, cappuccino, and orange) were profiled based on available studies and interviews with representatives of aromatising companies, which formed the basic basis of selection for the confectionery department in the biometric test. The results from the conscious feedback show that most respondents consider chocolate aroma to be the most pleasant smell for the confectionary department in a food shop (34%). The second most frequently indicated was coffee aroma (15%), and the least indicated aromas were those of orange (7%) and nougat (6%) (see Figure 4).

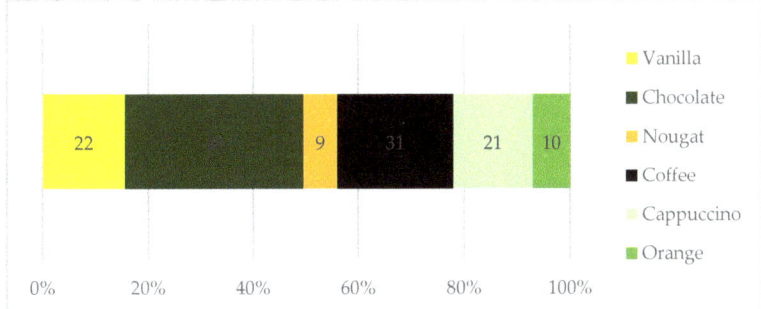

Figure 4. Selection of aromas for the confectionary department.

Control questions were also used in the test, where participants were asked to recommend on a scale from 0 to 10 (where 10 means the most appropriate) the aromas in question in the confectionery department. Each evaluated aroma was approached through a graphic visual. During the selection process, an emotional response was monitored through the respondents' facial biometrics. Differences in valence (polarity of emotions) is presented in Figure 5. If the valence values are positive, it is a positive perception. If the value is 0, it is a neutral perception, and in the case of negative values, there is a negative perception. The results show the most positive perception in the case of the vanilla aroma (0.04). The idea of chocolate (0.0015) and coffee (0.021) was equally positive. An interesting finding is that the nougat aroma, which was identified as being the least favourable aroma in the initial selection of the experiment and was only identified by 6 respondents as a suitable aroma for the department of confectionery, now achieved a better subconscious response (0.001) than the aroma of cappuccino (−0.01), which was previously recommended by 21 respondents.

Based on these findings in the online environment, we selected five aromas (vanilla, chocolate, nougat, coffee, and orange), which were tested in laboratory conditions in Experiment 2. Based on the results of the biometric association test, we conducted an experiment in laboratory conditions. The selected aromas were marked with the numbers 1 to 5 and placed in identical glass vials using a special aspirating paper. Those were tested by participants using a specialised aromatising box, which simulated the conditions of the confectionery department in the Kaufland shop in Nitra in terms of air quality. Following consultations with the company, the target sample represented a group of consumers responsible for the purchase of foodstuffs. A total of 52 respondents participated in the testing, but due to incorrect data recording, we had to exclude four of them. As shown in

Figure 6, the greatest degree of emotional engagement was recorded on the basis of the median of the elicited emotion in the case of the nougat aroma. This may be due to the more difficult recognition and odour imprint of several recognizable odours cumulated into this aroma and the efforts of the respondents to identify it. This assumption is confirmed by the fact that the citrus aroma of an orange reached the lowest level of bias, and respondents were also best able to identify it.

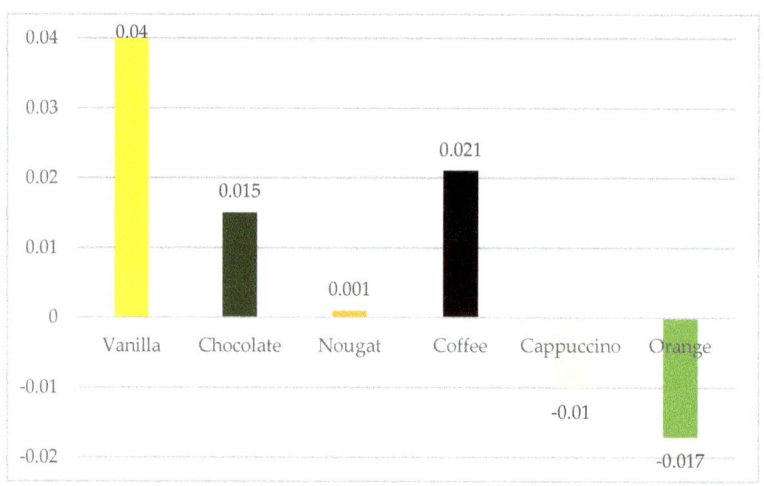

Figure 5. Emotional polarity when recommending aromas for the confectionery department.

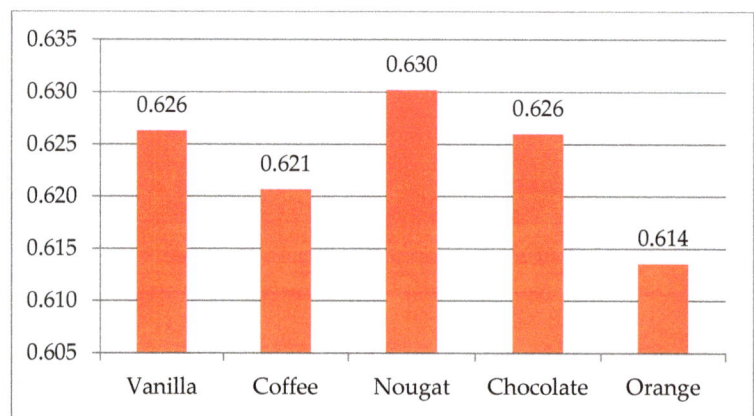

Figure 6. Engagement score in measuring the impact of the aromas on emotional engagement.

Using a single-factor variance analysis, we determined the statistically proven difference between the samples of aromatic compounds for the interest indicator. We tested the hypotheses at a significance level of 0.05.

Hypothesis 0 (H0). *Respondents perceive aromas in terms of emotional engagement in the same way;*

Hypothesis 1 (H1). *Respondents perceive aromas in terms of emotional engagement differently.*

Compared to the observed aromatic compounds on the emotional engagement indicator (interest), we attained a value ($p < 0.001$), based on which we can conclude that there is a statistically proven difference in perception in terms of engagement between the tested aromas. In a post hoc pair comparison of aroma pairs, differences between the nougat and orange aromas were demonstrated.

The highest frustration rate based on the average values was recorded in the coffee sample (0.50) (see Figure 7). It can be assumed that this result is due to the fact that respondents had difficulty identifying this aroma and not everyone was able to determine what it was immediately, which could have caused frustration. The reason may also be the method of smelling itself (distance of the nose from the test vessel) or the aromatic compound, which does not have an unambiguous composition and may remind participants of several types of aromas.

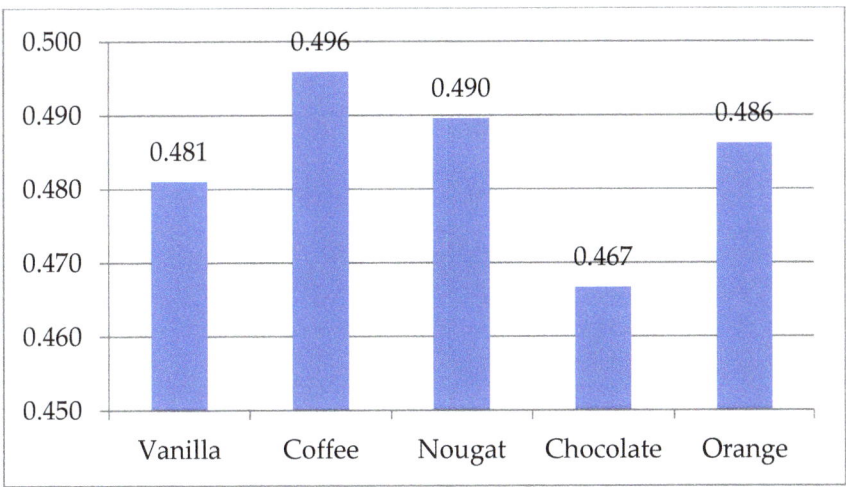

Figure 7. Frustration scores in measuring the impact of the aromas on emotional response.

Generally speaking, these are lower levels of frustration than those that are present in dealing with normal activities. At the same time, it should be stressed that frustration does not conflict with emotional engagement. We decided to also statistically verify these differences in frustration (concerns) for individual samples. We tested the hypotheses at a level of significance of 0.05.

Hypothesis 2 (H2). *Respondents perceive aromas in terms of frustration in the same way;*

Hypothesis 3 (H3). *Respondents perceive aromas in terms of frustration differently.*

As a result of the test, there is no evident difference in frustration that is dependent on the change of aroma ($p = 0.78$).

Excitement is an important emotion, as it denotes a certain degree of active involvement and anticipation. When a consumer is excited, other types of emotions that have a fundamental influence on the decision-making process are also more intense. Based on the median, we can see the highest rate of excitement for the aromas of coffee and nougat (0.47) in Figure 8. As mentioned above, this may have been due to a lower recognition capacity, but also could have been due to the associations that the aromatic compound invoked (coffee).

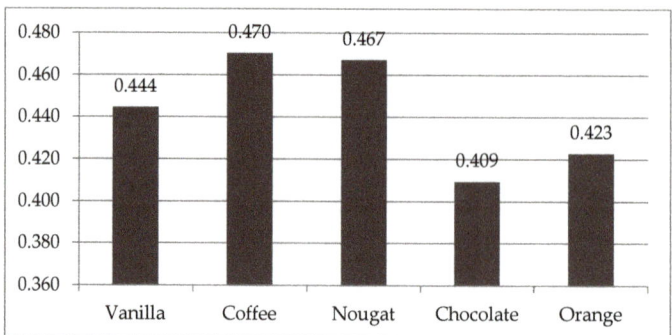

Figure 8. Comparison of excitement scores due to different aromas on emotional response.

We also statistically verified the observed differences in excitement for individual samples. We tested the hypotheses at a level of significance of 0.05.

Hypothesis 4 (H4). *Respondents perceive aromas in terms of excitement in the same way;*

Hypothesis 5 (H5). *Respondents perceive aromas in terms of excitement differently.*

A statistically proven difference was detected in the evaluation of excitement for individual aromas ($p = 0.0026$). Subsequently, paired post hoc tests were performed, and it was found that respondents reacted statistically differently with pairs of coffee–chocolate ($p = 0.01780$) and vanilla–chocolate ($p = 0.00545$).

Based on conscious feedback, respondents rated the vanilla aroma as the best (7.87) (see Figure 9). This finding is confirmed by the fact that vanilla is generally the most accepted aroma, and most people associate it with childhood (the scent of mother's milk). The worst was the orange citrus fragrance (5.67). An interesting finding is the assessment of the nougat aroma (6.76), which was better rated than the chocolate aroma (6.46).

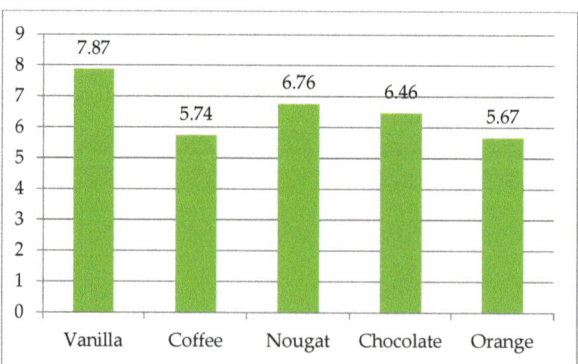

Figure 9. Conscious evaluation of tested aromas under laboratory conditions.

In addition to electroencephalography, unconscious feedback was taken by measuring microemotions based on facial expressions. By measuring emotions from facial expressions, we have obtained information about the valence (polarity of emotions) (see Figure 10). In this case, based on the mean medians, respondents were most positive about the nougat aroma (0.04) and felt the most negatively about the orange aroma (−0.02). However, it is necessary to note the possible distortion of the results by the fact that in some cases, some respondents smiled, probably because of the initial surprise, which in turn could artificially increase the rate of positive tuning in some samples, as the software evaluated the smile as positive feedback, as it recognises emotions based on facial expressions.

Based on a valence comparison using the Kruskal–Wallis test, we found that there are statistically significant differences between the aromas ($p = 0.0126$) in the emotions of the participants involved in the experiment. Differences have been confirmed between the orange and nougat aromas and between the chocolate and nougat aromas (see Table 1).

Table 1. Kruskal–Wallis test—comparison of the valence of individual aromas.

	Vanilla	Coffee	Nougat	Chocolate	Orange
Orange	H6	H6	H7	H6	
Chocolate	H6	H6	H6		
Nougat	H6	H7			
Coffee	H6				
Vanilla					

Testing at $\alpha = 0.1$.

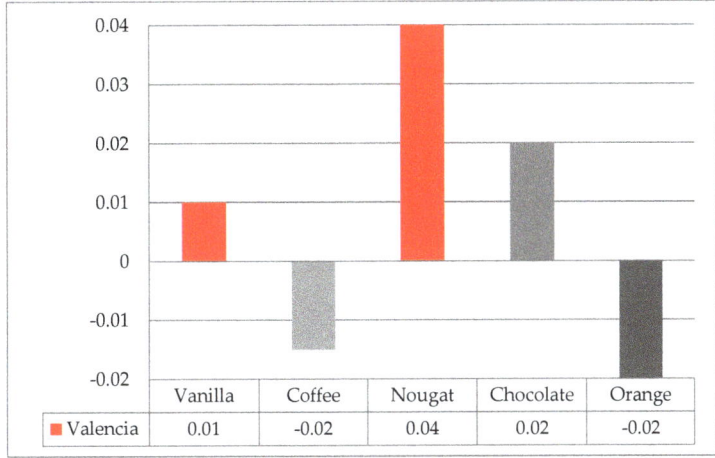

Figure 10. Valence due to tested aromas under laboratory conditions.

Hypothesis 6 (H6). *are equal = there is no difference.*

Hypothesis 7 (H7). *are different = there is difference.*

The results of the conscious aroma sample evaluation in question show that the respondents evaluated the aromas of vanilla and nougat the most positively. At the subconscious level, the most positive values of valence, but also of emotional engagement, were recorded with the nougat aroma. On the basis of these findings and the consultation with the managers of Kaufland Slovenská republika, v. o. s., we decided to use the nougat aroma in the real conditions of the confectionery department, which represents the third stage of this research.

The third stage of the research was significantly affected by the COVID-19 pandemic. Data collection under real conditions was limited to explicit feedback through a graphical scale. Implicit collection of data through facial biometrics could not be realised due to the obligation to cover the upper airways. This portion of the research was mainly intended to investigate the unconscious effect of aromatisation and air quality on the emotions of customers who visited the confectionery department. It follows from the above that the research under real conditions, in particular in terms of demonstrating an unconscious effect, was fundamentally limited.

A total of 6130 responses were recorded in the Kaufland Nitra shop from 10 November 2020 to 9 March 2021, with an average assessment of the atmosphere of confectionery department being 1.86. This included the monitoring of air quality at each minute. Given the extent of the obtained, only selected periods are compared with each other. From the data in Figure 11, you can see a conscious evaluation of the confectionery department over 20 days in the pre-Christmas period (from 10 November 2020 to 30 November 2020) with aromatisation and during the pre-Easter period (from 22 February 2021 to 14 May 2021) without aromatisation. The results based on average daily responses show approximately the same assessment of the atmosphere of the confectionary department as during the pre-Christmas period (average 1.80; 1580 responses) and the pre-Easter period (average of 1.88; 1216 responses). These results may be largely distorted due to the spread of the pandemic and the mandatory protection of the upper airways.

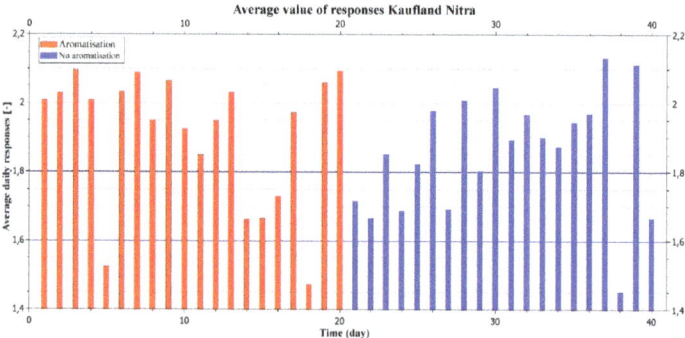

Figure 11. Comparison of evaluation of the atmosphere of the department during the experiment period with and without aromatisation.

4. Discussion

The aim of the conducted research phases was to verify the positive effect of aromatisation on the assessment of the atmosphere of a sales department, with which Vesecký [53] agrees and describes the unconscious perception of aromas as how the customer usually associates the aroma with something positive. Lindstrom [54] also stresses the fact that almost 75% of human feelings during the day are regulated by fragrances. Madzharov, Block, and Morrin [55] also highlight the choice of the right aroma for the use under real conditions. They state that traders are increasingly using the surrounding aroma as a strategic tool to distinguish themselves from competition, attract customers, stimulate sales, influence moods, and create overall pleasant and memorable shopping experiences. During the processes of decision making and choosing, a number of aspects affect the consumer, including mood or emotional state of mind [56,57]. The role of emotions in the consumer decision-making process is explained by the principle of neurological and cognitive frameworks, such as the somatic marker theory [58], which focuses on the so-called attention to negative impacts in decision making.

Despite the shortcomings, this research can be considered beneficial since there are few studies using biometric and neuroimaging methods to test the emotional impact of aromas, including taking into account surrounding environmental factors that have a fundamental impact on human perception [59].

The proof of this is that the application of consumer neuroscience tools in the food industry has recently gained considerable popularity in both academic and commercial fields. Large research companies such as Nielsen, Kantar, or Ipsos have also included these tools in their commercial offers [60]. Despite a number of critical aspects, such as questioning privacy limits and the concept of free will, mainstreaming these technologies and consumer behaviour and market research today constitute a significant part of understanding and meeting research objectives [61].

5. Conclusions

In the present paper, we looked at the impact of selected aromas on the consumer's active processes by using consumer neuroscience tools. The available studies and the following interviews with representatives from aromatising companies show that the smell of the confectionery department is most closely linked to the slightly sweet aroma of chocolate, nougat, various types of coffee, vanilla, but often also the fruit aroma of an orange. These findings formed the basis for the next association test using facial biometrics, the main task of which was to assess the suitability and recommendation of the aromas that were identified in the confectionary department. Of the six aromas from which respondents could choose as the most suitable for this department, the chocolate aroma (34%) and a coffee aroma (15%) had the greatest representation. The emotional response of the respondents was monitored for this question. The results show that the most positive subconscious perception in the case of the vanilla aroma (0.04). The idea of chocolate (0.0015) and coffee (0.021) was equally positive. An interesting finding was that the nougat aroma, which was identified as a suitable aroma for the department of confectionery by the least number of respondents (six) in the initial selection. In this case, however, it achieved a better subconscious response (0.001) than the aroma of cappuccino (-0.01), which was recommended by 21 participants.

The second stage consisted of research on the impact of selected aromas on human emotions using electroencephalography (EEG) and monitoring facial expressions (FA) in laboratory conditions. Of the six aromas that were subject to the association biometric test, five (vanilla, coffee, chocolate, nougat, orange) were selected on the basis of the results, which were tested using a special aromatising box at the FEM SUA in the Nitra Consumer Studies Laboratory. Despite the fact that based on the results of the previous online test, the cappuccino aroma achieved better results than the orange aroma, we decided to include it in the test because we assumed that there were more significant differences in implicit perception. At the same time, we decided to keep the coffee aroma in the test using two similar aromas (cappuccino and coffee). The test was conducted with 48 respondents who were subjected to an olfactory sensitivity test. Based on the brain activity measurements, the highest rate of emotional engagement based on the median of this emotion was observed with the nougat aroma (0.630). This may be due to the more difficult recognition and odour imprint of several recognizable odours that are cumulated into this aroma and the efforts of the respondents to identify it. In this context, using a single-factor dispersion analysis, we determined the statistically proven difference between samples of aromatic compounds from the point of view of emotional engagement, showing that there is a statistically significant difference in perception in terms of the engagement between the tested aromas. The highest frustration rate based on average values was observed in the coffee sample (0.50). It can be assumed that this result is due to the fact that respondents had difficulty identifying this aroma and not everyone was able to recognise it immediately, which could have caused frustration. We also decided to statistically verify these differences in frustration (concerns) for individual samples. However, there was no statistically significant difference in the perception of respondents in this case. The highest rate of excitement was noted for the coffee and nougat aromas (0.47). As with emotional engagement, a statistically proven difference was found in this case. In this context, pair post hoc tests were conducted, and it was found that respondents reacted statistically differently, especially with the coffee–chocolate and vanilla–chocolate pairs. On the basis of conscious feedback, respondents evaluated the vanilla aroma as the best (7.87), which is generally the most widely accepted aroma and most people associate it with childhood (the scent of mother's milk). The worst was the orange citrus aroma (5.67). An interesting finding is the assessment of the nougat aroma (6.76), which was better rated than the chocolate aroma (6.46). When asked which aroma seemed best suited for the confectionery department, the nougat (17 respondents) and vanilla (12 respondents) aromas were the most preferred in physical testing, which is in contrast to the biometric association test.

Differences in the development of the perception of aroma samples in terms of time have also been confirmed through a statistical test, and while some emotions have been more stable, others have changed.

In addition to electroencephalography, unconscious feedback was taken by measuring microemotions based on facial expressions. In this case, based on the mean median valence, respondents were most positive about the aroma of nougat (0.04) and the most negative about the orange aroma (−0.02). The statistical test also confirmed differences in perception between the aromas of orange and nougat and between the aromas of nougat and coffee. On the basis of these findings and after consultations with the managers of the retail company, we decided to use the aroma of nougat in the real conditions of the confectionery department.

The last stage (3) consisted of research on the impact of selected aromas on implicit and explicit linkages under the real conditions of a commercial operation. The solution to this part of the work was significantly influenced by the situation of the COVID-19 pandemic. Implicit data collection under real conditions was impossible, as the obligation to cover and protect the upper airways in the interiors of buildings prevented the detection of people and the recognition of emotions. In this context, data collection under real conditions was limited to explicit feedback. Last but not least, the pandemic also affected the validity of the data itself, as it can be assumed that different types of facial protection (respirator, face mask, scarf) more or less affected the perception of the aromas. In the light of the above, we have not been able to verify the presumption of the difference between implicit and explicit feedback under real conditions.

The results from obtaining a conscious feedback under real conditions show approximately the same assessment of the atmosphere of the confectionery department in the pre-Christmas period with aromatisation (average 1.80; 1580 replies) and in the pre-Easter period with no aromatisation (average 1.88; 1216 replies).

A pleasant atmosphere in stores or public spaces under the influence of a suitably chosen aroma can fundamentally affect the overall perception of people, which will ultimately have an impact on the economic results. The right choice of aroma also completes the overall atmosphere of the chosen sales department. Since the influence of aromas has mainly a subconscious effect, the choice of a suitable aromatic compound should not be limited to traditional forms of research. Therefore, we recommend sellers a combination of traditional research forms with the tools of consumer neuroscience, which provide a detailed view of real human emotions under the influence of particular aromas. This method will allow retailers to choose an aroma that will positively contribute to improving the perception of the environment not only for customers but also for employees. It should be taken into consideration that the research of preferences in the field of aromatization also requires special equipment which allows the testing of various fragrance compounds under laboratory as well as in real conditions.

It follows from the above that in the evaluation of emotional response, besides the use of classical feedback collection tools, it is important to extend these evaluations with measurements of subconscious reactions based on the monitoring of electrical brain activity (EEG) and facial expressions of the respondents—facial biometrics give a completely new insight into the actual perception of aromatic compounds as well as more efficient targeting and the use of corporate resources.

Based on empirical knowledge and limitations related to the pandemic, we plan to conduct a similar research project with an even larger sample of test respondents that will take the weather, season, olfactory sensitivity (anosmia, hyposmia, normosmia) and participant fatigue (start and end of the week) into account. Future research will be conducted under different air quality conditions (CO_2, VOC, temperature, humidity) in order to identify possible changes in the perception of aromas. Due to the need to cover the upper respiratory tract, the perception of aromas will also be simulated in order to quantify the impact of pandemic restrictions (mandatory upper respiratory protection in buildings) under real conditions. From the point of view of the technologies used in this study, we would like to conduct similar research with the 32channel Electroencephalograph (EEG) and its extension to the biometric method of measuring skin resistance (GSR).

Author Contributions: Conceptualization, J.B. and K.N.; data curation, K.N.; formal analysis, J.B. and K.N.; funding acquisition, J.B.; investigation, J.B., K.N., J.G. and A.M.; methodology, J.B. and K.N.; project administration, J.G.; resources, J.G. and A.M.; software, J.B.; supervision, J.B.; validation, J.B.; visualization, J.B.; writing—original draft, J.B., K.N., J.G. and A.M.; writing—review and editing, K.N. All authors have read and agreed to the published version of the manuscript.

Funding: This research was funded by the Erasmus+ KA2 Strategic Partnerships grant no. 2018-1-SK01-KA203-046324 "Implementation of Consumer Neuroscience and Smart Research Solutions in Aromachology" (NEUROSMARTOLOGY). The European Commission's support for the production of this publication does not constitute an endorsement of the contents, which only reflect the views only of the authors, and the Commission cannot be held responsible for any use which may be based on the use the information contained therein. The research was also funded by the research grant APVV-17-0564, "The Use of Consumer Neuroscience and Innovative Research Solutions in Aromachology and its Application in Production, Business and Services".

Institutional Review Board Statement: The entire testing process was governed by the Code of Ethics "Laboratory of Consumer Studies" of the Faculty of Economics and Management of the Slovak University of Agriculture in Nitra and by The NMSBA Code of Ethics for the Application of Consumer Neurosciences in Business.

Informed Consent Statement: Informed consent was obtained from all subjects involved in the study.

Data Availability Statement: Data are available upon request due to restrictions, e.g., privacy or ethics.

Conflicts of Interest: The authors declare no conflict of interest.

References

1. Felix, O.T.; Chile, T.S.; Abukari, O.R. Making Slogans and Unique Selling Propositions (USP) Beneficial to Advertisers and the Consumers. *New Media Mass Commun.* **2012**, *3*, 30–36.
2. Breuer, C.; Hallmann, K. Unique Selling Proposition. *Sage* **2011**, 1609–1611. [CrossRef]
3. Bao, Y.; Shao, A.T. Nonconformity advertising to teens. *J. Advert. Res.* **2002**, *42*, 56–65. [CrossRef]
4. Lieskovská, V.; Pavlov, P. The Impact of Selected Aspects of Neuroscience on the Quality of Senior Life. In *Reproduction of Human Capital—Mutual Links and Connections*; Oeconomica Publishing House, University of Economics: Praha, Slovakia, 2018.
5. Butcher, D. Aromatherapy—Its past and future. *DCI* **1998**, *162*, 22–23.
6. Tomi, K.; Fushiki, T.; Murakami, H.; Matsumura, Y.; Hayashi, T.; Yazawa, S. Relationships between lavender aroma component and aromachology effect. *Acta Hortic.* **2011**, *925*, 299–306. [CrossRef]
7. Wang, C.X.; Chen, S.L. Aromachology and its application in the textile field. *Fibres Text. East. Eur.* **2005**, *13*, 41–44.
8. Kumamoto, J.; Tedjakusuma, A.P. A study of the impact and effectiveness of scent used for promotion of products and services with low olfactory affinity. In *15th International Symposium on Management (INSYMA 2018)*; Atlantis Press: Chonburi, Thailand, 2018; p. 186.
9. Mitchell, D.J.; Kahn, B.E.; Knasko, S.C. There's Something in the Air: Effects of Congruent or Incongruent Ambient Odor on Consumer Decision Making. *J. Consum. Res.* **1995**, *22*, 229–238. [CrossRef]
10. Emsenhuber, B. Scent marketing: Subliminal advertising messages. In Proceedings of the INFORMATIK 2009—Im Focus das Leben, Beitrage der 39. Jahrestagung der Gesellschaft fur Informatik e.V. (GI), Lübeck, Germany, 28 September–15 October 2009.
11. Virkkunen, I. Consumers' Opinions on Scent Marketing Usage in Retail Environment. Master's Thesis, LUT University, Lappeenranta, Finland, 2015.
12. Sikela, H. Vôňa ako súčasť identity firmy. *Instoreslovakia* **2015**, *2*, 14–15.
13. Bradford, K.D.; Desrochers, D.M. The use of scents to influence consumers: The sense of using scents to make cents. *J. Bus. Ethics* **2009**, *90*, 141–153. [CrossRef]
14. Agarwal, S.; Dutta, T. Neuromarketing and consumer neuroscience: Current understanding and the way forward. *Decision* **2015**, *42*, 457–462. [CrossRef]
15. Berčík, J.; Paluchová, J.; Horská, E. Neuroeconomics: An innovative view on consumer's decision process. *J. Bus. Manag. Econ.* **2016**, *4*, 22–28.
16. Horská, E.; Berčík, J. *Neuromarketing in Food Retailing*; Wageningen Academic Publishers: Wageningen, Gelderland, 2017.
17. Samuhelová, M.; Šimková, L. Neuromarketing. Úvod do problematiky. *Mark. Sci. Inspir.* **2015**, *10*, 47–55.

18. Plassmann, H.; Venkatraman, V.; Huettel, S.; Yoon, C. Consumer neuroscience: Applications, challenges, and possible solutions. *J. Mark. Res.* **2015**, *52*, 427–435. [CrossRef]
19. Ariely, D.; Berns, G.S. Neuromarketing: The hope and hype of neuroimaging in business. *Nat. Rev. Neurosci.* **2010**, *11*, 284–292. [CrossRef]
20. Camerer, C.; Loewenstein, G.; Prelec, D. Neuroeconomics: How neuroscience can inform economics. *J. Econ. Lit.* **2005**, *43*, 9–64. [CrossRef]
21. Plassmann, H.; Ramsøy, T.Z.; Milosavljevic, M. Branding the brain: A critical review and outlook. *J. Consum. Psychol.* **2012**, *22*, 18–36. [CrossRef]
22. Plassmann, H.; Yoon, C.; Feinberg, F.; Shiv, B. Consumer Neuroscience. Chichester. *Wiley Int. Encycl. Mark.* **2010**, 115–122. [CrossRef]
23. Venkatraman, V.; Clithero, J.A.; Fitzsimons, G.J.; Huettel, S.A. New scanner data for brand marketers: How neuroscience can help better understand differences in brand preferences. *J. Consum. Psychol.* **2012**, *22*, 143–153. [CrossRef]
24. Miljkovi, M.; Alcakovic, S. Neuromarketing: Marketing research future? *Menadžment Mark. Trg.* **2010**, *7*, 274–283.
25. Karmarkar, U.R. *Note on Neuromarketing*; Harvard Business School: Boston, MA, USA, 2011.
26. Kenning, P.; Linzmajer, M. Consumer neuroscience: An overview of an emerging discipline with implications for consumer policy. *J. Fur Verbrauch. Und Leb.* **2011**, *6*, 111–125. [CrossRef]
27. Saint-Bauzel, R.; Fointiat, V. The sweet smell of coldness: Vanilla and the warm-cold effect. *Soc. Behav. Pers.* **2013**, *41*, 1635–1640. [CrossRef]
28. Doucé, L.; Poels, K.; Janssens, W.; De Backer, C. Smelling the books: The effect of chocolate scent on purchase-related behavior in a bookstore. *J. Environ. Psychol.* **2013**, *36*, 65–69. [CrossRef]
29. Madzharov, A.; Ye, N.; Morrin, M.; Block, L. The impact of coffee-like scent on expectations and performance. *J. Environ. Psychol.* **2018**, *57*, 83–86. [CrossRef]
30. Maison, D.; Pawłowska, B. Using the Facereader Method to Detect Emotional Reaction to Controversial Advertising Referring to Sexuality and Homosexuality. *Springer Proc. Bus. Econ.* **2017**, 309–327. [CrossRef]
31. Yu, C.-Y.; Ko, C.-H. Applying FaceReader to Recognize Consumer Emotions in Graphic Styles. *Procedia CIRP* **2017**, *60*, 104–109. [CrossRef]
32. Skoric, M.K.; Adamec, I.; Jerbić, A.B.; Gabelić, T.; Hajnšek, S.; Habek, M. Electroencephalographic Response to Different Odors in Healthy Individuals: A Promising Tool for Objective Assessment of Olfactory Disorders. *Clin. EEG Neurosci.* **2015**, *46*, 370–376. [CrossRef]
33. Chovancová, Ľ. *Vianočné Pozdravy. Prvý Čuchový Test Vianočných Vôní. EEG Meranie v Kombinácii s Facereaderom*; Paper Presentation; Agentúra 2muse: Bratislava, Slovakia, 2018.
34. ESOMAR. 36 Questions to Help Commission Neuroscience Research 2012. Available online: https://www.esomar.org/uploads/public/knowledge-and-standards/codes-and-guidelines/ESOMAR_36-Questions-to-help-commission-neuroscience-research.pdf (accessed on 10 June 2021).
35. Electrode Position Nomenclature Committee. Guideline thirteen: Guidelines for standard electrode position nomenclature. *J. Clin. Neurophysiol.* **1994**, *11*, 111–113. [CrossRef]
36. Nuwer, M.R.; Comi, G.; Emerson, R.; Fuglsang-Frederiksen, A.; Guérit, J.-M.; Hinrichs, H.; Ikeda, A.; Luccas, F.J.C.; Rappelsburger, P. IFCN standards for digital recording of clinical EEG. *Electroencephalogr. Clin. Neurophysiol.* **1998**, *106*, 259–261. [CrossRef]
37. Badcock, N.A.; Mousikou, P.; Mahajan, Y.; De Lissa, P.; Thie, J.; McArthur, G.; Abdullah, J. Validation of the Emotiv EPOC®EEG gaming system for measuring research quality auditory ERPs. *PeerJ* **2013**, *1*, e38. [CrossRef]
38. Duvinage, M.; Castermans, T.; Petieau, M.; Hoellinger, T.; Cheron, G.; Dutoit, T. Performance of the Emotiv Epoc headset for P300-based applications. *Biomed. Eng. Online* **2013**, *12*, 56. [CrossRef]
39. Hairston, W.D.; Whitaker, K.W.; Ries, A.J.; Vettel, J.M.; Bradford, J.C.; Kerick, S.E.; McDowell, K. Usability of four commercially-oriented EEG systems. *J. Neural Eng.* **2014**, *11*, 046018. [CrossRef] [PubMed]
40. Coelli, S.; Sclocco, R.; Barbieri, R.; Reni, G.; Zucca, C.; Bianchi, A.M. EEG-based index for engagement level monitoring during sustained attention. In Proceedings of the 37th Annual International Conference of the IEEE Engineering in Medicine and Biology Society (EMBC), Milan, Italy, 25–29 August 2015; Volume 2, p. 1.
41. Estikic, M.; Eberka, C.; Levendowski, D.J.; Rubio, R.F.; Etan, V.; Ekorszen, S.; Ebarba, D.; Ewurzer, D. Modeling temporal sequences of cognitive state changes based on a combination of EEG-engagement, EEG-workload, and heart rate metrics. *Front. Neurosci.* **2014**, *8*, 342. [CrossRef]
42. Berka, C.; Levendowski, D.J.; Lumicao, M.N.; Yau, A.; Davis, G.; Zivkovic, V.T.; Olmstead, R.E.; Tremoulet, P.D.; Craven, P.L. EEG correlates of task engagement and mental workload in vigilance, learning, and memory tasks. *Aviat. Space Environ. Med.* **2007**, *78*, 231–244.
43. Giraldo, S.; Ramirez, R. Brain-Activity-Driven Real-Time Music Emotive Control. In Proceedings of the 3rd International Conference on Music & Emotion, Jyväskylä, Finland, 11–15 June 2013; Geoff Luck & Olivier Brabant: Jyväskylä, Finland, 2013.
44. McMahan, T.; Parberry, I.; Parsons, T.D. Evaluating Player Task Engagement and Arousal Using Electroencephalography. *Procedia Manuf.* **2015**, *3*, 2303–2310. [CrossRef]
45. Abler, B.; Walter, H.; Erk, S. Neural correlates of frustration. *NeuroReport* **2005**, *16*, 669–672. [CrossRef]

46. DeVeney, C.M.; Connolly, M.E.; Haring, C.T.; Bones, B.L.; Reynolds, R.C.; Kim, P.; Pine, D.S.; Leibenluft, E. Neural Mechanisms of Frustration in Chronically Irritable Children. *Am. J. Psychiatry* **2013**, *170*, 1186–1194. [CrossRef]
47. Rich, B.A.; Holroyd, T.; Carver, F.W.; Onelio, L.M.; Mendoza, J.K.; Cornwell, B.R.; Fox, N.A.; Pine, D.S.; Coppola, R.; Leibenluft, E. A preliminary study of the neural mechanisms of frustration in pediatric bipolar disorder using magnetoencephalography. *Depress. Anxiety* **2010**, *27*, 276–286. [CrossRef]
48. Noldus Information Technology Reference Manual—FaceReader Version 7. 2010. Available online: http://sslab.nwpu.edu.cn/uploads/1500604789-5971697563f64.pdf (accessed on 10 June 2021).
49. Skiendziel, T.; Rösch, A.G.; Schultheiss, O.C. Assessing the convergent validity between the automated emotion recognition software Noldus FaceReader 7 and Facial Action Coding System Scoring. *PLoS ONE* **2019**, *14*, 233. [CrossRef]
50. Zimmerman, P.H.; Bolhuis, J.E.; Willemsen, A.; Meyer, E.S.; Noldus, L.P.J.J. The observer XT: A tool for the integration and synchronization of multimodal signals. *Behav. Res. Methods* **2009**, *41*, 731–735. [CrossRef]
51. Research Institute for Fragrance Materials. Available online: https://www.rifm.org/#gsc.tab=0 (accessed on 18 July 2021).
52. International Fragrance Association. Available online: https://ifrafragrance.org/ (accessed on 18 July 2021).
53. Vesecký, Z. Vyzkoušejte Aroma Marketing, Váš Úspěch je ve Vzduchu. 2015. Available online: http://www.podnikatel.cz/clanky/vyzkousejte-aroma-marketing-vas-uspech-je-ve-vzduchu/ (accessed on 10 June 2021).
54. Lindstrom, M. *Brand Sense: Sensory Secrets Behind the Stuff We Buy*; Free Press: New York, NY, USA, 2010; p. 175.
55. Madzharov, A.V.; Block, L.G.; Morrin, M. The cool scent of power: Effects of ambient scent on consumer preferences and choice behavior. *J. Mark.* **2015**, *79*, 83–96. [CrossRef]
56. Lawless, H.T.; Heymann, H. *Sensory Evaluation of Food: Principles of Good Practice*; Springer: New York, NY, USA, 2010; p. 175.
57. Schiffman, L.G.; Wisenblit, J. *Consumer Behavior*, 12th ed.; Pearson English Readers: London, UK, 2019; p. 512.
58. Reimann, M.; Bechara, A. The somatic marker framework as a neurological theory of decision-making: Review, conceptual comparisons, and future neuroeconomics research. *J. Econ. Psychol.* **2010**, *31*, 767–776. [CrossRef]
59. Berčík, J.; Paluchová, J.; Vietoris, V.; Horská, E. Placing of aroma compounds by food sales promotion in chosen services business. *Potravinarstvo* **2016**, *10*, 672–679. [CrossRef]
60. Moya, I.; García-Madariaga, J.; Blasco, M.-F. What Can Neuromarketing Tell Us about Food Packaging? *Foods* **2020**, *9*, 1856. [CrossRef] [PubMed]
61. Feinberg, F.M.; Kinnear, T.C.; Taylor, J.R. *Modern Marketing Research: Concepts, Methods, and Cases*, 2nd ed.; South-Western College Pub: Mason, OH, USA, 2013; p. 720.

Review

Aromachology Related to Foods, Scientific Lines of Evidence: A Review

Dámaris Girona-Ruíz, Marina Cano-Lamadrid, Ángel Antonio Carbonell-Barrachina, David López-Lluch and Sendra Esther *

Centro de Investigación e Innovación Agroalimentaria y Agroambiental (CIAGRO-UMH), Miguel Hernández University, 03312 Orihuela, Spain; damarisgruiz@gmail.com (D.G.-R.); marina.cano.umh@gmail.com (M.C.-L.); angel.carbonell@umh.es (Á.A.C.-B.); david.lopez@umh.es (D.L.-L.)
* Correspondence: esther.sendra@umh.es

Abstract: Smell is the second-most used sense in marketing strategies in the food industry. Sensory marketing appeals to the senses with the aim of creating sensory experiences and converting them into specific emotions associated with a specific product. There is a strong relationship between sensory marketing, aromachology, and neuroscience. In this review, studies were searched on the use of scents in food experiences such as restaurants and food establishments, and a critical evaluation was performed on their aims, target population, place of the study, scents tested, foods tested, and measured parameters, and the main findings were reviewed. Case studies carried out by private companies are also presented. A small number of scientific studies on aromachology related to food are available, and most of them are conducted in artificial laboratory conditions. Methodological procedures largely diverge among studies, making them very difficult to compare and extrapolate results. There is a clear need for research on aromachology related to food in the fields of sensory marketing and appetite modulation. After a brief presentation of the state of the art, we briefly mention future improvements and ideas for future research.

Keywords: scent; neuroscience; sensory marketing; consumer

1. Introduction

Smell/aroma is directly related to human emotions; it is the main trigger for human emotions after sight. In fact, it has been reported that 75% of human emotions are created through smell/aroma [1]. The olfactory bulb is part of the brain's limbic system (seat of emotions, desires, and instincts), and that is why smells can trigger strong emotional reactions. This explains the strong link between smells, emotions, and memories. In practice, it is possible to use this evidence to influence and promote certain feelings [2]. Herz [3] reviewed scientific studies on the mechanisms mediating the effect of odours on mood, physiology, and behaviour. Two main types of studies were reported—one investigating pharmacological and the other psychological mechanisms of action. The author concluded that the psychological interpretation of odour effects was the most comprehensive interpretation, showing that odours have clear psychological effects.

Scents use has been evaluated for different purposes such as sensory marketing of different goods or services, well-being, cosmetics, etc. [4]. Regarding our field of interest, foods and food-related stores and environments, scents have been tested for several purposes: to study their impact on appetite, food consumption, food sales, evaluating shopping experience, etc. Sensory marketing can be defined as marketing that involves the senses of consumers and studies the perception, emotion, learning, preference, choice, evaluation, knowledge, judgment, and purchasing behaviour based on the senses [5]. Sensory marketing appeals to the senses with the aim of creating sensory experiences and converting them into specific emotions associated with a specific product.

Smell is the second-most used sense in marketing strategies in the food industry [6]. Therefore, aromas play an important role in marketing strategies [6]. The memory of smell is the most intense of all the senses, and only about 20% of olfactory sensations are forgotten. Human beings even maintain very old memories and feelings related to smell [1]. Aroma marketing has two main modalities: (i) the use of the unique smell/aroma of the product itself, with the possibility of creating an aroma that identifies the company with the product/brand and (ii) the use of an ambient smell/aroma in spaces (restaurants, supermarkets, small shops, public spaces) [2].

Ambient scent is defined as a scent that is present in the environment but does not emanate from a particular object [2]. These ambient scents have been classified based on (i) the affective quality of the aroma (how pleasant the aroma is), (ii) the level of arousal of the aroma (how likely is it to elicit a physiological response), and (iii) the intensity of the aroma (how strong it is). Several authors pointed out that stores that use ambient scents give their customers the feeling that they spend less time looking at products and trying them [7,8].

In the 1970s, fragrances began to gain prominence as a tool for retailers aiming to improve the indoor environment by introducing specific scents [9]. Origins of olfactory marketing seem to be in the 1980s when British supermarkets realised that fresh baking bread aromas increased selling bread and other products [10]. This moved them to introduce bakery as a new department area. However, the difficulty of introducing aromas in a supermarket for increasing sales can be illustrated by the fact that customers can smell fresh bread aromas and buy the bread but can prevent them from buying other goods [6]. This reduction in their willingness to buy is due to the fact that their sensory perception and emotions are, to some extent, satisfied by purchasing the bread [2]. That is a case based on the scent of a product itself. However, most recent studies have focused on ambient aroma, and analysed the influence of aroma on the purchase intention of consumers [2].

In 1982, the Olfactory Research Fund coined the term 'aromachology', relevant to marketing. This area of expertise deals with the temporary effects of fragrances on human behaviour, feelings, well-being, moods, and emotions [11]. Aromachology, as defined by the Sense of Smell Institute in 1982, is the scientific discipline studying psychological and physiological effects of inhaling aromas and examining, feelings and emotions elicited by odours stimulating olfactory pathways. Aromachology research must follow empirical scientific methodology—goals, hypothesis, materials and methods (aroma, subject population number and representativity as well as the control group), and proper statistical data analysis—and be published in peer-reviewed reputable journals [11]. Under these premises, if a study is conducted using the internet, many publications that may be found regarding odour effects on mood and behaviour should not be taken into consideration since they do not follow such premises, and their results may not be taken as scientifically sound. In the present review, only studies following the requirements have been included. At present, focusing on the general scientific literature on aromachology, there are many scientific lines of evidence reporting that inhaling aromas may elicit feelings such as relaxation, sensuality, happiness, or exhilaration [12–15]. There are also scientific lines of evidence on the physiological effect of scents. As an example, in a study on rats, Shen et al. [16] presented evidence that the scent of grapefruit oil excited sympathetic nerves, innervating white and brown adipose tissues and the adrenal gland, inhibiting the vagal nerve innervating the stomach, increasing lipolysis and heat production (energy consumption), and reducing appetite and body weight in rats; the opposite effect was observed for lavender, mainly due to linalool, which enhanced appetite and body weight [16].

The most common use of scents is for marketing purposes. Scent sensory marketing is about much more than simply spreading a pleasant fragrance in a space. It may be, starting from the brand identity of a company (and its values) and studying its target consumer, to create an aroma that exemplifies company identity (and values). The expression 'scent marketing' has been used to describe the use of essences to create an environment, and promote products or position a brand, and therefore, scent marketing can be defined as the strategic use of the olfactory experience and essences in relation to commercial products [17]. There are three types of scents used in environments [6,18] known as (i) head, (ii) heart, and (iii) basic. Head scents are generally small, light molecules that give a refreshing and invigorating sensation. These are typically fresh citrus or green notes, including lemon, lime, neroli, bergamot, grapefruit, and cooler herbal notes such as lavender, thyme, and basil. The molecules responsible for heart-like scents tend to be larger and can take anywhere from five minutes to an hour to develop. They can include different ingredients, such as flowers, spices, woods, resins, and grasses. Lastly, the basic-type scent molecules are the largest and heaviest. They are aromas such as woods, resins, oakmoss, vanilla, amber, and musk [2].

The use of aromas in food is regulated (R1334/2008 in the European Union), and all aromas need to be approved by public authorities after following strictly regulated procedures. In the present review, we do not consider food aromas but scents used in food-related environments. Scents should also comply with safety and quality standards that are supervised by independent laboratories leading to safety certificates, such as the International Fragrance Association (IFRA) Conformity Certificate, assessed by a panel of experts from the Research Institute for Fragrance Materials (RFIM). The safety of scents is evaluated according to the intended use (odorant, skin contact, etc.).

Classical data collection on consumer studies are questionnaires to consumers; however, they cannot assess the complex set of factors affecting decision making (emotions, feelings, etc.) [19]. It is in this scenario that neuroscience tools entered the field of consumer marketing studies. Neuromarketing aims to use psychological and neuroscience tools to study subconscious processes during decision making in order to provide scientific explanations of consumer's preferences and behaviours. Main neuroscience tools used in neuromarketing are biometric measurements (body reaction measures: eye movements, facial expressions) and brain measurements. Using such techniques to measure respondents' subconscious reactions in addition to classical feedback collection techniques may provide a comprehensive perspective on consumers' perception [19]. In the present review, we will focus only on scents, even though visual factors (packaging, design, portion size, the gastronomic service used, etc.) also influence consumers' perception and food appeal. Both senses are closely related; however, little is known about their complex interactions [20], and only a few studies combine the evaluation of both factors.

Regarding sensory marketing in the food business, one may differentiate between food stores (food is sold, not consumed) and restaurants (gastronomic facilities where food is consumed). To this second situation applies the concept of neurogastronomy; neuroscientist Gordon M. Shephard [19] first summarised the neuroscientific research on the gastronomic experience in the brain (perception and processing of taste, etc.).

Taking all above mentioned into account, it can be said that there is a strong relationship between sensory marketing, aromachology, and neuroscience as consumers' responses can be measured in two ways, namely, (i) explicit tests: through direct consultation with consumers through surveys/questionnaires and (ii) implicit tests: using biometric parameter measurement equipment, for example, using eye trackers. These three applied sciences (sensory marketing, aromachology, and neuroscience) are closely interrelated.

Scent branding is quite popular in non-food stores, and one may recall certain brand scents, but it is not that common in food stores and restaurants. Most developments in this area have been driven by companies' needs, and carried out by private companies, with little knowledge shared with the public and scientific community [19]. The present work was carried out within the framework of the Erasmus + KA2 project NEUROSMARTOLOGY GY Strategic partnership Project No. 2018-1-SK01-KA203-046324. Implementation of Consumer Neuroscience and Smart Research Solutions in Aromachology. Very little information is available in the scientific literature regarding aromachology and much less on aromachology related to food. The present review aims to evaluate scientific evidence and knowledge on aromachology related to food. For this purpose, a literature review was conducted, focusing on the use of scents in restaurants, food establishments, and artificial laboratory conditions. A critical evaluation was performed on their aims, target population, place of the study, scents tested, foods tested, and measured parameters, and main findings were reviewed. Case studies carried out by a scent company are also presented. Results of the review may provide the scientific community with the state of the art on aromachology in food-related environments and a critical evaluation of the applied experimental procedures. The study may also help scientists, scent providers, food businesses, and consumers in understanding and developing solutions to better suit consumer needs and demands (enhanced customer experience related to food purchase or consumption, appetite modulation, etc.).

2. Literature Review Methods

2.1. Scientific Literature Review

The review is organised as a research paper. A scoping review was used to synthesise the evidence and assess the scope of the 18 studies on the topic. This review was based on the PRISMA Extension (PRISMA-ScR) approach [21] for Scoping Reviews. A comprehensive literature search—Scopus and ScienceDirect—was performed in April 2021 and was limited to articles published in English since 1990 (Figure 1). Text words and controlled vocabulary for several concepts (food, consumer, aroma, behaviour) within the titles, abstracts, and keywords, were used. Scopus, Web of Science, and Google Scholar were used for the literature search. Terms such as sensory marketing, scent marketing, aromachology, behaviour, consumers and food, etc., were used. The main focus was given to studies published in journals included in Journal Citation Reports, as well as sensory and aroma marketing books published by highly relevant publishers and only focused on food and food business. Only research papers including experimental design and data treatment were selected. The structure of the review allows dissection of how published studies have been conducted: population under study, number of participants, tested scents, location of the study (real or artificial laboratory conditions), foods evaluated, measured parameters (customer ballots, biometrics, etc.), aims of the studies, and major findings.

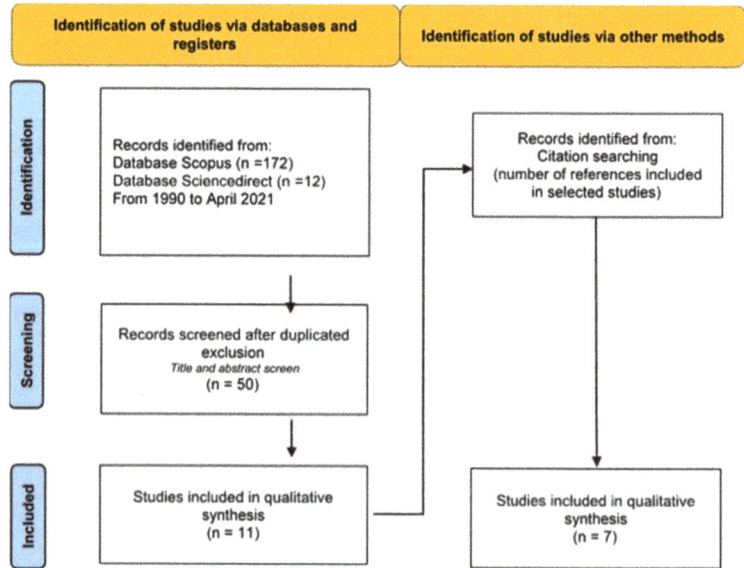

Figure 1. Flow diagram describing study selection process of scientific literature.

Table 1 presents the codification of the studies; the numbers given to each study are used in supplementary tables to cite them. Literature review methodology, objectives, and findings are presented in the table and briefly described to allow further discussion.

Table 1. Coding of revised manuscripts found linked to neuromarketing and aromachology in restaurants and food establishments, with its objectives and finding of the revised scientific evidence. Basic data on the experiments on reviewed papers: number of participants, characteristics of participants, and food/non-food used.

Study		Main Objectives	Findings	N	Characteristics of Participants	Material	Data Collected
			OBJECTIVE REAL BEHAVIOUR				
1	Guéguen and Petr [22]	To know the effect of two classical aromas diffused in a restaurant in order to test their effect on consumers' behaviour.	Lavender—but not lemon aroma—increased the length of stay of customers and the amount of purchasing, possibly linked to lavender relaxing effect.	88	Restaurant customers	Lemon and lavender scents in a pizzeria 17 pizzas, 4 types of meat, 3 fishes, and 4 salads.	Length of time and money spent at the pizzeria
2	Wada et al. [23]	To explore whether the ability to bind olfactory and visual information in object recognition is developed in infancy. The study explored the ability of infants to recognise the smell of daily foods, including strawberries and tomatoes.	Infants showed a preference for the congruent odour when they smelled the strawberry picture when they smelled the strawberry season. This olfactory-visual binding effect disappeared while strawberries were out of season.	Study 1: 37 Study 2: 26	Babies (6–8 month) Females	Non food (Digital photos of tomatoes and strawberries were taken for visual stimuli) Pieces of chocolate, cake and stroopwafel, beef croquette, cheese cubes and crisps, slice of melon, an apple and strawberries, piece of cucumber, tomato salad and raw carrot, bread, croissants, and pancake.	Infant looking time as assessed by recording Infant looking time as assessed by recording
3	Berčík et al. [24]	How aroma influences customer purchasing decision (preferences) in chosen service provider through the tracking of daily sales of baked baguettes (Paninis) with using of aroma equipment: Aroma Dispenser.	The acquired values were baked baguettes sales in a chosen period including aromatic stimulus, as a form of sales promotion, provides only a minimal effect. Nevertheless, an effect of specific odour was noticed on total sale of Paninis but only a small increase, which cannot be considered as economically efficient.	Unknown (real restaurant customers)	Customers of sports bar	Baguettes (Panini) released scents: 'crunchy bread' and 'chicken soup'	Sales and preference for specific baguettes measured in real conditions
4	Leenders et al. [25]	To test the effects of a pleasant and congruent ambient scent at different intensity levels in a real supermarket on shoppers' mood and their evaluations and in-store behaviours. To explore the moderating effects of shopper characteristics such as age and gender.	Shoppers tend to overestimate the amount of time spent shopping at lower intensity levels and underestimate time spent shopping at high scent intensity levels. The nature of the shopping trip is important because shoppers may be more or less aware of the ambiguous scent presence. In this case, grocery shoppers, there was ample variety in time pressure and age.	Unknown (real conditions)	Supermarket customers	Melon scent in a supermarket	Questionnaire: mood, overall evaluation of the store, and store environment. Real time spent in the store. Questionnaire on time pressure and pleasantness of the scent.

Table 1. Cont.

Study		Main objectives	Findings	N	Characteristics of Participants	Material	Data collected
5	Biswas and Szocs [26]	This research examines the effects of food-related ambient scents (indulgent and non-indulgent) on children's and adults' food purchases/choices. It aims to evaluate whether the perception of a food scent may induce reward and so reduce the need to seek rewards from gustatory food consumption.	Extended exposure (of more than two minutes) to an indulgent food-related ambient scent (e.g., cookie scent) leads to lower purchases of unhealthy foods compared with no ambient scent or a non-indulgent food-related ambient scent (e.g., strawberry scent). The effects seem to be driven by cross-modal sensory compensation, whereby prolonged exposure to an indulgent/rewarding food scent induces pleasure in the reward circuitry, which in turn diminishes the desire for actual consumption of indulgent foods. Notably, the effects reverse with brief (<30 s) exposure to the scent.	Study 1: 900	Middle School Students (middle school cafeteria)	Apple scent Pizza scents No scent	Sales of indulgent and non-indulgent foods under the three scenting conditions
				Study 2: 61	Laboratory consumer study	Cookies' scent Strawberry scent	Questionnaire to choose either cookies or strawberries under both scenting conditions
				Study 3: Unknown	Customers at a supermarket	Chocolate chip cookies scent Strawberry scent	Collecting customer receipts to register items purchased
				Study 4: Unknown (Students from a major University)	University students	Cookies' scent Strawberry scent	Questionnaire on food choice between indulgent and non-indulgent food
				Study 5: Unknown (Students with parental consent)	Middle School Students (middle school cafeteria)	Cookies' scent Apple scent	Questionnaire about feelings and reward
				Study 6: Unknown (Students from a major University)	University students	Cookies' scent Strawberry scent Tested for: high and low exposure time	Questionnaire on food choice between indulgent and non-indulgent food
				Study 7: Unknown (Students from a major University)	University students	Cookies' scent Strawberry scent No scent	Scent identification capability Food choice scale between pizza and salad
OBJECTIVE PHYSIOLOGICAL DATA							
6	Krishna et al. [27]	Effect of scent, image, and both in consumer response. Consumer response is measured by salivation change (studies 1 and 2), actual food consumption (study 3), and self-reported desire to eat (study 4).	Imagined odours can enhance consumer response but only when the consumer creates a vivid visual mental representation of the odour referent. The results demonstrate the interactive effects of olfactory and visual imagery in generating approach behaviours to food cues in advertisements. Scents can enhance consumers' responses.	Study 1: 59	Undergraduate students	Non food (Advertised food products: chocolate chip cookies)	Salivation.
				Study 2: 142	Undergraduate students	Non food (Advertised food products: chocolate chip cookies)	Salivation
				Study 3: 226	Undergraduate students	Non food (visual sensory input with a special focus on imagining pictures on food consumption). Cookies provided after the test	Food consumption
				Study 4: 170	Undergraduate students	Scent of chocolate chip cookies with a picture of chocolate chip cookies in the print ad.	Self-reported desire to eat

Table 1. Cont.

Study		Main objectives	Findings	N	Characteristics of Participants	Material	Data collected
7	Lin [28]	The focus of this dissertation is to understand the role of olfaction (sense of smell) in consumer behaviour.	Unpleasant odours raised stronger emotions than pleasant ones. Enhanced olfactory sensitivity (Hyperosmics) and normal individuals reacted in different ways to pleasant and unpleasant odours. Odour conditions affected food choices in both groups of individuals. Scenting enhanced preference for healthier food choices.	Study 1: 26	Students	Scents released from manufactured smell kits, Sniffin Sticks (Burghart, Germany), are utilised as odour stimuli. Twenty different odours are included.	Neuroimagery and questionnaire chemical sensitivity scale
				Study 2: 60	Students	15 pleasant odour-associated pictures, 15 unpleasant odour-associated pictures and 10 non-odour-associated pictures.	Neuroimagery and questionnaire chemical sensitivity scale
				Study 3: 19	Students	Non food (images of snacks)	Food choices questionnaire
				Study 4: 80	Students	Non food (images of snacks)	Food choices questionnaire
SUBJECTIVE DATA COLLECTION (EXPLICIT TEST)							
8	Knasko [29]	Two hypotheses were proposed: (i) subjects exposed to pleasant odours will spend more time looking at the food slides and give the slides better scores and (ii) when the odour of the room is conceptually congruent with a food slide, the slide will be viewed longer and be given higher ratings.	The thematic relationship between the ambient room-odour and the content of the photographic food slides did not play a role in this study. Rather, the results suggest that pleasant odours may have some general effects on humans due to their hedonic value. Congruency enhances pleasantness.	120	Age between 18–35	Non food (Slides with pictures: 6 chocolate items and 12 control slides of pine trees)	Questionnaires: mood, pleasantness, arousal, health symptoms (hunger and thirst)
9	Mitchell et al. [30]	To investigate the effects of pleasant ambient odours within two different decision-making contexts: (i) to examine how the congruency of the effects of ambient odour on the brands chosen and the related decision process and (ii) to investigate the effects of scent on multiple decisions.	Experiments 1 and 2 provided that the congruency of the odour with the target product class influences consumer decision making. When ambient odour was congruent with the product class, subjects spent more time processing the data.	77	Pennsylvania University Students	Chocolate assortments, and non-food test (flowers)	Questionnaires: memory and choice among chocolate assortments
10	Morrin and Ratneshwar [31]	To examine the relationship between ambient scent and brand memory in incidental learning task in which subjects were exposed to brand information through digital food photographs on a computer screen. Ambient scent was manipulated and stimulus viewing time was included.	It demonstrates that for studying the effects of ambient scent in marketing and consumer research settings, theory and methodological tools from cognitive psychology can be successfully adapted and applied to brand and product stimuli.	90	Students with good English level	Food spices plus non-food (brand recognition, other scents)	Questionnaire on food spices for pleasantness, liking, and appropriateness for food and beverages

Table 1. Cont.

Study		Main objectives	Findings	N	Characteristics of Participants	Material	Data collected
11	Bosmans [32]	To research the effects of pleasant ambient scents on evaluations: (i) the congruence of the scent with the product, (ii) the salience of the scent, and (iii) consumers' motivation to correct for extraneous influences.	Ambient scents strongly influenced customer evaluations. As long as ambient scents are congruent with the product, scents continue to affect consumers' evaluations, even when their influence becomes salient or when consumers are sufficiently motivated to correct for extraneous influences.	Study 1: 80	Undergraduate students	Orange	Questionnaire on product evaluation
				Study 2: 118	Undergraduate Students	Orange	Questionnaire on product evaluation
				Study 3: 75	Undergraduate students	Banana, apple, or tomato	Questionnaire on product evaluation
12	Yamada et al. [33]	To investigate whether olfactory information modulates the categorisation of visual objects and whether the preference for visual objects that correspond to olfactory information stems from the categorisation bias. Additionally, to elucidate these issues by using perceptible and imperceptible odour stimuli.	The authors employed morphed images of strawberries and tomatoes combined with their corresponding odorants as stimuli. Visual preference for novel fruits was based on both conscious and unconscious olfactory processing regarding edibility. There is an interaction between visual and olfactory information: odours did not affect categorisation but preference.	56	Students	Non food (pictures of tomato and strawberry) and scent release from subliminal to supraliminal	Questionnaire on evaluation and odour detection
13	Firmin et al. [34]	To assess the effect of the olfactory sense on chocolate craving in college females as influenced by fresh (criatmint) or sweet (vanilla) scents	Inhaling a fresh scent reduced females' craving levels; similarly, when a sweet scent was inhaled, the participants' craving levels for chocolate food increased. These findings are potentially beneficial for women seeking weight loss.	92	Student age 18–22	Non food (12 digital, coloured photographs of chocolate foods in the categories of chocolate cake, chocolate muffin, chocolate ice cream, and chocolate brownie). Fresh and sweet scents released for the evaluation	Place a ballot indicating craving level for chocolate
14	Zoon et al. [35]	To replicate the influence of olfactory cues on sensory-specific appetite for a certain taste category and extend those findings to energy-density categories of foods. Additionally, whether the hunger state plays a modulatory role in this effect.	Exposure to food odours increases appetite for congruent products, in terms of both taste and energy density, irrespective of hunger state. Food odours steer towards the intake of products with a congruent macronutrient composition.	29	Females	Pieces of chocolate, cake and stroopwafel, beef croquette, cheese cubes and crisps, slice of melon, an apple and strawberries, piece of cucumber, tomato salad and raw carrot, bread, croissants, and pancake.	Study conducted both under hunger and satiety conditions. Rating odour intensity, general appetite, and specific appetite for 15 foods
15	Ramaekers et al. [36]	To investigate how switching between sweet and savoury odours affects the appetite for sweets and savoury products	The appetite for the smelled food remained elevated during odour exposure, known as sensory-specific appetite, whereas the pleasantness of the odour decreased over time, previously termed olfactory sensory-specific satiety. The first minute of odour exposure may be of vital relevance for determining food preference.	30	Women	Cups with banana, meat, or water (no smell). Combinations (odourless/banana, odourless/meat, meat/banana, and banana/meat.)	Sequential exposure to two aromas, followed by appetite questionnaire and food preference

Table 1. *Cont.*

Study		Main objectives	Findings	N	Characteristics of Participants	Material	Data collected
		REVIEWS					
16	Krishna [5]	This review article presents an overview of research on sensory perception. The review also points out areas where little research has been conducted; therefore, each additional paper has a greater chance of making a bigger difference and sparking further research.	Still remains a tremendous need for research within the domain of sensory marketing, and such research can be very impactful.				
17	Paluchová [2]	This chapter is a summary of how the smell sense works through odour perception and its impact on consumer emotions and purchase decisions. Smell and memory are close terms, and their relationship is explained.	Either in a laboratory or in real conditions, air quality has to be respected and adapted for research and for spending time in each store.				
18	Spence and Carvalho [37]	Review: To summarise the evidence documenting the impact of the environment on the coffee-drinking experience. To demonstrate how many different aspects of the environment influence people's choice of what coffee to order/buy as well as what they think about the tasting experience.	The coffee-drinking experience (what we choose to drink and what we think about the experience) are influenced by product-extrinsic factors. There is a need to examine cross-cultural differences in consumers' choices of coffee to determine motivations for coffee consumption in different cultures.				

2.2. Case Studies from Scent Company

In addition to the scientific literature, case studies provided by REIMA Airconcept Company, which is a partner of the above-mentioned project are presented. On a regular basis, they develop scents and conduct studies in real conditions with their customers in order to provide solutions for customer needs, most of them protected by confidentiality agreements. Providing two case studies was the only contribution of the company; they did not take part in the manuscript. After reviewing the scientific literature and case studies provided by REIMA, a critical discussion is presented, aiming to point to future research needs on this field and detect fields that may benefit from an in-depth research on aromachology related to food.

3. Results and Discussion

3.1. Revision of Scientific Literature

Regarding aromachology focused on food, Table 1 shows the scientific manuscripts (reviews and articles) linked with the topic of this review, their main objectives, and findings. Only 18 studies related to aromachology on food were available, most of them on marketing or consumer studies journals, and most of them published within the last 10 years. Therefore, this a new field of scientific studies, with scarce background on the procedures, methodology, and an absence of standardised procedures, as we will discuss below.

What were the main aims of such studies? Some published studies reported results from more than one experiment. If we focus on real experiments, a total of 30 were reported. Twelve of the experiments explored food preferences or choices [26,28,30,32,33,36]; seven evaluated appetite modulation/effect [27,34–36]; three evaluated food sales ([24,26]; five evaluated odour–emotion mechanisms [26,28,29,31], and one the shopping experience (Table 1). The interest in aromachology comes from different fields, aroma marketing is probably the main field; however, scents as factors affecting appetite are an especially interesting field given that it can be useful to prevent obesity epidemics [26].

What were the methodologies used in the studies? Table 1 shows the main characteristics of the methodologies used in the reviewed studies: number of participants, characteristics of participants, food/non-food used, and type of collected data. 'Non food' means that pictures and slides were used to present food. Uneven details on participants have been provided in different studies; as an example, the number of participants is not given in several studies (unknown), mainly in studies performed in real conditions, when it is difficult to assess real numbers of customers. The number of participants ranged from 19 [28] to up to 900 [26]. Most available studies have been conducted with university students as participants, whereas just three on real restaurant or store customers [22,26,35,38]. Among the experiments reported in the selected papers, only eight were conducted in which real foods were present, i.e., real food choices could be made. In the others, only the scents or some pictures were used to recall the idea of food. Both types of studies are probably useful given that there are two types of scenarios: stores and gastronomic facilities. In some of the experiments, more than one type of data was collected (Table 1). Seventeen experiments collected subjective assessments in questionnaires. Nine of the experiments measured objective real behaviour: time measurement in five studies [22,23,25], sales in three studies [24,26], and food consumption in one study [27]). Finally, five studies measured objective physiological data: salivation in three experiments [27] and neuroimaging in two [28].

As previously commented, most studies relied on students as participants, and although valuable information was obtained from students, it is not clear to which extent a more complex population (diversity of ages, educational level, income level, etc.) will perceive or react to the tested scents in the same way, and therefore, if the results may be translated to market conditions. There are no standardised procedures to set target populations of consumer groups to conduct scent marketing studies, and some studies have been carried out only in women, mainly those regarding effects on appetite and food choices [23,35,36].

It is important to highlight that one of the aspects related to the aroma of an establishment is the number of people in it at any given time. In this, some studies in real conditions included air quality assessment [24] which is somehow related to the influx of visitors, among other factors; however, store influx has not been taken into consideration in the reviewed studies, where only three had been performed in real conditions [24–26]. In future studies in real conditions, air quality assessment should be considered. Chebat and Michon [39], in the context of a field experiment, varied the aroma along with the retail density (how crowded the mall was) and examined the perceptions of the buyers about the quality of the product, mall environment, and positive effect. They found a positive effect of ambient scent on shoppers' perceptions of the mall's atmosphere only at the medium retail density level. In addition, a favourable perception of the retail environment influenced the perception of product quality. Buyers' moods did not have a significant direct effect on perceptions of product quality.

What data were collected in the experiments? At present, almost 50 per cent of aromachology studies on food are based on subjective assessments collected under controlled conditions (questionnaires), and there is little evidence on the real effect of aromatisation on physiological responses and behaviour. Very little use of neuroscience tools has been reported so far in the scientific literature [28], and the measurement of physiological data is very limited [27]. Studies reviewed are a collection of individual contributions with scarce coincidences on methodology, and therefore, collected results are quite difficult to compare. Given the diversity of methods employed and parameters evaluated such studies cannot be compared or discussed as a whole. Another relevant point is that most studies are directed to evaluate food choices or appetite. The aims of scent use are not always directed only to enhance customer satisfaction, as in non-food stores, but mainly to modulate food consumption or to provide knowledge on understanding the effect of odour on consumer mood or behaviour. Given that the scent can modulate consumer behaviour, many types of studies with different purposes may be planned and may need different methodology and measured parameters.

Where did the studies take place? Most of the studies were conducted under artificial laboratory conditions (79%) mainly collecting data by computer-based assessments, and only three were conducted in real conditions with real customers (restaurant, store) (details in Table S1).

What were the most tested scents? Fruit scents were the most popular in the reviewed studies. The scents used in the scientific studies were grouped as follows into five distinct groups: sweets, fruits, salty, floral, and spices. Among the aroma groups used, the most commonly used were 'fruits' (31.4%), and 'floral' (29.4%), followed by 'salty' (17.6%), 'sweet' (15.7%), and 'spices' (5.9%) (details in Table S2). Flowers were tested in studies evaluating congruent aromas [30].

What were the main findings of the reviewed studies? Table 1 presents findings from individual studies that are summarised in this section. The use of pleasant scents enhanced pleasantness, and unpleasant odours raised stronger emotions than pleasant ones [28]. The use of ambient scents modified behaviour (time spent at stores or viewing food images) [22,23,25]. The presence of scent in general stores can slow the flow of customers in the store and therefore increase the time spent in the store [2]. Scenting affected consumer choices, and the effect of scents was enhanced by the congruency of the odour with the images, products, or even seasons [23,29,30,32,35]. Scents, hence olfactory perceptions, interact with visual perceptions or imagery [27,33]. Appetite was affected by odour exposure; however, nonconclusive results can be obtained from the reviewed studies. Knasko [29] reported that exposure to chocolate scent reduced the perceived hunger, and other pleasant scents (baby powder) also reduced hunger perception. Some authors reported that exposure to food odours increases the appetite for congruent foods, including sweets, [34,35] and that fresh scents reduced the craving for sweets. Some authors even concluded that exposure to food odours may promote overeating and therefore contribute to obesity [35]. Mechanisms explaining the appetite for congruent foods have not been elucidated; a theory has been proposed that cephalic phase responses mediated by the vagal nerve that prepare the body for intake and digestion may be involved [36,40]. It has been reported that the pleasantness of food odours (banana and savoury meat) was reduced during odour exposure, whereas the specific appetite for the congruent food remained unchanged, and hunger/general appetite was unaffected [36], This decreased odour pleasantness may be related to olfactory sensory-specific satiety (SSS), defined by Rolls et al. [41] as the decrease in the pleasantness of, or desire to, eat recently consumed foods, relative to uneaten foods, which suggest a lack of appetite for the smelled food; this does not match results obtained by previously cited studies. In this sense, Ramaeckers et al. [36,40] have coined the opposite term: sensory-specific-appetite (SSA), pointing to an enhanced appetite for the congruent food that is possibly explained by the fact that smelling the food anticipates food intake; these authors hypothesise that the extended exposure to the odour stimulates chemical senses and reduces the appeal for the odour but not for the taste, and therefore, different mechanisms would underlie both processed SSS and SSA. It is also hypothesised that the largest changes in food preferences may occur within the first minute to odour exposure; thus, it is of main relevance to study behaviour changes during that first minute. Several authors report that such effect depends on the exposure time to the scent: short times of exposure to sweet scents may enhance appetite for the food, whereas long times decreases the appeal for sweet foods and enhances the appeal for healthy or other choices [26,36,41,42]. This may be caused by cross modal sensory compensation; the scent provides enough reward and reduces the desire for consumption of indulgent foods, such as an olfactory sensory-specific satiety. Another factor to be considered is that the intensity of the scent is either subthreshold or recognisable, as different effects can be reported [20,43]. Fresh scents are thought to be associated with health care, good hygiene, and cleanliness, rather than being associated with sweets consumption [29,34]. Most of the published studies only collected and reported craving sensation or appeal, which are not truly food consumption; it needs to be clearly differentiated whether the studies report subjective measurements anticipating food intake (appetite, food choice) or actual food consumption (intake satiety), given that they cannot be directly extrapolated [20]; therefore, more studies are needed in real situations that measure actual consumed food to determine how to use scents to either prevent obesity or ameliorate malnutrition.

Reported results have similarities with those reported in non-food stores. Numerous studies have been carried out evaluating the effect of applying scents in non-food store environments [1,8,14,39,44–46]. Those studies reported that product sales increased between 14.8% and 15.9%, the time that customers spent in the store also increased by 18.8%, and interest on the purchased products and the request for information also increased [45]. Therefore, scents are used in stores to create a positive shopping environment with the aim of increasing purchase intention or increasing the time spent in the establishment [24]. All these factors are expected to lead to an increase in sales and in the degree of customer satisfaction [6]. Stores that use scents have been reported to give their customers the feeling that they spend less time looking at products and trying them [7,8,47]. Spangenberg et al. [47] exhaustively tested 26 individual essences and separated them into the affective dimension and the exciting or activating dimension. They found that the affective dimension explained most of the effects that scent produced in people. In parallel, they combined the effect of aroma (neutral versus pleasant) and its intensity (low, medium, high) and studied it with an additional control group. The authors found that whether the aroma was neutral or pleasant did not matter how intense the aroma was, as compared to the control group that had no aroma. Furthermore, they observed that subjects in the scented group reported noticing that they had spent less time in the store, compared to the unscented control group. On the other hand, subjects in the unscented group reported spending much more time in the store than they actually had. Subjects in the scent group did not show this discrepancy. Evaluations of the store, in general, and the store environment were more positive when the store was scented than if it was not. Most results obtained in the reviewed studies have been positive, presenting a clear correlation between the aroma used and the sensation produced in consumers, which is beneficial, because it leads to an increase in stay in supermarkets or restaurants, in addition to an increase in consumption or purchase of food as already found [45].

What are the reasons or mechanisms behind this positive response? The two most commonly used explanations can be separated by whether odour primarily influences unconscious effects, such as mood, or whether an odour primarily influences cognition. In the area of the commercial atmosphere, Mehrabian and Russell [48] discussed mood as a mediating factor between environmental cues and behaviour. Environmental psychologists claim that shoppers react to environmental cues with focus (desire to stay in the environment, explore, etc.) or avoidance behaviours (desire to leave) and that mood mediates this relationship. However, in the marketing literature, this explanation has not received strong support. Bone and Ellen [44] found that only a small percentage of the studies (16.1%) showed any influence of smell on mood. Another explanation for the process is that smell influences cognitive processes. Morrin and Ratneshwar [31] found no effect of scent on mood, but they found that scent increased attention to brands, as measured by display times for various brands [31,49]. Mitchell, Kahn, and Knasko [30] found that smell influenced the extent of information processing and cognitive elaborations. Chebat and Michon [39] tested various process theories and concluded that cognitions related to product quality and the shopping environment are influenced by smell, which in turn influenced the buyer's mood. As mentioned before, Herz [3] concluded that the most comprehensive theory was based on psychological mechanisms mediating the effect of odours on mood, physiology, and behaviour.

Another relevant factor is the congruence between the products offered by an establishment and its aroma. In this sense, Mitchell, Kahn, and Knasko [30] studied the effect of an ambient aroma congruent with a product category: a chocolate aroma was combined with an assortment of sweets and a floral aroma with a flower arrangement. If the aroma was congruent with the product, the subjects spent more time processing the data, generated more self-references, and were more likely to make additional inferences and exhibit a search behaviour for other purchase options. In general, cognitive elaboration was higher in congruent conditions. According to Berčí-k, Palúchová, Vietoris, and Horská [24], a pleasant aroma can affect the perception of the passage of time. It can also affect visual and taste perceptions [7,45] or create a generally pleasant environment for clients [46,50]. Another example is that the results of Guéguen and Petr [22] confirmed the hypothesis that scents have an influence on restaurant customers' behaviour. The study found that both the length of time and amount of money spent were positively affected by lavender in pizzeria restaurants (small choice of dishes: 17 pizzas, 4 types of meat, 3 fishes, and 4 salads). However, the lemon aroma was found to have no effect on either of the above two variables.

3.2. Case Studies

In addition to data from the scientific literature, we had access to real data from customer applications from a scent company, thus in the specific application of sensory marketing.

One of the studies was conducted in a small cafe with a patisserie serving and selling both chocolates and cakes located at Gottingen (Germany). In this café, the scent Coffee & Cake (REIMA Airconcept) was used. Due to the existing outdoor area in front of the cafe, the fragrance device was placed in the entrance area. This allowed the scent to waft outside a little bit as well. During the test period (7 weeks: half of the period scented and the other half without scent), customers had handy questionnaires requesting their age, sex, date of visit, time spent, and opinion on the atmosphere. In total, 30 people took part in the survey. One of the participants was not considered because the survey was not completed, in addition to another three who did not indicate the date of the cafe visit.

Therefore, 26 participants were left. The range of ages of the participants was 33–46 years (17 females and 9 males). Nine of them (30%) were in the range between 30–40 years. The average length of stay at the café was 1 h and 8 min. During the fragrance phase, 16 people participated in the survey, while in the non-perfumed phase, 10 people participated. The rating was performed according to the German school grading system (GPA): from 1—very good/completely to 6—insufficient/not at all right. The perfumed phase was rated at 1.65 and the non-perfumed one at 1.95. Looking at the sexes, there was a small difference between the grading of the two phases among women. However, men rated the two periods much more clearly. Here, the rating during scenting was 1.61. Subsequently, men rated the atmosphere only with a grade of 2.78. This is a clear divergence and could be an indication of the influence of the fragrance. Another peculiarity can be seen by dividing the whole group by age. Odour perception was most pronounced between the ages of 30 and 40. This can be justified based on the fact that the participants between 30 and 40 years assessed the atmosphere during the scented phase with 1.72 and the unscented with 2.83. This clear difference cannot be determined in the other age groups, with a tiny difference of only 0.11 points. As another aspect observed in this age range, male participants gave much better marks than female ones. In conclusion, the most positive evaluation of the café atmosphere was obtained during the fragrance phase and especially by men.

A second food establishment was an eatery, which was part of a larger chain, offering Tex-Mex dishes, burgers, and snacks, as well as cocktails and desserts. In addition to a large guest room inside the restaurant, which extended over two floors, there was also a large outdoor area with lounge character. The interior was rustic style. The restaurant had an open kitchen, through which odours from the kitchen can waft in the guest room (fatty and roasted aromas). Two devices of the type AromaStreamer 750 with the intensity level 3 (REIMA Airconcept) were placed in the guest room (interior about 250 m^2). The scent curry-pepper marinade was used to match the kitchen flavours (REIMA Airconcept). During the test period (7 weeks: first half scented, second non-scented) a questionnaire was provided to consumers asking: date, age, sex, residence time, rate the atmosphere if (pleasant, cozy, stimulating, unpleasant) and the question: how well do you feel today? In total, 54 people participated in the survey (36 females and 18 males). The range of ages 29–68 years (34 (63%) 20–30 years; 10 (18.5%) 30–40 years; 5 (9.3%) 40–50 years; 2 (3.7%) 50–60 years; 3 (5.6%) not specified). The high participation, as compared to the experience at the café, was probably due to the fact that there was a coupon worth EUR 30 to win. Four participants were excluded: three because their survey was not completely finished and one that specified a residence time of 20 h. Overall, this resulted in the usable participation of 50 people. The rating was performed according to the German school grading system, as in the previous study. In the evaluation of the data of this restaurant, there were sometimes clear differences in the rating but sometimes very marginal. The overall average of the criteria 'pleasant', 'cozy', and 'stimulating' showed that the participants rated these criteria better (average 2.33), during the scenting phase than afterwards (2.42). There were only small differences between sexes, both before and after scenting experiment, although there was a tendency for women to rate the atmosphere slightly better than men. The criterion 'unpleasant' showed only a difference of 0.08 points: during the scenting experiment, this criterion was rated at 5.42, followed by 5.50 during the non-scent phase, meaning that on both phases customers disagreed or strongly disagreed with the description of the restaurant as 'unpleasant'. A relatively large difference was seen in the question 'How well do you feel?': during the perfumed phase, the restaurant reached a mark of 1.96, while after the perfumed phase, the average rate was 2.50. The difference became clearer when splitting the ratings between women and men. Men averaged 2.07 during and 3.00 after the fragrance phase. For women, the difference with the grade 1.91 to 2.00 was only 0.09 points. This shows a markedly differentiated rating between the two periods, which is an indication of the actual effect of the scenting. The average length of stay in the restaurant was 2 h and 13 min during, and 2 h and 15 min after the scent period. Again, the difference was very marginal. Thus, it could not be proven whether the scenting had an effect on the length of stay of the guests; the only clear trend is that men felt better during the scenting phase.

Those are two real examples provided by a company in which data were collected through questionnaires for consumers. The company carries out many more types of studies to develop real applications, but the effectiveness of the scents is directly evaluated by their clients through real sales of food products, with no need of contacting customers. Such case studies are confidential and cannot be shared to be published. We can still analyse the two case studies presented and the main difficulties of studies performed in real conditions. The present cases are evaluations of applications for a small business. Gathering 30 to 50 surveys within 7 weeks is considered quite low numbers for conducting reliable research. From the results, one may guess that the youth and men are more influenced and better discriminate whether the atmosphere is scented or not, but still, total numbers are low. In addition, it cannot be proven to what extent those participants represent regular customers of the establishment, which is probably the reason why in real conditions, total sales are the best indicators for food business, and, if possible, implicit measurements of neuroscience-related and physiologically based sensations should be considered. Small businesses need to measure whether the investment in aromatisation unit plus scents is worthwhile in the short term.

3.3. Improvements, Trends, and Future Research on Aromachology Related to Food

Aromachology related to foods may have different applications; the most active fields are sensory marketing and appetite modulation. Although extensively used in non-food businesses, scent marketing would be also of great interest to food businesses, and purposes such as brand identity or specific developments to suit needs and enhance consumer satisfaction would be of interest. Much more interesting would be the use of scents for modulating appetite, which will be an interesting tool to be included in anti-obesity strategies.

Scents in sensory marketing: Copyright of a scent as food establishment identity. Transferring laboratory findings into products is neither an easy nor a quick process, and it is now starting to see the development of products and marketing campaigns that are properly incorporating scents into food establishments and/or experiences. Should it be possible to copyright or trademark a scent? From the perspective of marketers, an affirmative response will increase the scent marketing industry. Currently, only scents that are non-functional can be trademarked, and it is still not easy to obtain a scent trademark. As a clear example, an orange juice company could not trademark the scent of oranges, but if the same scent were adopted by an automobile or electronics company, that company might be able to prevent its competitors from copying that aroma [51]. One relevant factor to consider in scent marketing is the opinion and well-being of employees. They are exposed to the scent during their entire working session, and they should be able to feel comfortable under such conditions. Air turnover also needs to be considered, as well as air quality and airflow. Scents need to be congruent with the store location and not interfere with the scent of fresh food to avoid masking, confusing, or generating off-flavours. All those considerations are taken into account by scent companies when developing applications for their customers.

Research effect of scents to suit specific needs: the example of food consumed in aeroplanes. Scent branding is a well-established practice in airports and planes [52], but it requires careful consideration. While some may find aromas soothing, others find them intrusive, and some passengers may have an unpleasant flight experience. A Spanish aircraft company has introduced an aroma called 'Mediterráneo', which mainly has notes of lemon, bergamot, and citrus blossoms. Heathrow Airport (London) applied this concept at Terminal 2, giving passengers a whiff of exotic destinations within reach of the airport [52]. There is an issue regarding airlines' food service: Food consumed on airplanes does not taste as that consumed on land. Recent studies suggested that various factors such as low pressures, the decrease of the level of humidity, and the noise perceived inside the plane may be responsible for the decreased perception. The degree of decreased perception has been determined for sweet and salty tastes: salty taste is reduced up to 30% and sweet up to 20% when foods are consumed during flights [53]. However, real causes are currently unknown, and more studies are needed under real conditions for a better knowledge of the condition. Aromachology may be explored to provide solutions to overcome such a decrease in taste perception.

Generating general accurate scales for scent in restaurants/food establishments: data collection procedures. Regarding methodology, the collection of data through questionnaires shows clear limitations under real conditions. Wrzesniewski et al. [54] developed a scale measuring individual differences in the affective impact of odours on places, objects, and people. Among others, one promising direction for future research would be to develop a general scale measuring the susceptibility of an individual to using scent as an input for decisions and evaluations. Efforts can be made to enhance the reliability of questionnaires; however, collecting objective data (implicit tests) would be much more helpful and reliable. In this sense, the use of neuroscience tools and physiological measurements needs to gain a place in the methodology applied to aromachology on food.

Future needs. Most relevant future needs include in-depth research on scents use as appetite modulators (either to tackle malnutrition or obesity), which is not the main topic of this review but a matter of high interest for consumers, and the use of neuroscience tools and physiological measurements to gather human responses trying to avoid subjective data. Regarding marketing studies in the scientific literature, they may benefit from the development of standard methodology and recommended experimental designs (number of participants, place, time, etc.), and there is a clear need of conducting studies in real conditions (stores, restaurants, food business) with real food, as most of the available studies were conducted in artificial conditions. It has been pointed out that very few studies have been carried out in real store environments, and those studies had limitations: reduced number of participants, uneven participation during different phases, and the fact that explicit measurements have also limitations (are they given by the most representative customers? are they influenced by other factors such as noise?). Such observations point to the need of using implicit measurements (assessed by tools measuring body responses neuroscience and physiological-related parameters) and other measurements such as sales of different goods (either related or unrelated to the scent). Additionally, data collected from the stores should be compared between scented and unscented periods, as well as with data collected from the same period from the previous years or similar establishments during the same period. Air quality assessment during the studies will provide valuable information on the level of occupation of the establishment and proper ventilation conditions and health conditions for employees and customers (CO_2 concentration, particles in suspension, and volatiles in the air). Other points in need of attention are ethical issues, whether consumers agree with the use of food scents in food environments, and if they had to be regulated to avoid the use of scents that may mask unwanted flavours or enhance the scent of low-quality products.

4. Conclusions

A small number of scientific studies on aromachology related to food are available, and most of them are conducted in artificial laboratory conditions. The most common aim is food preference and choice, followed by the study of the effects of odour on appetite; other interests are sales, shopping experience, and the study on mechanisms connecting odour and emotions. Participants through questionnaires provide most of the data collected, with a scarce number of studies using neuroscience and physiological tools and measurements. Methodological procedures largely diverge among studies, making them very difficult to compare and extrapolate results. The reviewed literature points to a greater effect of scents when they are congruent with the food, to the fact that unpleasant scents raise stronger emotions than pleasant ones, to a clear effect of scents on food preference and appetite mediated by the scent and the exposure time, as well as other effects on human behaviour. There is a clear need for research on aromachology related to food in the fields of both sensory marketing and appetite modulation. At present, the effect of odours on appetite/food intake is not clear and consistent among studies and may depend on exposure time to scents. This field is in need of studies evaluating the effect of scent exposure during the first minute on real food intake, not just on appetite or preferences. Only when the real effect of scent on food intake is determined may scents be potentially used in anti-obesity strategies. The methodology for scent studies is in clear need of improvement by working in real conditions and introducing neuroscience tools and real physiological measurements.

Supplementary Materials: The following are available online at https://www.mdpi.com/article/10.3390/app11136095/s1. Table S1: Type of place in which the study was carried on each reviewed study, Table S2: Scents used in the reviewed studies.

Funding: This publication has been supported by the Erasmus+ KA2 Strategic Partnerships Grant No. 2018-1-SK01-KA203-046324 'Implementation of Consumer Neuroscience and Smart Research Solutions in Aromachology' (NEUROSMARTOLOGY). The European Commission's support for the production of this publication does not constitute an endorsement of the contents, which reflect the views only of the authors, and the Commission cannot be held responsible for any use which may be made of the information contained therein.

Institutional Review Board Statement: Not applicable.

Informed Consent Statement: Not applicable.

Data Availability Statement: Not applicable.

Acknowledgments: REIMA AirConcept GmbH, Meerane (Germany) for providing information on real case studies.

Conflicts of Interest: The authors declare no conflict of interest. The funders had no role in the design of the study; in the collection, analyses, or interpretation of data; in the writing of the manuscript, or in the decision to publish the results.

References

1. Lindstrom, M. Brand sense: How to build powerful brands through touch, taste, smell, sight and sound. *Strateg. Dir.* **2006**, 22. [CrossRef]
2. Paluchová, J.; Berčík, J.; Horská, E. The sense of smell. In *Sensory and Aroma Marketing*; Sendra-Nadal, E., Carbonell-Barrachina, Á.A., Eds.; Wageningen Academic Publishers: Wageningen, The Netherlands, 2017; p. 33.
3. Herz, R.S. Aromatherapy facts and fictions: A scientific analysis of olfactory effects on mood, physiology and behavior. *Int. J. Neurosci.* **2009**, *119*, 263–290. [CrossRef]
4. Ferdenzi, C.; Delplanque, S.; Barbosa, P.; Court, K.; Guinard, J.-X.; Guo, T.; Craig Roberts, S.; Schirmer, A.; Porcherot, C.; Cayeux, I.; et al. Affective semantic space of scents. Towards a universal scale to measure self-reported odor-related feelings. *Food Qual. Prefer.* **2013**, *30*, 128–138. [CrossRef]
5. Krishna, A. An integrative review of sensory marketing: Engaging the senses to affect perception, judgment and behavior. *J. Consum. Psychol.* **2012**, *22*, 332–351. [CrossRef]
6. Mendlikova, P. Smyslový a Emoční. Master's Thesis, University of Economics in Prague, Prague, Czechia, 2011.
7. Levy, M.; Weitz, A.B.; Grewal, D. *Retailing Management*, 8th ed.; MC Graw-Hill: New York, NY, USA, 2021; p. 675.
8. Peck, J.; Childers, T.L. Effects of sensory factors on consumer behavior: If it tastes, smells, sounds, and feels like a duck, then it must be a... In *Handbook of Consumer Psychology*; Taylor & Francis Group/Lawrence Erlbaum Associates: New York, NY, USA, 2008; pp. 193–219.
9. Schifferstein, H.N.J.; Blok, S.T. The signal function of thematically (in)congruent ambient scents in a retail environment. *Chem. Senses* **2002**, *27*, 539–549. [CrossRef] [PubMed]
10. Hanlon, M. Citroen Adds a Sense of Smell to the New c4. 2 June 2005. Available online: https://newatlas.com/citroen-adds-a-sense-of-smell-to-the-new-c4/3643/ (accessed on 29 June 2021).
11. Clark, P.; Esposito, M. *Running Head: Management Overview of Scent as a Marketing Communications Tool*; SMC Working Paper; Swiss Management Center: Hong Kong, 2009.
12. Butcher, D. Aromatherapy—Its past and future. *Drug Cosmet. Ind.* **1998**, *162*, 22–25.
13. Henshaw, V.; Medway, D.; Warnaby, G.; Perkins, C. Marketing the 'city of smells'. *Mark. Theory* **2016**, *16*, 153–170. [CrossRef]
14. Teller, C.; Dennis, C. The effect of ambient scent on consumers' perception, emotions and behaviour: A critical review. *J. Mark. Manag.* **2012**, *28*, 14–36. [CrossRef]
15. Verissimo, J.; Pereira, R.A. The effect of ambient scent on moviegoers' behavior. *Port. J. Manag. Stud.* **2013**, *18*, 67–79.

16. Shen, J.; Niijima, A.; Tanida, M.; Horii, Y.; Maeda, K.; Nagai, K. Olfactory stimulation with scent of lavender oil affects autonomic nerves, lipolysis and appetite in rats. *Neurosci. Lett.* **2005**, *383*, 188–193. [CrossRef] [PubMed]
17. Vlahos, J. Scent and Sensibility. The New York Times 2007. Available online: https://www.nytimes.com/2007/09/09/realestate/keymagazine/909SCENT-txt.html (accessed on 29 June 2021).
18. Štetka, P. Scent Marketing Alebo Aromamarketing. Útok Predajcov na Ďalší náš Zmysel. Štetka, P. 2012. Available online: https://peterstetka.wordpress.com/2012/12/09/scent-marketing-alebo-aromamarketing-utok-predajcov-na-dalsi-nas-zmysel/ (accessed on 29 June 2021).
19. Berčík, J.; Paluchová, J.; Neomániová, K. Neurogastronomy as a tool for evaluating emotions and visual preferences of selected food served in different ways. *Foods* **2021**, *10*, 354. [CrossRef]
20. Boesveldt, S.; de Graaf, K. The differential role of smell and taste for eating behavior. *Perception* **2017**, *46*, 307–319. [CrossRef] [PubMed]
21. Page, M.J.; McKenzie, J.E.; Bossuyt, P.M.; Boutron, I.; Hoffmann, T.C.; Mulrow, C.D.; Shamseer, L.; Tetzlaff, J.M.; Akl, E.A.; Brennan, S.E.; et al. The prisma 2020 statement: An updated guideline for reporting systematic reviews. *BMJ (Clin. Res. Ed.)* **2021**, *372*, n71.
22. Guéguen, N.; Petr, C. Odors and consumer behavior in a restaurant. *Int. J. Hosp. Manag.* **2006**, *25*, 335–339. [CrossRef]
23. Wada, Y.; Inada, Y.; Yang, J.; Kunieda, S.; Masuda, T.; Kimura, A.; Kanazawa, S.; Yamaguchi, M.K. Infant visual preference for fruit enhanced by congruent in-season odor. *Appetite* **2012**, *58*, 1070–1075. [CrossRef]
24. Berčí-k, J.; Palúchová, J.; Vietoris, V.; Horská, E. Placing of aroma compounds by food sales promotion in chosen services business. *Potravin. Slovak J. Food Sci.* **2016**, *10*, 672–679. [CrossRef]
25. Leenders, M.A.A.M.; Smidts, A.; Haji, A.E. Ambient scent as a mood inducer in supermarkets: The role of scent intensity and time-pressure of shoppers. *J. Retail. Consum. Serv.* **2019**, *48*, 270–280. [CrossRef]
26. Biswas, D.; Szocs, C. The smell of healthy choices: Cross-modal sensory compensation effects of ambient scent on food purchases. *J. Mark. Res.* **2019**, *56*, 123–141. [CrossRef]
27. Krishna, A.; Morrin, M.; Sayin, E. Smellizing cookies and salivating: A focus on olfactory imagery. *J. Consum. Res.* **2013**, *41*, 18–34. [CrossRef]
28. Lin, M. Individual Differences in the Impact of Odor-Induced Emotions on Consumer Behavior. Ph.D. Thesis, Iowa State University, Ames, IA, USA, 2014.
29. Knasko, S.C. Pleasant odors and congruency: Effects on approach behavior. *Chem. Senses* **1995**, *20*, 479–487. [CrossRef]
30. Mitchell, D.J.; Kahn, B.E.; Knasko, S.C. There's something in the air: Effects of congruent or incongruent ambient odor on consumer decision making. *J. Consum. Res.* **1995**, *22*, 229–238. [CrossRef]
31. Morrin, M.; Ratneshwar, S. Does it make sense to use scents to enhance brand memory? *J. Mark. Res.* **2003**, *40*, 10–25. [CrossRef]
32. Bosmans, A. Scents and sensibility: When do (in)congruent ambient scents influence product evaluations? *J. Mark.* **2006**, *70*, 32–43. [CrossRef]
33. Yamada, Y.; Sasaki, K.; Kunieda, S.; Wada, Y. Scents boost preference for novel fruits. *Appetite* **2014**, *81*, 102–107. [CrossRef]
34. Firmin, M.W.; Gillette, A.L.; Hobbs, T.E.; Wu, D. Effects of olfactory sense on chocolate craving. *Appetite* **2016**, *105*, 700–704. [CrossRef]
35. Zoon, H.F.A.; de Graaf, C.; Boesveldt, S. Food odours direct specific appetite. *Foods* **2016**, *5*, 12. [CrossRef]
36. Ramaekers, M.G.; Luning, P.A.; Lakemond, C.M.M.; van Boekel, M.A.J.S.; Gort, G.; Boesveldt, S. Food preference and appetite after switching between sweet and savoury odours in women. *PLoS ONE* **2016**, *11*, e0146652. [CrossRef] [PubMed]
37. Spence, C.; Carvalho, F.M. The coffee drinking experience: Product extrinsic (atmospheric) influences on taste and choice. *Food Qual. Prefer.* **2020**, *80*, 103802. [CrossRef]
38. Spence, C. Book review: 'Neurogastronomy: How the brain creates flavor and why it matters' by gordon m. Shepherd. *Flavour* **2012**, *1*, 21. [CrossRef]
39. Chebat, J.-C.; Michon, R. Impact of ambient odors on mall shoppers' emotions, cognition, and spending: A test of competitive causal theories. *J. Bus. Res.* **2003**, *56*, 529–539. [CrossRef]
40. Ramaekers, M.G.; Boesveldt, S.; Lakemond, C.M.; van Boekel, M.A.; Luning, P.A. Odors: Appetizing or satiating? Development of appetite during odor exposure over time. *Int. J. Obes.* **2014**, *38*, 650–656. [CrossRef]
41. Rolls, B.J.; Rolls, E.T.; Rowe, E.A.; Sweeney, K. Sensory specific satiety in man. *Physiol. Behav.* **1981**, *27*, 137–142. [CrossRef]
42. Nowlis, S.; Shiv, B.; Wadhawa, M. *Smelling Your Way to Satiety: Impact of Odor Satiation on Subsequent Consumption Related Behaviors*; Angela, Y., Ed.; Advances in Consumer Research Volume 35; Association for Consumer Research; Lee and Dilip Soman: Duluth, MN, USA, 2008; pp. 169–172.
43. Gaillet-Torrent, M.; Sulmont-Rossé, C.; Issanchou, S.; Chabanet, C.; Chambaron, S. Impact of a non-attentively perceived odour on subsequent food choices. *Appetite* **2014**, *76*, 17–22. [CrossRef] [PubMed]
44. Bone, F.P.; Ellen, S.P. Scents in the marketplace: Explaining a fraction of olfaction. *J. Retail.* **1999**, *75*, 243–262. [CrossRef]
45. Bradford, K.D.; Desrochers, D.M. The use of scents to influence consumers: The sense of using scents to make cents. *J. Bus. Ethics* **2009**, *90*, 141–153. [CrossRef]
46. Kardes, F.R.; Cronley, M.L.; Cline, T.W. *Consumer Behavior*, 2nd ed.; Cengage India: Noida, India, 2014.
47. Spangenberg, E.R.; Grohmann, B.; Sprott, D.E. It's beginning to smell (and sound) a lot like christmas: The interactive effects of ambient scent and music in a retail setting. *J. Bus. Res.* **2005**, *58*, 1583–1589. [CrossRef]

48. Mehrabian, A.; Russell, J.A. *An Approach to Environmental Psychology*; The MIT Press: Cambridge, MA, USA, 1974.
49. Morrin, M.; Ratneshwar, S. The impact of ambient scent on evaluation, attention, and memory for familiar and unfamiliar brands. *J. Bus. Res.* **2000**, *49*, 157–165. [CrossRef]
50. Tarczydło, B. Scents and elements of aroma marketing in building of an appropriate brand image. In Proceedings of the International Scentific Conference of the College of Management and Quality Sciences of the Cracow University of Economics, 4–6 June 2014; Andrzej Jaki, B.M., Ed.; Foundation of the Cracow University of Economics: Crakow, Poland, 2014; pp. 97–107.
51. Office, Legal Patent Meyer-Dulheuer MD Legal Patentanwälte PartG mbB U.P.A.T. Protecting Scent Trademarks (1): Practically Possible in the Us—Rather Difficult in the EU. 2012. Available online: https://legal-patent.com/trademark-law/scent-trademark-us-and-eu/ (accessed on 29 June 2021).
52. APEX. *Scents of Place: Airlines Apply Aromas for Passenger Comfort*; The Airline Passenger Experience Association: New York, NY, USA, 2016; Available online: https://apex.aero/articles/scents-place-airlines-apply-aromas-passenger-comfort/ (accessed on 29 June 2021).
53. Zumaya, N.; Reyes, P.A.; Baruch Díaz Ramírez, J. La ciencia de la comida en los aviones. *Rev. Cienc.* **2021**, *68*, 7.
54. Wrzesniewski, A.; McCauley, C.; Rozin, P. Odor and affect: Individual differences in the impact of odor on liking for places, things and people. *Chem. Senses* **1999**, *24*, 713–721. [CrossRef]

Systematic Review

Aromachology and Customer Behavior in Retail Stores: A Systematic Review

Davide Giacalone [1,*], Bartłomiej Pierański [2] and Barbara Borusiak [2]

1. Department of Technology and Innovation, University of Southern Denmark, Campusvej 55, 5230 Odense M, Denmark
2. Department of Commerce and Marketing, Poznan University of Economics and Business, Al. Niepodległości 10, 61-875 Poznan, Poland; bartlomiej.pieranski@ue.poznan.pl (B.P.); barbara.borusiak@ue.poznan.pl (B.B.)
* Correspondence: dg@iti.sdu.dk

Citation: Giacalone, D.; Pierański, B.; Borusiak, B. Aromachology and Customer Behavior in Retail Stores: A Systematic Review. *Appl. Sci.* **2021**, *11*, 6195. https://doi.org/10.3390/app11136195

Academic Editor: Maurizio Faccio

Received: 4 May 2021
Accepted: 28 June 2021
Published: 3 July 2021

Publisher's Note: MDPI stays neutral with regard to jurisdictional claims in published maps and institutional affiliations.

Copyright: © 2021 by the authors. Licensee MDPI, Basel, Switzerland. This article is an open access article distributed under the terms and conditions of the Creative Commons Attribution (CC BY) license (https:// creativecommons.org/licenses/by/ 4.0/).

Abstract: Interest in the use of scents in retail environments for creating better customer experiences is growing. Yet, knowledge of the effectiveness of aromachology to affect actual customer behavior and ultimately increase turnover is incomplete, as published results present inconsistencies and are often based on highly controlled environments rather than actual store environments. Situated within this context, this paper offers a systematic review on research in aromachology with a focus on effects on actual customer behavior in actual retail environments. As expected, the available research on actual environments (relative to laboratory-based studies) is limited, with only 20 articles meeting the inclusion criteria. While reported results are, overall, indicative of the positive effects of scent on customers' emotional states and on their in-store behavior (dwell time, product choices) and attitudes (purchase intention, intention to revisit), several critical issues with the available literature emerged. These pertain primarily to a lack of sufficient methodological details (specifically on the scents, their compositions, intensity and methods of delivery), a narrow focus on scents without considering interactions with other atmospherics factors, and a general disregard of individual differences in olfaction. The review provides suggestions for addressing these shortcomings and improving the quality and actionability of this line of research.

Keywords: aromachology; scent marketing; retailing; customer behavior

1. Introduction

For centuries, scents have been used for religious purposes, in traditional treatments as well as in everyday life. From the very beginning of civilization, people realized that scents regarded as pleasant may have a good influence on their mood, health, and their social position perception [1]. Nowadays, scents are also widely used for business purposes and have become an interesting field of study focusing on factors influencing consumer behavior and well-being [2–4]. This, to a large extent, is a result of the growing interest in environmental psychology, which deals with interrelationships between individuals and their physical settings, and the way individual behaviors and experiences are affected by environmental factors [5]. An often applied approach to examine the impact of the environment on people experiences is Stimulus-Organism-Response model, which emerged in the middle of 1960s [6]. It was developed later by Mehrabian and Russell [7], who focused on three dimensions expressing the emotional state of an individual (pleasure, arousal and dominance), which results in approach or avoidance responses. That model received a lot of attention from researchers as a promising method to detect how to induce a desirable behavior in people by design of environmental settings [8]. Both service and retail companies are highly interested in creating strong and appealing in-store experiences, and the use of scents is, in this context, generally regarded as a potential source of competitive advantage [9]: for example, scents may be used to differentiate the brand in an increasingly competitive market where the usual marketing mix is not sufficient (an example being major clothing chains such as Abercrombie & Fitch and hotel companies such as Marriot being noted for their signature scents), as well as generally to provide better in-store experiences to their customers and increase their spending and likelihood of revisiting the store.

The customer experience is a complex construct mainly because it is affected by numerous elements, only some of which are controlled by the retailer. It is based on the set of interactions between a customer and a product or/and a company and also between a customer and other customers, which generate a reaction [10–12]. Schmitt [13] distinguishes five types of experiences: sensory (sense), affective (feel), cognitive (think), physical (act), and social-identity (relate). Sensory experience is created by the retail outlet atmosphere (referred to as "atmospherics" and regarded as a marketing tool), which is based on the sensory channels: sight, sound, touch, and smell [14]. Additionally, the current concept of retail atmospherics—design–ambient–social–trialability (DAST)—acknowledges odors as an important ambient factor and potentially powerful instrument used for customer experience building [15].

The term "aromachology" first appeared in 1982 to denote the science that is dedicated to the study of the relationship between psychology and scents to elicit a variety of specific emotions, such as relaxation, exhilaration, sensuality, happiness and well-being. Indeed, the sense of smell is considered to be the one most closely related to emotional reactions, as the olfactory bulb is directly connected to the areas of the brain (collectively known as the limbic system) that deal with emotion and memory [16,17]. Moreover, the sense of smell is emotionally processed and, unlike other sensory modalities, does not require consciously attending to any stimulus and instead exerts emotional consequences without conscious perception of the odor itself [18,19]. Due to these characteristics, interest in the use of scents to affect human behavior has been steadily increasingly [4,20]. In recent years, several studies have been published concerning usage of aromas in a retail environment (shops, restaurants, etc.), and interest in aromachology (as well as retail atmospherics more generally) has been steadily increasing [2–4,20,21].

Historically, the majority of studies who have sought to explain the effect of scents on customer behavior have considered one or both of the following two theoretical frameworks:

1. The already mentioned Stimulus-Organism-Response (S-O-R) paradigm [1,7,22], in which scents generate affective and cognitive responses in consumers (e.g., pleasantness, arousal), which, in turn, affect approach or avoidance behaviors towards products. From an applied perspective, if retailers introduce a positively valenced scent, customers' experience with the store, dwelling time and ultimately purchases will be enhanced;
2. A thematic congruency theory [23–25] proposing that the effect of scents on behavior depends on their perceived congruency with their target product; in this framework, scents can become a signal or facilitator for drawing attention towards specific products, meaning that when there is a match between the product and the scent, an effect can be expected.

It is apparent and should be emphasized that these theories are not mutually exclusive. Schifferstein and Blok [26] explain this with anecdotal example, involving the smell of freshly baked bread, which both gives consumers a pleasant experience (fresh bread smells good), but it also communicates information about the presence and the characteristics of the products, for example, it signals that the bread is fresh and probably still warm. This means that the smell of bread can have consequences for customer behavior in general and for the behavior towards the focal product (bread) and related products (e.g., bakery items).

The available literature offers some degree of support for both theories. Several of the available studies reported positive effects of scent applied in a shop on customers' emotional states and on their in-store behavior, measured in terms of dwell time and product choices [27], as well as on stated attitudes such as purchase intention and likelihood to revisit the store [2,28]. Some studies also suggested that scent may influence the amount of money spent [2], although other studies indicated that this relationship may be more complex. For instance, Herrmann and collaborators [29] found that a simple scent increased actual spending, whereas a more complex scent had no such effect. Such effects are often moderated by the congruency of the scent with the object, in accordance with the second theory [30].

Nevertheless, several "null" results have also been reported (e.g., [26]). This is possibly due to differences in the type of product and environments considered, as well as in variation in methodological aspects—for example, the intensity of the scent and whether it was consciously experienced or not, which is very important because the emotional effects of odors are different depending on whether or not they are consciously perceived [18]. Moreover, according to some (e.g., [31]), in a retail context the ambient scent could have negative effects if they were perceived by consumers as a marketing tool to influence their behavior (at least in absence of elements justifying the presence of that smell). These inconsistencies in the results, however, suggest that the knowledge of the effects of aromachology in retailing is still incomplete.

While promising findings have sparked interest in the use of scents in retail environments, much (most) of the available literature is based on studies conducted in controlled settings, such as laboratories or simulated environments (e.g., [30]), and/or is based on attitudinal data such as product and store evaluations (e.g., [32–34]). It is therefore uncertain how much of these findings correspond to actual behaviors in actual retail environments.

Against this backdrop, the present paper presents a systematic review of the literature on aromachology with a focus on customer behavior in actual retail environments. The main research question this review seeks to answer is, therefore, the following: "what is the evidence for aromachology effects on actual customer behavior in actual retail environments?" To the best of the authors' knowledge, this is the first review paper to do so in a systematic way. The main contribution of the paper is threefold: first, to summarize the available evidence on the topic, secondly, to critically evaluate the available literature, and, finally, to provide recommendations for future research on aromachology.

2. Methods

Since this review focuses on the application of aromachology in retailing and its effects on consumer behavior, the main inclusion criteria were that studies should present experimental data on ambient scents of retail areas and include at least one behavioral variable. By contrast, studies were excluded if (1) they were not based in actual retail environments (e.g., exclusively lab-based studies or using mock-ups and simulated environments), (2) they focused on food products, (3) they focused on scents originating from the product itself rather than the environment (e.g., [17]), (4) focused on the general experience of the retail environment but did not include any behavioral variables, and finally (5) if they did not include any experimental data (e.g., reviews, editorials, etc.). The reason for excluding food-related studies was twofold: first, because the use of scents on food-related behavior has received more attention in the literature, especially in the context of how to use to scents to direct consumers towards making healthier choices, and secondly because using scents in food establishments presents some specific technical issues (e.g., safety/hygiene regulations, interaction between ambient scents and odors originating from food items), which are not necessarily shared by other retail environments. Readers interested in applications of aromachology in food stores are directed to the review paper by Girona-Ruiz and collaborators also appearing in this special issue [35].

The protocol for the systematic review was informed by the PRISMA guidelines [36] and is shown in Figure 1. A literature search was performed using two databases—Web of Science (Core Collection) and Scopus. The search in the aforementioned databases was performed during April 2021. No time limits were applied to the search itself. Search terms were initially identified by discussion between the authors, and the list was subsequently refined after conducting a preliminary set of scoping searches from the focal databases. Keywords used for the search were *retail atmospherics*, *aroma marketing*, *ambient scents*, *consumer behavior*, and *aromachology* using Boolean operators. A wildcard asterisk (*) was applied to all word stems in order to retrieve all articles that included terms starting with each word stem. The following Boolean search terms were defined based on the outlined research requirements:

TS = ((retail atmospheric* OR aroma marketing* OR ambient scent* OR scent* OR aromachology*) AND (consumer* OR customer*)).

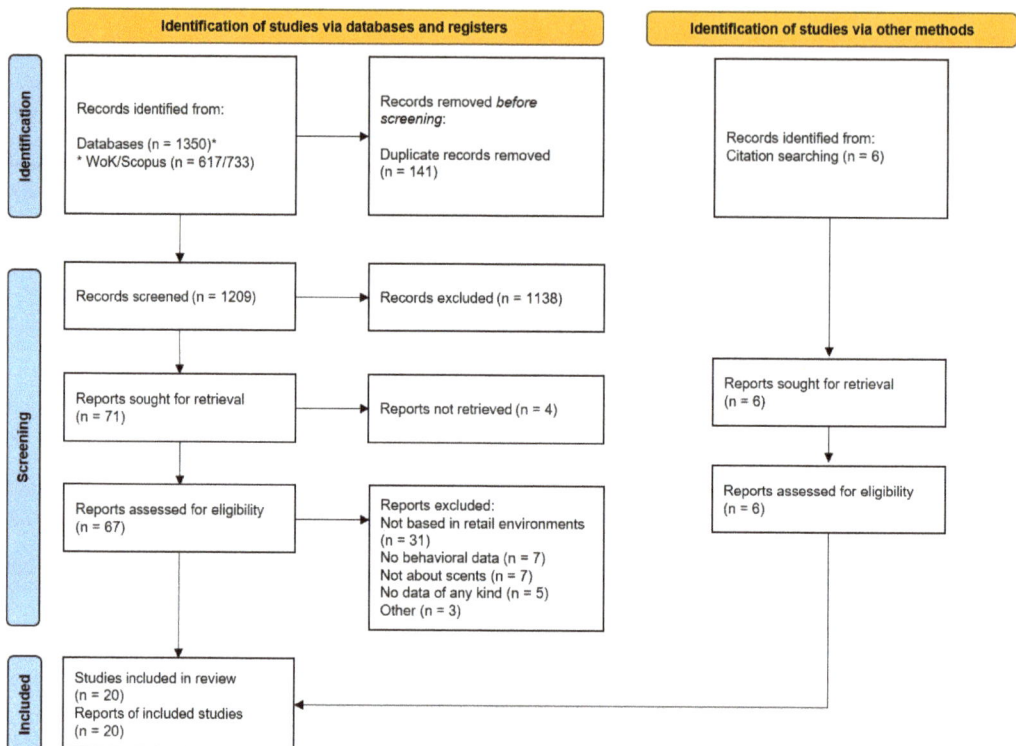

Figure 1. PRISMA flow diagram for the systematic review of aromachology and customer behavior.

The search yielded, respectively, 617 records on Web of Science and 733 records on Scopus. The records came from a wide variety of research fields, with business, management, food science and technology being the fields most represented (Figure 2). The database search further supplemented by a manual search using the "snowballing" method, from which additional six records were found (Figure 1). Complete documentation on this process and the full list of records are available as supplementary materials to this paper.

The initial list was screened and duplicate records were removed. After excluding duplicates, the titles and abstracts of each record were inspected to assess their relevance according to the inclusion criteria. Studies that met the inclusion criteria were analyzed in-depth with a focus on the following theoretical and methodological aspects: type of retail environment, product category, hypotheses and findings, type of scents used and method of delivery in the retail environment, number of subjects and target behavioral variable.

Figure 2. Treemap of literature pertaining to aromachology, showing breakdown by scientific fields (N = 617, Source: Web of Science, Clarivariate Analytics, Core collection, Search terms: see Section 2). Fields with fewer than 15 records were omitted to improve legibility.

3. Results and Analysis
3.1. Overview of Included Literature

Twenty studies met the inclusion criteria and were included in this review (Table 1). The most common reason for exclusion was that studies were not based on actual retail environments (Figure 1), although it should be mentioned that most papers included laboratory-based assessments in addition to the actual retailing environment (e.g., [27,29]), usually to isolate causal mechanisms and/or to document the perceptual properties of the target odors in controlled conditions. In such cases, only the results involving actual retail environments were included for the in-depth review.

All studies but two [27,37] included a control (without scent) condition, so that the effect of adding a scent could be benchmarked against the usual (odorless) store environment. Regardless of whether or not a control condition was included, most papers tested two distinct scents so as to test the effects of both the mere presence of a scent and its specific characteristics (Table 2). Common outcome measures included attitudinal measures via surveys and behavioral records such as in-store dwelling time and sales figures (Table 1).

Table 1. Overview of the literature included in this review, listed chronologically. [1] S = Sales volume, T = Dwell time, A = Attitude survey, O = Observations.

Source	Environment	Target Product	Behavioral Measures [1]
Knasko (1989) [38]	Jewerly store	Jewelry	S, T, O
Hirsch (1995) [39]	Casino (gambling area)	Slot machines	S
Mattila and Wirtz (2001) [40]	Gift shop	Misc. gift items	S, T, O
Schifferstein and Blok (2002) [26]	Bookstore	Magazines	S
Chebat & Michon (2003) [41]	Shopping mall	Non-grocery	S
Spangenberg et al. (2006) [37]	Fashion store	Clothing	S, T, A
Ward et al. (2007) [1]	Electrical store (cookers and laundry area)	Household appliances	T, A
Parsons (2009) [24]	Bookstore	Books	S, T
Morrison et al. (2011) [42]	Fashion store	Clothing	S, T, A
Doucé and Janssens (2013) [43]	Clothing store	Clothing and Jewelry	A
Doucé et al. (2013) [44]	Bookstore	Books	S, O
Herrman et al. (2013) [29]	Home decor	Plates, candles, baskets, etc.	S, A
Jacob et al. (2014) [22]	Florist shop (indoor)	Plants and flowers	S
Bouzaabia (2014) [45]	Fashion store	Sportswear	S, T
Madzharov, Block and Morrin (2015) [27]	Optics store	Sunglasses and prescriptions glasses	S
Carrijo et al. (2016) [46]	Fashion store(s)	Childrenswear	S, A
Helmefalk & Hultén (2017) [25]	Furnishing store	Furniture and accessories	S, T
Berčík et al. (2018) [21]	Travel agency	Tour sales	S, O
Errajaa et al. (2020) [47]	Clothing store	Menswear	S
Cao & Duong (2021) [2]	Fashion store	Clothing	S, T, A

Table 2. Experimental conditions in the reviewed literature. N/R = not reported.

Source	Type(s)	Valence	Intensity	Delivery Method	Subjects N
Knasko (1989) [38]	Fruity/floral and Spicy	Positive	N/R	N/R	N/R
Hirsch (1995) [39]	N/R	Positive	Above awareness threshold	N/R	N/R
Mattila and Wirtz (2001) [40]	Lavender and Grapefruit	Positive	N/R	Four ceramic diffusers	247
Schifferstein and Blok (2002) [26]	Sunflower and grass	Neutral	Slightly above threshold	Air cleaner system (model reported)	N/R
Chebat and Michon (2003) [41]	Citrus fruits	Positive	Around threshold	10 scent diffusers (model N/R)	592
Spangenberg et al. (2006) [37]	Essential oils: rose maroc and vanilla	Positive	Mild intensity (not specified further)	Scent diffuser (model N/R)	181
Ward et al. (2007) [1]	Apple pie w. cinnamon (cookers) and clean washing (laundry)	N/R	N/R	N/R	429
Parsons (2009) [24]	Rose and coffee	Positive	N/R	N/R	N/R
Morrison et al. (2011) [42]	Vanilla	Positive	N/R	Scent diffuser (model N/R)	263
Doucé and Janssens (2013) [43]	"Fresh office" (slightly minty lemon)	Positive	Below spontaneous detection threshold	N/R	194
Doucé et al. (2013) [44]	Chocolate	Positive	Below spontaneous detection threshold	Two dispensers (entrance and middle of the store)	201
Herrman et al. (2013) [29]	Orange (simple) and orange basil with green tea (complex)	Positive	Above detection threshold	N/R	402
Jacob et al. (2014) [22]	Lavender	Positive	N/R	Electric fragrance diffuser (model N/R)	100
Bouzaabia (2014) [45]	Ylang ylang (flower)	Positive	N/R	Scent diffuser, connected to central A/C system	400
Madzharov, Block and Morrin (2015) [27]	Cool (Peppermint) vs. Warm (cinnamon)	Positive (equally valenced)	Adjusted to "unobstrusive level"	Commercial scent diffuser (model not reported)	154
Carrijo et al. (2014) [46]	N/R	Positive	N/R	N/R	671
Helmefalk and Hultén (2017) [25]	Positive	N/R	N/R	Scent diffuser (model N/R)	245
Berčík et al. (2018) [21]	"North sea", "Apple" Rock N Roll	Positive/Neutral	N/R	Scent diffuser (model reported)	N/R
Errajaa et al. (2020) [47]	(woody-like), Rose	Neutral	"Not aggressive" (not specified further)	Scent diffuser (model N/R)	203
Cao & Duong (2021) [2]	Vanilla	Positive	N/R	N/R	205

3.2. Retail Environments and Product Categories

The included studies covered a rather diverse range of retail stores, showing that scents can affect consumer behavior towards very different product categories. Clothing was the product category most frequently considered in the included literature, which fits expectations as the use of scents is popularly associated with some clothing brands and their stores (e.g., Abercrombie & Fitch). Other product categories included accessories (e.g., jewelry items, glasses), books and magazines, household appliances, slot machines, and travel packages (Table 1). Accordingly, very different retail environments, ranging from general-purpose stores to specialized ones such as fashion, optics, and book stores. All included studies focused on customer behavior towards tangible goods except for two which focused on, respectively, money gambled on slot machines in a Las Vegas Casino [39], and tour sales in a travel agency [21]. One study [22] was conducted on a florist shop, although it involved a product category (flowers) that naturally emits scents; in that study, the target scent (lavender) was diffused by way of an electric fragrance diffuser, so it met our criterion that scents should originate from the environment and not the product itself.

The duration of the studies, i.e., the time during which scents were diffused in the store, varied significantly among studies, ranging from a few days (e.g., [39]) to several weeks (e.g., [21,26]). Very short time spans pose some problems as customer behavior is known to be affected by a variety of factors, such as weather and time of the day [48,49], which may act as a confounder. Accordingly, most studies included an experimental period of at least one week and/or limited the data collection to a set time of the day.

Finally, all studies but two had an exclusive focus on the effect of scents in a retail environment, and accordingly sought to minimizing variation in other store atmospherics. The two exceptions were two studies which also considered the effect of in-store music and its interactions with scents [40,42].

3.3. Scent Characteristics and Delivery Methods

As already mentioned, nearly all studies included some form of pre-test for evaluation of the perceptual properties of the target scents, principally their pleasantness, which was most often assessed via rating scales, and in one case using consumer biometrics (specifically, facial expression analysis [21]). In this regard, it should be noted that all studies used positively or neutrally valanced scents (Table 2). No studies reported using unpleasant scents. This is not surprising and likely due to constraints placed by the store managers who would otherwise be unwilling to participate in the study. A few studies purposefully selected perceptually different, but equally valenced scents in order to investigate whether qualities other than valence may affect customer behavior ([26,39]). Other perceptual odor characteristics considered during pre-tests were familiarity, intensity, complexity [26,28], as well as conceptual associations such "cool/warm" [27] or "masculine/feminine" [37] (Table 2) to assess congruency with specific products.

Methodological reporting pertaining to the actual scents and methods of delivery is quite poor. Most papers simply mentioned the commercial or lay name for the scent (e.g., "rose", "coffee", "sunflower", see Table 2), but their chemical constituent(s) was rarely reported in the literature. Additionally, while several studies reported whether consumers were consciously aware and/or attended to any ambient scents, the specific intensity of the scent in the retail environment was generally not reported or only qualitatively described with terms such as "mild", "unobstrusive", "not aggressive", etc. No study explicitly considered measuring the concentration of the scent, the airflow conditions, or any other aspects of air quality that may have affected the concentration of the scented particles in the store environments. Likewise, many studies do not mention the device used for diffusing scents but just refer to a generic "dispenser" or "diffuser"; only three studies [21,26,43] mentioned the specific models and/or technical characteristics of the devices (Table 2). Finally, while the store area is usually reported, the number and the positioning of the scent unit(s) was rarely given; thus, in many cases, it was not clear whether the scent was perceived throughout the entire store or only close to the target products.

3.4. Reported Effects on Customers' Behaviors and Theoretical Accounts

Consistent with the expectations, the vast majority of studies built on the S–O–R and the the mathic congruency theory to explain the effect of scents on behavior often considered both frameworks within the same study. For instance, Doucé et al. [44] studies the effect of adding a chocolate scent on general store behavior (such as length of stay, interaction with the staff, etc.) in a bookstore, which would reflect the S-O-R view, but also the effect on sales for thematically congruent items (cookbooks and romantic novels), which would reflect the thematic congruency theory.

Generally, support for the S-O-R theory seems to be found in the literature at least when it comes to attitudinal outcomes: accordingly, almost all studies included in this review report a positive effect of adding a pleasant scent on, e.g., engagement with the store, satisfaction with the experience, intention to revisit, etc. However, evidence of an effect on actual customer behavior is not always straightforward. For example, Ward [1] found that addition of a pleasant scent made the in-store environment more engaging, but with no differences in actual behavior between scented and control conditions. More to the point, studies that employed two qualitatively different but equally valenced scents reported that only one out of the two actually affected customer behavior, meaning that valence/pleasantness in and of itself is not enough to produce the expected effect on customers' behaviors. For example, Hirsch [39] reported that only one of two scents introduced in a Las Vegas casino increased the amount gambled on slot machines, whereas results for a second scent were not different from the control (no odor) conditions. Similarly, Parsons [24] in a bookstore study found that addition of in-store browsing and sales figures were slightly higher for a congruent scent (coffee) than for an incongruent scent (rose) of equal valence. Finally, Madzharov et al. [27] investigated the effect of adding warm vs. cool scents (equally pleasant) to an optics stores, and found that shoppers were more likely to purchase premium brands and to purchase more items in the warm scent condition. Overall, the literature evidences that valence (pleasantness) is a necessary but not sufficient condition for the effectiveness of scents to affect customer behavior.

This could suggest that other perceptual characteristics of the scents, such as congruency with the product category, are more important in terms of affecting customer behavior. Yet, support for the thematic congruency hypothesis is also limited, with studies reporting mixed results. Perhaps the best support for this theory is in the study on clothing by Spangenberg and collaborators [37], which found a positive impact of adding a "masculine" or "feminine" scent on sales of, respectively, men's and women's clothing items. Douce et al. [44] found that adding a chocolate scent to a bookstore increased buying behavior towards thematically congruents books, but only when controlling for gender (the addition of the scent worked for women but not for men). Schifferstein and Blok [26] investigated whether the degree of thematic congruency between an ambient odor and a magazine affected magazine sales in bookstores by using two odors (a grass odor, congruent with soccer, animal/nature and gardening magazines, and a sunflower odor, congruent with personal care and women's magazines), but found that the ambient scent did not increase sales for thematically congruent magazines, nor did it decrease sales for incongruent magazines. Similarly, Ward and collaborators [1] reported no differences in product-related behavior (e.g., dwelling time) in a different electrical retailer store when a congruent scent was present (vs. a control condition). Schifferstein and Blok [26] explain these inconsistencies by pointing out that it is not enough that a scent is thematically congruent with a product (say, a grass scent with a gardening magazine) to enhance its sales: experience of the association is required on the part of the consumer to effectively pair scents and products. Moreover, even if the scent triggers the intended association with a product, it may not be enough to affect that product's sales, so that ultimately the effect of scents on individual product categories may be rather small [26]. An alternative explanation for the lack of support for the thematic congruency theory is that the presence of a pleasant smell may distract customers from their specific shopping goals towards enjoying the overall shopping experience (in accordance with the tenet of S-O-R theory). This explanation is supported by the results of Doucé and collaborators [44], who found that addiction of a chocolate scent in a bookstore increased the general approach behavior but not goal-directed behavior (general books sales increased, but sales of thematically congruent book genres, such as cookbooks and romantic novels, did not).

4. Discussion

4.1. Do Scents Affect Actual Customer Behavior in Retail Stores?

Situated in the context of a growing interest in the field of aromachology, this paper has presented a systematic review of the available literature documenting the effects of using scents to create better customer experiences and affect their in-store behavior. Despite promising results from laboratory and controlled environment studies, suggesting that the addition of scents may affect product and store evaluations positively [27], the complexity and highly context-dependent nature of the sense of smell do not guarantee results will translate to actual retail environments. In fact, evidence from actual retail environments is remarkably limited, which only 20 studies meeting the inclusion criterion. This number is remarkably low in light of the fact that the relevance of scents for customer behavior has long been recognized [7,14] and that the much larger number of laboratory-based studies published within the same period. This indicates that the application of aromachology in actual retail environments is still an under-researched area. This might possibly be due to practical difficulties in setting up field studies which require, on the one hand, researchers to step out of their familiar habits and, on the other, cooperative store managers interested and willing to let the study happen and share the data with the researchers.

To date, much of the published research on the effects of aromachology has relied upon the S-O-R theoretical framework [7], the core of which suggests that a pleasant scent triggers a positive affective state in the consumer, which in turn evokes approach behaviors [28]. Another often considered framework is the thematic congruency of the scent with the store's offerings, on the premise that a match between the two is a necessary condition for an effect to occur [23,31].

While the literature offers some degree of support for both, neither the S-O-R nor the thematic congruency frameworks are consistently supported by the available data, suggesting that current theoretical explanations on the effects of scents on customer behavior may need updating. Yet, explanations beyond the notions of pleasantness and congruency were rarely considered in the literature. One exception was the study by Hermann and collaborators [29] that considered a processing fluency viewpoint, based on the work by Lévy, MacRae and Köster [50], suggesting that the effect of scents on behavior depends on the perceived complexity of the scent. The finding of that study, involving a home decor store, supported this, as they showed that, whilst keeping valence and familiarity constant, the addition of a simple scent (i.e., fewer components, easy to process) led to increased actual spending, whereas a more complex scent had no such effect. This indicates that there is still much we do not know, and that future research should, in particular, consider how scent properties other than pleasantness and congruency might influence customers' behaviors in ways that are relevant to the retail sector, and try to elucidate the causal mechanisms by which such properties might do so.

4.2. A Roadmap for Future Research in Aromachology

What would, then, be the most important future avenues for future research? A good starting point is to look at the shortcomings of the available literature that may explain these inconsistent results. There appears to be at least three areas that should productively be explored in future research.

Firstly, nearly all studies have dealt with the experimental data at the aggregated level, basically by simply comparing averaged data (e.g., dwell time, sales) against a control condition. This is notwithstanding the large and growing scientific evidence pointing at substantial individual differences in odor perception—due to genetics, demographics, habits, etc. [51–56]. This variability pertains to all aspects of olfaction, such as the specific quality of the perception (how does a scent test to different consumers), its perceived intensity (how strong it will be experienced as), and its valence (is it going to be perceived as pleasant or unpleasant). For example, the aging process is known to affect odor sensitivity. Ability to perceive and identify smells peaks with early childhood and declines steadily afterwards so that, generally, older individuals can be expected to be less sensitive to odors than younger ones [55,57]. This may be an issue of the prevalent practice of using students for selecting scenting and pre-testing their intensity, as students are generally young individuals whose olfactory functioning may not be representative of that of the end consumers (for instance, a scent may be experienced as strong by a 20-year-old person but may be very faint, or even undetectable, to a person aged 60). Likewise, men and women are known to differ in their sensitivity to smells [56,58–60], and accordingly, several studies report significant findings only when analyzing the results for men and women separately [37,44]. The differences are due to the individual genetic makeup, most of which are likely still unknown, that may cause individual differences in the possibility to perceive certain odors [54]. While the latter may not be relevant in the context of studies in actual retailing, phenotypical differences as a minimum have to be expected and accounted for. Finally, even if one could keep these perceptual differences invariant, there might still be differences in the importance different consumers ascribe to smells in the context of the shopping experience [61]. Therefore, the first recommendations for future research in aromachology are to move away from aggregate-level analyses in favor of analyses that account for individual differences, and secondly to ensure that the characteristics of the individuals involved in pre-testing and scent selecting match as much as possible those of the final consumers.

Secondly, nearly all papers included for review focused on varying ambient scents while minimizing variation in other store atmospherics factors. This suggests that the external validity of current research in aromachology may be limited due to the multitude of other environmental factors (such as lightning, decor, musical background, etc.) and sensory inputs that may influence the customers' in-store experience [3,4,9,14]. It is telling here that out of the only two studies that investigated additional factors, both reported significant interactions between in-store atmospherics. The study by Morrison and collaborators [42] found a significant two-way interaction between scent (presence vs. absence) and music (high vs. low volume) on arousal and ultimately time and money spent in the store. The study by Mattila and Wirtz also manipulated scent and music and found that when scent and music are congruent with each other, customers rated the environment significantly more positively and bought more than when these store atmospherics factors were at odds with each other [40]. Therefore, in light of these results, future research is advised to increasingly consider more complex designs when more aspects of store atmospherics can be systematically varied (on this topic, readers are also referred to the recent paper by Spence [4] who warns that *"ultimately (...) only limited progress will be made in understanding the impact of ambient scent on well-being, or anything else (e.g., store sales), by considering the sense of smell in isolation from the other senses"* (p. 9)). Admittedly, this is much be easier to do in a lab than in a retail environment, where store owners may object to manipulating certain aspects of the store environment. On a related note, studies should report and account for environmental changes (e.g., day-to-day weather changes) and ideally be conducted over the course of several weeks (e.g., [21,26]) to be robust against these confounders.

Lastly, a common thread across the reviewed literature is that methodological conditions appear quite poorly reported. Notably, most papers simply mentioned the commercial or lay name for the scent but their chemical composition and intensity are rarely reported.

While several studies at least tried to estimate whether consumers were consciously aware and/or attended to any ambient scents, any reporting was exclusively based by a qualitative assessment by the experimenter. No study explicitly considered measuring the concentration of the scent, the airflow conditions, or any other aspects of air quality in the store environments (e.g., temperature, CO_2 levels, volatile compounds from other sources) that would have likely affected the perception of the scents during the experimental period. Likewise, many studies did not mention the device used for diffusing scents but just referred to a generic "dispenser" or "diffuser"; only three studies [21,26,43] mentioned the specific models. Finally, while the store area was usually reported, the number and the positioning of the scent unit(s) was rarely given; thus, in many cases it was not clear whether the scent was perceived throughout the entire store or only close to target products. Taken collectively, such omissions seriously limit the reproducibility of such research and may explain inconsistencies in the results. This disregard for the chemistry of scents reflects the fact that the available literature on the effect of scents on customer behavior comes from the business field. This is in stark contrast with reporting in aromachology papers coming from other fields such as analytical chemistry (where identification and quantification of key compounds is the primary focus), and building science (where evaluation of indoor air quality follows set standards). In the latter, however, behavioral effects of scents are seldom reported or even mentioned, suggesting that collaborations across disciplines should be encouraged in future studies. In particular, considering air quality and scent concentration/intensity is needed to increase the quality and actionability of this line of research.

5. Conclusions

Interest in the use of scents in retail environments is growing due to the possibility to create better customer experience and potentially increase turnover. Situated within this context, this paper offers a systematic review on research in aromachology with a focus on research documenting effects on actual customer behavior in actual retail environments. The paper contributes to the literature by summarizing and assessing the available evidence pertaining to the effects of aromachology on customer behavior. As expected, the available research on actual environments (as opposed to laboratories and simulated environments) is limited, with only 20 articles meeting the inclusion criteria. While reported results are indicative of a positive effects of scent on customers' emotional states and on their in-store behavior (dwell time, product choices) and attitudes (purchase intention, intention to revisit), results were not always consistent, indicating that theoretical explanations for the effect of scents on behavior are insufficient. As additional contributions, we identified several critical issues with the available literature and provided suggestions for addressing these shortcomings. In particular, (i) focusing to a much higher degree on individual differences in olfaction (as opposed to aggregated level analyses), (ii) moving away from a narrow focus on scents to considering interactions with other atmospherics factors, and, (iii) improving the level of methodological reporting (specifically on the scents, their compositions, intensity and method of delivery) were identified as key areas for improving the quality and actionability of this line of research.

Supplementary Materials: The full list of records retrieved (whether from databases or manually) and the list of records assess for eligibility are available online at https://www.mdpi.com/article/10.3390/app11136195/s1.

Author Contributions: Conceptualization, D.G.; methodology, D.G., B.P. and B.B.; validation, B.P. and B.B.; investigation, D.G., B.P. and B.B.; data curation, D.G.; writing—original draft preparation, D.G.; writing—review and editing, D.G., B.P. and B.B.; visualization, D.G. All authors have read and agreed to the published version of the manuscript.

Funding: This research was funded by Erasmus+ KA2 Strategic Partnerships of the European Union, grant number 2018-1-SK01-KA203-046324 (Project "Neurosmartology"), which also covered the APC.

Institutional Review Board Statement: Not applicable.

Informed Consent Statement: Not applicable.

Data Availability Statement: Not applicable.

Conflicts of Interest: The authors declare no conflict of interest. The funders had no role in the design of the study; in the collection, analyses, or interpretation of data; in the writing of the manuscript, or in the decision to publish the results.

References

1. Ward, P.; Davies, B.J.; Kooijman, D. Olfaction and the retail environment: Examining the influence of ambient scent. *Serv. Bus.* **2007**, *1*, 295–316. [CrossRef]
2. Cao, M.T.; Duong, Q.N. Effect of Ambient Scents and Behavior Responses of Customer. *Rev. Argent. Clínica Psicológica* **2021**, *30*, 133.
3. Krishna, A. An integrative review of sensory marketing: Engaging the senses to affect perception, judgment and behavior. *J. Consum. Psychol.* **2012**, *22*, 332–351. [CrossRef]
4. Spence, C. Using ambient scent to enhance well-being in the multisensory built environment. *Front. Psychol.* **2020**, *11*, 598859. [CrossRef]
5. Gifford, R.; Steg, L.; Reser, J.P. Environmental psychology. In *IAAP Handbook of Applied Psychology*; Martin, P.R., Cheung, F.M., Knowles, M.C., Kyrios, M., Littlefield, L., Overmier, J.B., Prieto, J.M., Eds.; Wiley Blackwell: Hoboken, NJ, USA, 2011.
6. Jacoby, J. Stimulus-organism-response reconsidered: An evolutionary step in modeling (consumer) behavior. *J. Consum. Psychol.* **2002**, *12*, 51–57. [CrossRef]
7. Mehrabian, A.; Russell, J.A. The basic emotional impact of environments. *Percept. Mot. Ski.* **1974**, *38*, 283–301. [CrossRef]
8. Bakker, I.; Van Der Voordt, T.; Vink, P.; De Boon, J. Pleasure, arousal, dominance: Mehrabian and Russell revisited. *Curr. Psychol.* **2014**, *33*, 405–421. [CrossRef]
9. Lemon, K.N.; Verhoef, P.C. Understanding customer experience throughout the customer journey. *J. Mark.* **2016**, *80*, 69–96. [CrossRef]
10. Grewal, D.; Levy, M.; Kumar, V. Customer experience management in retailing: An organizing framework. *J. Retail.* **2009**, *85*, 1–14. [CrossRef]
11. Puccinelli, N.M.; Goodstein, R.C.; Grewal, D.; Price, R.; Raghubir, P.; Stewart, D. Customer experience management in retailing: Understanding the buying process. *J. Retail.* **2009**, *85*, 15–30. [CrossRef]
12. Verhoef, P.C.; Lemon, K.N.; Parasuraman, A.; Roggeveen, A.; Tsiros, M.; Schlesinger, L.A. Customer experience creation: Determinants, dynamics and management strategies. *J. Retail.* **2009**, *85*, 31–41. [CrossRef]
13. Schmitt, B. Experiential marketing. *J. Mark. Manag.* **1999**, *15*, 53–67. [CrossRef]
14. Kotler, P. Atmospherics as a marketing tool. *J. Retail.* **1973**, *49*, 48–64.
15. Roggeveen, A.L.; Grewal, D.; Schweiger, E.B. The DAST framework for retail atmospherics: The impact of in-and out-of-store retail journey touchpoints on the customer experience. *J. Retail.* **2020**, *96*, 128–137. [CrossRef]
16. Horská, E.; Sedik, P.; Bercik, J.; Krasnodebski, A.; Witczak, M.; Filipiak-Florkiewicz, A. Aromachology in food sector-aspects of consumer food products choice. *Żywność Nauka Technologia Jakość* **2018**, *25*, 33–41.
17. Wang, C.; Chen, S.L. Aromachology and its application in the textile field. *Fibres Text. East. Eur.* **2005**, *13*, 41–44.
18. Köster, E.P.; Møller, P.; Mojet, J. A "Misfit" Theory of Spontaneous Conscious Odor Perception (MITSCOP): Reflections on the role and function of odor memory in everyday life. *Front. Psychol.* **2014**, *5*, 64. [CrossRef]
19. Soars, B. Driving sales through shoppers' sense of sound, sight, smell and touch. *Int. J. Retail. Distrib. Manag.* **2009**, *37*, 286–298. [CrossRef]
20. Roschk, H.; Loureiro, S.M.C.; Breitsohl, J. Calibrating 30 years of experimental research: A meta-analysis of the atmospheric effects of music, scent, and color. *J. Retail.* **2017**, *93*, 228–240. [CrossRef]
21. Berčík, J.; Paluchová, J.; Gálová, J.; Neomániová, K.; Hladíková, L. Aroma Marketing—A Modern Marketing Phenomenon. *Int. Sci. Days* **2018**, 586–598.
22. Jacob, C.; Stefan, J.; Guéguen, N. Ambient scent and consumer behavior: A field study in a florist's retail shop. *Int. Rev. Retail. Distrib. Consum. Res.* **2014**, *24*, 116–120. [CrossRef]
23. Gulas, C.S.; Bloch, P.H. Right under our noses: Ambient scent and consumer responses. *J. Bus. Psychol.* **1995**, *10*, 87–98. [CrossRef]
24. Parsons, A.G. Use of scent in a naturally odourless store. *Int. J. Retail. Distrib. Manag.* **2009**, *37*, 440–452. [CrossRef]
25. Helmefalk, M.; Hultén, B. Multi-sensory congruent cues in designing retail store atmosphere: Effects on shoppers' emotions and purchase behavior. *J. Retail. Consum. Serv.* **2017**, *38*, 1–11. [CrossRef]
26. Schifferstein, H.N.; Blok, S.T. The signal function of thematically (in) congruent ambient scents in a retail environment. *Chem. Senses* **2002**, *27*, 539–549. [CrossRef] [PubMed]
27. Madzharov, A.V.; Block, L.G.; Morrin, M. The cool scent of power: Effects of ambient scent on consumer preferences and choice behavior. *J. Mark.* **2015**, *79*, 83–96. [CrossRef]
28. Spangenberg, E.R.; Crowley, A.E.; Henderson, P.W. Improving the store environment: Do olfactory cues affect evaluations and behaviors? *J. Mark.* **1996**, *60*, 67–80. [CrossRef]

29. Herrmann, A.; Zidansek, M.; Sprott, D.E.; Spangenberg, E.R. The power of simplicity: Processing fluency and the effects of olfactory cues on retail sales. *J. Retail.* **2013**, *89*, 30–43. [CrossRef]
30. Mitchell, D.J.; Kahn, B.E.; Knasko, S.C. There's something in the air: Effects of congruent or incongruent ambient odor on consumer decision making. *J. Consum. Res.* **1995**, *22*, 229–238. [CrossRef]
31. Lunardo, R. Negative effects of ambient scents on consumers' skepticism about retailer's motives. *J. Retail. Consum. Serv.* **2012**, *19*, 179–185. [CrossRef]
32. Spangenberg, E.R.; Grohmann, B.; Sprott, D.E. It's beginning to smell (and sound) a lot like Christmas: The interactive effects of ambient scent and music in a retail setting. *J. Bus. Res.* **2005**, *58*, 1583–1589. [CrossRef]
33. Biswas, D.; Labrecque, L.I.; Lehmann, D.R.; Markos, E. Making choices while smelling, tasting, and listening: The role of sensory (Dis) similarity when sequentially sampling products. *J. Mark.* **2014**, *78*, 112–126. [CrossRef]
34. Bosmans, A. Scents and sensibility: When do (in) congruent ambient scents influence product evaluations? *J. Mark.* **2006**, *70*, 32–43. [CrossRef]
35. Girona-Ruíz, D.; Cano-Lamadrid, M.; Carbonell-Barrachina, A.A.; López-Lluch, D.; Sendra, E. Aromachology related to foods, scientific lines of evidence: A Review *Appl. Sci.* **2021**, *11*, 6095.
36. Page, M.J.; McKenzie, J.E.; Bossuyt, P.M.; Boutron, I.; Hoffmann, T.C.; Mulrow, C.D.; Shamseer, L.; Tetzlaff, J.M.; Moher, D. Updating guidance for reporting systematic reviews: Development of the PRISMA 2020 statement. *J. Clin. Epidemiol.* **2021**, *134*, 103–112. [CrossRef] [PubMed]
37. Spangenberg, E.R.; Sprott, D.E.; Grohmann, B.; Tracy, D.L. Gender-congruent ambient scent influences on approach and avoidance behaviors in a retail store. *J. Bus. Res.* **2006**, *59*, 1281–1287. [CrossRef]
38. Knasko, S.C. Ambient odor and shopping behavior. *Chem. Senses* **1989**, *14*, 719.
39. Hirsch, A.R. Effects of ambient odors on slot-machine usage in a Las Vegas casino. *Psychol. Mark.* **1995**, *12*, 585–594. [CrossRef]
40. Mattila, A.S.; Wirtz, J. Congruency of scent and music as a driver of in-store evaluations and behavior. *J. Retail.* **2001**, *77*, 273–289. [CrossRef]
41. Chebat, J.C.; Michon, R. Impact of ambient odors on mall shoppers' emotions, cognition, and spending: A test of competitive causal theories. *J. Bus. Res.* **2003**, *56*, 529–539. [CrossRef]
42. Morrison, M.; Gan, S.; Dubelaar, C.; Oppewal, H. In-store music and aroma influences on shopper behavior and satisfaction. *J. Bus. Res.* **2011**, *64*, 558–564. [CrossRef]
43. Doucé, L.; Janssens, W. The presence of a pleasant ambient scent in a fashion store: The moderating role of shopping motivation and affect intensity. *Environ. Behav.* **2013**, *45*, 215–238. [CrossRef]
44. Doucé, L.; Poels, K.; Janssens, W.; De Backer, C. Smelling the books: The effect of chocolate scent on purchase-related behavior in a bookstore. *J. Environ. Psychol.* **2013**, *36*, 65–69. [CrossRef]
45. Bouzaabia, R. The effect of ambient scents on consumer responses: Consumer type and his accompaniment state as moderating variables. *Int. J. Mark. Stud.* **2014**, *6*, 155. [CrossRef]
46. Carrijo, M.C.; Minciotti, S.A.; Mazzon, J.A.; Prearo, L.C. Aromas: Influência do comportamento de compra em lojas no Brasil. *Espacios* **2016**, *37*, 23–43.
47. Errajaa, K.; Daucé, B.; Legoherel, P. Consumer reactions to olfactory congruence with brand image. *J. Retail. Consum. Serv.* **2020**, *52*, 101898. [CrossRef]
48. Dacko, S.G. Time-of-day services marketing. *J. Serv. Mark.* **2012**, *26*, 375–388. [CrossRef]
49. Murray, K.B.; Di Muro, F.; Finn, A.; Leszczyc, P.P. The effect of weather on consumer spending. *J. Retail. Consum. Serv.* **2010**, *17*, 512–520. [CrossRef]
50. Lévy, C.; MacRae, A.; Köster, E. Perceived stimulus complexity and food preference development. *Acta Psychol.* **2006**, *123*, 394–413. [CrossRef]
51. Bensafi, M.; Rouby, C. Individual differences in odor imaging ability reflect differences in olfactory and emotional perception. *Chem. Senses* **2007**, *32*, 237–244. [CrossRef]
52. Croy, I.; Buschhüter, D.; Seo, H.S.; Negoias, S.; Hummel, T. Individual significance of olfaction: Development of a questionnaire. *Eur. Arch. Oto Rhino Laryngol.* **2010**, *267*, 67–71. [CrossRef]
53. Mantel, M.; Ferdenzi, C.; Roy, J.M.; Bensafi, M. Individual differences as a key factor to uncover the neural underpinnings of hedonic and social functions of human olfaction: Current findings from PET and fMRI studies and future considerations. *Brain Topogr.* **2019**, *32*, 977–986. [CrossRef]
54. McRae, J.F.; Jaeger, S.R.; Bava, C.M.; Beresford, M.K.; Hunter, D.; Jia, Y.; Chheang, S.L.; Jin, D.; Peng, M.; Gamble, J.C.; et al. Identification of regions associated with variation in sensitivity to food-related odors in the human genome. *Curr. Biol.* **2013**, *23*, 1596–1600. [CrossRef]
55. Song, X.; Giacalone, D.; Johansen, S.M.B.; Frøst, M.B.; Bredie, W.L. Changes in orosensory perception related to aging and strategies for counteracting its influence on food preferences among older adults. *Trends Food Sci. Technol.* **2016**, *53*, 49–59. [CrossRef]
56. Dijksterhuis, G.B.; Møller, P.; Bredie, W.L.; Rasmussen, G.; Martens, M. Gender and handedness effects on hedonicity of laterally presented odours. *Brain Cogn.* **2002**, *50*, 272–281. [CrossRef]

57. Sorokowska, A.; Schriever, V.A.; Gudziol, V.; Hummel, C.; Hähner, A.; Iannilli, E.; Sinding, C.; Aziz, M.; Seo, H.; Negoias, S.; et al. Changes of olfactory abilities in relation to age: Odor identification in more than 1400 people aged 4 to 80 years. *Eur. Arch. Oto Rhino Laryngol.* **2015**, *272*, 1937–1944. [CrossRef]
58. Koelega, H.S.; Köster, E. Some experiments on sex differences in odor perception. *Ann. N. Y. Acad. Sci.* **1974**, *237*, 234–246. [CrossRef]
59. Zucco, G.M.; Aiello, L.; Turuani, L.; Köster, E. Odor-evoked autobiographical memories: Age and gender differences along the life span. *Chem. Senses* **2012**, *37*, 179–189. [CrossRef] [PubMed]
60. Olofsson, J.K.; Nordin, S. Gender differences in chemosensory perception and event-related potentials. *Chem. Senses* **2004**, *29*, 629–637. [CrossRef] [PubMed]
61. Dörtyol, İ.T. Do consumers need to smell? Scale development and validation. *J. Sens. Stud.* **2021**, *36*, e12630. [CrossRef]

Review

Review of the Potential of Consumer Neuroscience for Aroma Marketing and Its Importance in Various Segments of Services

Jakub Berčík [1], Katarína Neomániová [1,*], Anna Mravcová [2] and Jana Gálová [3]

[1] Department of Marketing and Trade, Faculty of Economics and Management, Slovak University of Agriculture, 949 76 Nitra, Slovakia; jakub.bercik@uniag.sk

[2] Department of Social Science, Faculty of Economics and Management, Slovak University of Agriculture, 949 76 Nitra, Slovakia; anna.mravcova@uniag.sk

[3] Center for Research and Educational Projects, Faculty of Economics and Management, Slovak University of Agriculture, 949 76 Nitra, Slovakia; jana.galova@uniag.sk

* Correspondence: katarina.neomaniova@uniag.sk

Citation: Berčík, J.; Neomániová, K.; Mravcová, A.; Gálová, J. Review of the Potential of Consumer Neuroscience for Aroma Marketing and Its Importance in Various Segments of Services. *Appl. Sci.* **2021**, *11*, 7636. https://doi.org/10.3390/app11167636

Academic Editor: Alexander E. Hramov

Received: 29 June 2021
Accepted: 17 August 2021
Published: 19 August 2021

Publisher's Note: MDPI stays neutral with regard to jurisdictional claims in published maps and institutional affiliations.

Copyright: © 2021 by the authors. Licensee MDPI, Basel, Switzerland. This article is an open access article distributed under the terms and conditions of the Creative Commons Attribution (CC BY) license (https://creativecommons.org/licenses/by/4.0/).

Abstract: In the current era of a strongly competitive business environment, it is more difficult for companies to attract customers. Consumer neuroscience has growing potential here, as it reveals internal consumer preferences by using innovative methods and tools, which can effectively examine consumer behavior and attract new customers. In particular, smell has a great ability to subconsciously influence customers and, thus, support profitability. This paper examines the importance of consumer neuroscience and its modern technologies used for exploring human perceptions to influence customers and benefit from the aromatization of business spaces. We focused our analysis on various service sectors. Despite the potential of the examined issue, there are a limited number of studies in the field of service providers that use neuroscience tools to examine the effect of aromas on human emotions. Most studies took place in laboratory conditions, and the used methodological procedures varied widely. Our analysis showed that, in spite of the positive impact of aromatization in the majority of aromatized spaces, service companies still do not use the potential of consumer neuroscience and aroma marketing to a sufficient degree. Innovative methods and tools, in particular, are still very underused.

Keywords: consumer neuroscience; neuromarketing tools; aroma marketing; human perception; services; aromatization impact; scents

1. Introduction

The marketing industry, as well as other sectors, is increasingly facing the problem of visual and information overload. This has caused consumers to become increasingly resistant to traditional marketing actions, thus registering them in a state of so-called perceptual blindness [1–4]. Hence, it is becoming more difficult to attract customers at the point of sale, which is the last chance to potentially reverse a person's decision to purchase a product. This is the main reason why there is an increased interest in targeting several senses at the same time to affect shopping behavior. One option for marketers is to focus on smell as it has great potential in this field.

Traditional research tools, including questionnaires, tend not to provide enough relevant information, and those that have already been applied are no longer sufficient to determine the exact needs of consumers. This is due to several reasons, including, to a large extent, the hectic time we live in, since people in these surveys either do not have the time to think properly on what they are asked about, do not understand the question, simply do not want to answer truthfully, especially when it comes to sensitive questions, or their response is in accordance with what society expects [5]. These factors lead to the use of advanced methods which can detect active parts of the brain when monitoring stimuli, thereby determining what emotions are evoked in the consumer [6].

Compared to the aforementioned traditional research methods based on questionnaires and interviews, neuromarketing and consumer neuroscience research provides more accurate information about consumer perception [7]. It has also been proven to offer information on consumer preferences that cannot be obtained using conventional methods [8]. Consumer neuroscience is an interdisciplinary field that combines knowledge from various scientific disciplines while trying to study how the human brain responds to external marketing stimuli [9]. At the same time, the neuro-approach can help solve potential problems in businesses that were previously invisible or ignored due to limitations stemming from traditional approaches [10].

Consumer neuroscience tools applied in consumer surveys have helped gain new insight into different aspects of brand perception [11–15], product packaging [16,17], emotional response to advertisements [18,19], and new product development [8]. Last but not least, it has enabled to survey the impact of different aromas on affective and cognitive processes [20,21].

In the context of smell significance, another field in marketing is also becoming more important. This is known as aroma marketing, based on aromachology, which is a science that studies the psychological and physiological effects of inhaling aromas and examines, with the use of fragrance technology, feelings and emotions produced by scents stimulating olfactory pathways [22,23]. Aroma marketing refers to the usage of scents to set a mood, promote products, or position a brand. The main goal of aroma marketing is the creation of a pleasant atmosphere in order to encourage customers to stay in stores longer and, accordingly, buy more products and raise their final consumption [24].

Neuromarketing research is justified in the field of aromachology in the services segment. A pleasant atmosphere within the field of services, in a workplace, or in a public space can fundamentally affect the overall perception of people if impacted by a properly chosen aroma, which will ultimately affect the economic results. The question is how to choose the right aroma, as its effect is mainly unconscious. One of the options is the use of biometric and neuroimaging tools, which provide a more detailed view of human emotions under the influence of particular aromas. Thus, an aroma can be chosen that will positively contribute to improving the perception of the environment, not only of customers but also of employees.

2. Materials and Methods

It is an undeniable fact that consumer neuroscience has attracted the attention of academic researchers, as well as practitioners. Since it is quite a new topic in marketing (especially aroma marketing), there are currently only a limited number of studies in this field at present, while a considerable increase in their number is expected in the near future. Therefore, related studies were reviewed and are presented to gain an understanding of this phenomenon and its potential impacts.

The present work was carried out within the framework of the Erasmus + KA2 Strategic partnership project NEUROSMARTOLOGY (no. 2018-1-SK01-KA203-046324), which aims to increase the amount of knowledge and information that is available in the scientific literature regarding aromachology, especially in relation to services, not retailing in general, where companies usually carry out private investigations and do not share the gathered findings with the public and/or the scientific community.

The research objective in the present study was to explore the potential application of consumer neuroscience in aroma marketing and the field of various service providers. The present study aimed to highlight potential new possibilities for monitoring the specific effect of aromas on human emotions by using consumer neuroscience tools. It is, thus, possible to make a more relevant aroma selection for the space in question and eliminate the risk of inappropriate selection.

For the study of the literature within the area of scientific interest, we chose the most frequently used scientific information databases and search engines globally, such as Google Scholar, SCOPUS, Web of Science, and ResearchGate. In deciding the selection of keywords, we relied primarily on our previous experience and the area of research (see studies mentioned in Section 1). Since this review focuses on the application of aromachology in various segments of services, the main inclusion criteria were studies that presented experimental data on ambient scents of different service areas (HORECA segment, medical facilities, cultural facilities, financial institutions, travel agencies, and telecommunication companies) in relation to consumer behavior.

Thus, the initial search included more keywords (including "ambient scent", "aroma marketing", "aromachology", "consumer behavior", and the individual selected types of services) and their modifications in publication titles, abstracts, and keywords, which resulted in us finding several articles outside the main field of interest (e.g., within chemistry and medicine).

The next step was to define the criteria for which of inclusion of the available articles in the analysis. The inclusion criteria for the study were as follows:

1. Articles written in English;
2. Articles published since 2005 and before May 2021;
3. Articles from peer-reviewed scientific journals or conference proceedings;
4. Articles focused on the area of scent marketing in various segments of services;
5. Articles related to aroma and neuroscience;
6. Articles including experimental design;
7. Articles in short or full version (not only an editorial or abstract).

The articles found were then screened until the end of May 2021 in order to exclude those unsuitable regarding their topics and contents (not from the field of business, management, marketing, food sciences, and economics). Finally, from the 2360 results from different databases, 33 full-text articles were selected on the basis of the relevance of their data and findings to this study. Those selected articles were analyzed in depth including type of environment, laboratory or real conditions, tested scents, sample subjects, sample size, used methodology (traditional vs. neuromarketing research tools), measured parameters, and main findings. The contribution of this detailed analysis was to point out the currently used tools of consumer neuroscience in aromachology research in the various service segments and possible implications for further research.

3. Results and Discussion

3.1. Potential of Consumer Neuroscience for Aroma Marketing

Consumer neuroscience combines knowledge from neuroscience, psychology, economics, and information technology and, using modern tools, investigates the emotions that influence consumer behaviour [25]. Neuromarketing examines the mind and brain of the consumer and can identify their needs and opinions about a particular company, advertisement, or product [6]. Therefore, "neuromarketing or consumer neuroscience can be understood as a subarea of neuroeconomics that addresses marketing-relevant problems with methods and insights from brain research. With the help of advanced techniques of neurology, which are applied in the field of consumer neuroscience, a more direct view into the "black box" of the organism should be feasible" [26]. However, consumer neuroscience should not be seen as a challenge to traditional consumer research; instead, it constitutes a beneficial complementary advancement for further investigation of specific decision-making behavior [26].

Accordingly, it is possible to divide the research tools and techniques of neuromarketing into two main categories (Table 1): biometric measurement (measuring the reactions of the body) and brain measurement (measuring the response of the brain) under the influence of aroma/marketing stimuli [27]. Each approach captures a different type of signal, and each brings a number of various advantages and disadvantages depending on the used measurement technique.

Table 1. Neuromarketing measures from the body and the brain.

Neuromarketing Measures			
Body Measures		**Brain Measures**	
Somatic (SNS) measures	Automatic (ANS) measures	Blood flow measures	Electrical measures
Facial expressions	Electrodermal activity (EDA)	Blood oxygenation (fMRI)	Electrical fields (EEG)
Facial muscle movements	Heart rate	Positron emissions (PET)	Magnetic fields (MEG)
Eye movements and fixations	Blood pressure	-	-
Eye blinks and the startle reflex	Respiration	-	-
Behavioral response times	Pupil dilation	-	-

There are many studies around the world that used neuroimaging and biometric methods to demonstrate the effect of odors on brain activity, which analyzed human response using the EEG signal [28] or the effect on emotions from a mood and physiology perspective [29–31]. In general, consumer neuroscience has helped gain new insights into consumer research by examining the effects of different aromas on affective and cognitive processes [20,21,32]. More detailed knowledge about brain processes influenced by scents was provided by a study [33] using functional magnetic resonance (fMRI). A prerequisite for applying consumer neuroscience in the selection of scents is that their influence is manifested mainly at the unconscious level. This statement was also confirmed by [34,35], which emphasized the fact that almost 75% of the feelings that occur during a day are regulated by scents. This assumption was surveyed in a study evaluating several floral, herbal, and fruity scents and their effect on emotions, which showed that the most popular scents were those that were the most pleasant [36]. There are several studies that used consumer neuroscience tools to demonstrate the effect of particular aromas. In an experiment [37], the effects of eucalyptus aroma, which is considered as an energizing one [38], and linalool, which is considered a sedative one [39,40] were tested. The aim was to find out whether it is possible to influence the attention of participants by simultaneously aromatizing the space with contrasting scents. Secondary outputs of the research were traditional data (potentials) related to the response to events and the strength of the oscillating activity of the brain. Another study [20] focused on surveying the emotions caused by odor stimuli and how odors play a role in evoking emotions in individuals with different olfactory abilities. Participants were presented with fragrances and then asked to identify them by choosing from five options, which included an "empty" option displayed on a computer screen. Their brain activity was monitored by EEG throughout the process. EEG uses electrodes applied to the upper part of the skull (scalp) and records a very low electric current from brain fields 2000 times per second, generated by the rapid movement of neurons due to nerve impulses [20,41,42]. In fact, it is a measurement of a very weak signal that permeates the skull and soft tissue to the surface of the head; however, the EEG can amplify this signal and filter out noise [43]. It is a dynamic test of frequency, which changes with brain maturation, alertness level, age, and drug use. EEG frequencies can be varied either diffusely or locally, by transient, fixed, or progressive change [44]. The results indicated that normal individuals do not pay as much attention to odor information unless specifically asked to do so. On the other hand, olfactory-sensitive individuals seem to implicitly pay a certain level of attention to odor information that evokes a natural state (passive odor). Another study [21] was focused on examining the effect of stimulation duration and time of response (TR) in the form of blood-oxygen-level-dependent imaging, or BOLD contrast imaging, in the activation pattern of four olfactory brain areas: the anterior and the posterior piriform cortex, the orbitofrontal cortex, and the insula. BOLD fMRI, which is dependent on neural activation in the olfactory cortex, has facilitated, in particular, the identification of cortical and subcortical structures of the brain involved in olfactory processing [45]. A time-course analysis of the activation of the general linear model (GLM) in these olfactory brain areas revealed that short TR is associated with a more pronounced relative increase in signal compared to long TR. Long stimulation was associated with a longer time-to-peak signal and an oscillating BOLD response. Accordingly, the traditional GLM analysis confirmed that the combination of short stimulation and short TR can lead to visually more extensive activation in the olfactory cortex. The question whether masked body odors influence any decision-making role or whether their influence is specific to moral dilemmas was also researched in another experiment [46]. This one focused on examining how the emotional response is represented in the human brain during the cross-interaction between odors and trigeminal stimuli and whether the degree of agreement between the two types of stimuli affects these emotional responses and their neural processing. fMRI is a derived variant of MRI. Its concept is based on a conventional MRI scanner, but it also records two other phenomena—blood perfusion (flow) and oxygen supply [47]. This method is a popular tool of academic researchers, and it can currently be considered the most widespread in the research of cognitive functions, emotions, and personal qualities.

There are several studies in neuroscience focusing on the sense of smell and its direct connection to the limbic system and memory centers in the brain. An example is the phenomenon of Proustian memory [48]. The Proust phenomenon is the basis for the hypothesis that odor-evoked memories are more emotional than memories evoked by other stimuli. Currently, there is descriptive and laboratory-based support for this proposition. Descriptive autobiographical memory studies have shown that odor-evoked memories are highly emotional, as measured by both self-report and heightened heart rate responses [49–51]. Several cross-modal laboratory experiments have further demonstrated that memories associated with odors are more emotional than memories associated with cues perceived through other modalities (vision, tactile, and verbal) [52]. The sample size for such surveys ranges from 15 to 30 respondents. The effect of aromas was examined using electroencephalography (EEG) on a sample of 16 respondents in Croatia [53]. A commercial research agency in Slovakia monitored the effect of Christmas scents on consumer emotions in a sample of 20 respondents [54]. The European Society for Opinion and Marketing Research (ESOMAR) argues that most research agencies which use consumer neuroscience have much smaller samples of respondents than in traditional market research, with 15–30 respondents sufficient to achieve quality results [55].

In addition to the use of these technologies to determine the specific effect of scents on human brain activity, the selection of the right aroma for real-world use also comes to the fore. Marketers are increasingly using ambient scents as a strategic tool to differentiate themselves from the competitors, attract customers, stimulate sales, influence moods, and create an overall pleasant and unforgettable shopping experience [56]. Several aspects affect the consumer's decision making and choice, including mood or emotional state [57,58]. The role of emotions in the consumer decision-making process is explained by the principle of neurological and cognitive frameworks, such as the theory of somatic markers [59], which focuses on the so-called attention to the negative effects of decision making.

Proof of that is the application of consumer neuroscience tools in the food industry which has recently gained considerable popularity in academia and commerce. Large research companies such as Nielsen, Kantar, or Ipsos have included these tools in their commercial offerings [60]. Despite many critical aspects, such as questioning the privacy limit or the concept of free will, the incorporation of these technologies into consumer behavior and market research currently forms an essential part of understanding and meeting research goals [61].

The development of consumer neuroscience in food and retail also faces some concerns about the interpretation and findings of some commercial studies conducted so far [62], due to the fact that some companies even make controversial claims without evidence-based citations [63,64]. Thus, it should be noted that academic studies are based on strict protocols and adherence to methodological procedures [65], which allows for a new perspective on unconscious consumer perception. Nevertheless, there are some critical views on the existence of strong unconscious influences on decision making and related behavior [66].

Usually, traditional surveys are used for understanding the perception of aromas, but these approaches require larger samples of respondents to obtain reliable results and are based on the assumption that participants are able to express their preferences [67]. However, it should be highlighted that food stimuli can also affect preferences and eating habits on an unconscious level [68]; therefore, the use of neuroscientific methods has its justification in this area. Their main goal is to measure crucial aspects of consumer perception not only in the unconscious (attention, emotional response, and memory), but also in the declarative area (attitudes and preferences) [69,70], so that the findings can be applied in managerial decision making in the creation of effective sales strategies [60].

3.2. Importance of Aroma Marketing in Various Segments of Services

The current era is characterized by intensifying competition of individual business environments and entities. The acquisition and the maintenance of customers are becoming more challenging, not excluding the area of services. Therefore, in this marketing environment, new strategies and approaches have also been expanding, which focus on the use of various and innovative technologies to explore consumer behavior and the possibilities of its influencing. Therefore, in the service sector, communications focused on human senses and, in our case, especially on the sense of smell in the form of consumer neuroscience, are also of great importance, because they help to reveal consumer decision-making processes in their subconsciousness [71]. The intangible nature of services makes it significantly more difficult for customers to evaluate their offer before the actual consumption. According to Goldkuhl and Styvén [72], aroma marketing using scents and various innovative technologies offers an effective tool for increase the tangibility of services. Examining customer behavior is becoming more important and a frequent purpose of research and studies in every area of today's operations. It focuses mainly on the attractiveness of the premises in which customers move, as well as the attractiveness of the services provided to consumers. Therefore, much research is focused directly on the use of aroma marketing in services such as cafés or restaurants, hotels, travel agencies, transport, medical facilities, financial institutions, and many others, as well as on the effects of aromatization on customer behavior [25].

3.3. Gastro Sector

Specifically, we can look at the restaurant segment. There are many scents for this service industry that are suitable for application to a given space. These are mainly the aromas related to the dominant offered item. Thus, it is often a food aroma. When entering service areas (as well as other services), the first impression is particularly important, which decides whether customers will feel comfortable, which of course will affect their spending and possibly whether they will come back. According to many surveys of aromatization already carried out, we can observe that it is advantageous for gastronomic establishments to aromatize their premises, thus influencing their customers and increasing their spending, because various aromas (such as the smell of chocolate, fresh bread, or even beef and many others) also increase salivation and, thus, the overall appetite (see, for example [73]).

The important role that aroma marketing plays, especially in such facilities, is also the neutralization of negative odors. Another very important impact that the aromatization of services has, as demonstrated through realized research, is the visible positive economic effect. Furthermore, Errajaa et al. [74] claimed, according to their research focused on the gastro services and experiment realized in a French café, that, when the scent is perceived as congruent with the brand image, reactions in the store are more favorable. It is not only about the use of scent, but also whether it is congruent with the environment. However, the scent must be perceived by consumers as consistent with the brand image. This improves guest satisfaction, intention to revisit, and perceptions of the product and service. These findings highlight the importance for services to use scents to generate a positive impact on their guests. One of the studies important to us was carried out in Slovakia, which examined the effect of aromatization used in the SportPub restaurant in Brezno and the effect of smell on consumer preferences when selling baked baguettes, i.e., paninis. Two different aromas were applied to the space—"chicken soup" and "crunchy bread". The results, after comparing sales in the period with and without aromatization, showed that the aromatization of the restaurant was beneficial. On average, more paninis were sold in the period with aroma [25]. Another experiment that was carried out, also using the innovative neuroscience technology (specifically, the FaceReader device), examined aromatization in the Sport Café in Nitra. The research consisted of testing in laboratory conditions, where a group of respondents—customers of a given cafe—were surveyed on the basis of conscious and unconscious feedback in choosing the appropriate aroma. The selected aroma was a coffee house. It was then tested in real conditions, implemented in the space of the café. The results of testing confirmed the assumption that the aromatization used in the selected café increased coffee sales. An increase of approximately 30% was observed during the testing period [5]. Further research focused on the effect of aromatization in the gastro segment was carried out in a pizzeria in Brittany, France. Two different aromas were dispersed in the restaurant environment in different places: lavender and lemon. The sales results from the aromatization period were compared with the sales results before the aromatization. They showed that the lavender aroma increased the length of stay of the customers and the amount of food they ordered. Lavender had a relaxing effect on people, which led them to stay in the aromatized area longer. In the pleasant relaxing atmosphere, customers ordered additional items and, thus, increased the final amount spent. However, in the case of lemon aroma, such an impact and increased sales were not demonstrated [75], which highlights the need to choose the appropriate aroma for scenting. Because, when the aroma and its intensity are not chosen correctly, such aromatization may have the opposite effect. A similar experiment was carried out in Maltese restaurants [76]. The objective was to assess if lavender and lemon scents impact the customer's dining experience in terms of money and length of time spent in mid-range restaurants in Malta. The experiment was conducted in three restaurants. However, their findings suggest that scents did not statistically impact the time and money spent in restaurants by consumers. Gaillet et al. [77] presented a study conducted in Dijon, France, where groups of participants were exposed to the scent of melon (as a typically entrée-related aroma in France) to the scent of pear (a typically dessert-related aroma). Both were presented at a very low and imperceptible level. They compared the impact of these scents to the experiment with no scent. The results showed that those who were exposed to the melon scent tended to choose more salads and less fatty entrées than those who were not exposed to this scent. Furthermore, those exposed to the pear aroma chose more fruit desserts than those in the no scent group [77]. Research about the impact of aromatization on customers was also carried out, for example, in the KFC fast food network in Mauritius. The campaign aimed at smelling their unique spice was realized. The restaurants delivered this aroma with food orders to companies at lunch time. The shipment contained chicken, byproduct, and biscuit. The intention was to release the aroma of fried chicken throughout the office and to evoke a taste for the food in busy research participants. According to the survey, 46.3% of participants felt excited about the aroma, 31.3% of participants felt very happy, 12.7% of participants felt nothing, and 9% felt relaxed [78,79], which points to the positive impact of aroma on customers. The study was based mainly on surveys conducted through questionnaires submitted to 133 random respondents—customers of KFC—to find out how sensory marketing affects the consumption level of rational individuals. The study confirmed that our five senses have a tremendous impact on how consumers purchase and experience products, services, and brands, as well as contribute to a company's strategic marketing. The result was that the smell of the restaurant motivated customers to choose the KFC restaurant without planning [80]. Another experiment was realized in restaurants in Sri Lanka. For the study, Randiwela and Alahakoon [81] chose the world-known restaurants McDonalds, KFC, and Manhattan Fish Market. Through the questionnaire, they collected data and realized a limited number of interviews to explore in-depth information. Data were collected from respondents (guests of the restaurants), as well as through several in-depth interviews. Findings supported the assumption that sensory marketing has a strong impact on customers, whereby smell was one of the strongest factors. We can find many other experiments realized by sellers and various concerns with using the power of smell and scents which had a positive impact, mostly on sales. We can also mention, for example, the world-famous company focused on selling donuts (Dunkin' Donuts), the company focused primarily on selling coffee (Starbucks), the Cinnabon bakery network, the Subway or Burger King fast-food chains, and many others (see more in [71]).

3.4. Traveling and Travel Agencies

The transport industry is also making progress in finding new ways to increase the wellbeing and comfort of passengers, with the primary focus on increasing profits. One of the strategies that is increasingly used is aroma marketing. Whether the goal is to achieve customer loyalty or brand awareness, aromatization has proven to be beneficial. Today, it is also becoming a common strategy in this segment of services. Thanks to the right choice of aromatization, such companies can induce in passengers a pleasant feeling of traveling, as well as a feeling of luxury or a relaxing environment.

Travel agencies are also among the service sectors in which aroma marketing plays an important role. Until recently, they only used holiday catalogs, brochures, and pictures to attract customers and promote sales. At present, this area of services is increasingly using the potential of aromas, where it uses scent to try to induce in its customers a holiday feeling the moment they enter the office. Studies have shown that specially designed exotic scents directly evoke the right holiday atmosphere in potential customers in the travel agency, affect their time spent in the office, and affect their desire to book additional holidays and spend more money than originally planned (see more in [71]). In such operations, the smell of coconut, which evokes the atmosphere of an exotic holiday, the smell of orange, which is reminiscent of a holiday in the Mediterranean, or the smell of the sea breeze, which is associated, for example, with sea cruises, are used most often.

As an example, we can mention the use of aromatization within one of our experiments in the travel agency AVOCADO, whose space was aromatized with two selected scents—North Sea and apple. The results confirmed the positive impact of the effectiveness of aroma deployment on the customers and on the economic indicators of the agency, because, in the period of aromatization, there were obviously more sales than before and after the aromatization [71].

The senses are also widely used to attract tourists during traveling in various ways. For example, in Finland, research was conducted in buses and ferries carrying tourists. It was examined whether the senses, mainly smell, can raise the number of sold trips. In buses, pinewood resin was disseminated via a scent machine. Sales increased during this period by 51%. Multiple sensory studies were conducted; however, smell was found to strongly affect sales. In ferry, scents and sounds were applied. The scent used was fresh linen. However, in this study, the scent stimulus did not affect visitor perception. The reason may have been the bad position of the scent machine, which was placed in the corner of the ferry [82].

Another study focused on aroma marketing in the field of tourist services. The study [83] identified the forms and ways of influencing people's senses in the process of selling consumer goods, providing some examples from this sector of services. The popularity of using sensory marketing was also mentioned in Luxurious cruise ships, for example, the Voyager of the Seas operated by Royal Caribbean International, which uses numerous multisensory facilities for the guests. There is a large casino, theater, basketball field, golf course, rock-climbing wall, ice-skating rink, and numerous themed restaurants including an Italian-style Portofino, which evokes the atmosphere of restaurants from the 1960s where the managers try to stun all human senses, whereby smell is a highly effective one. This is very beneficial for the company.

Public transport is also increasingly being aromatized by individual companies to attract more passengers and increase their turnover. Quite large field experiments in this area were done by Girard et al. [84] on railways to examine the effect of aroma on customers. The researchers examined the short-term and long-term effects of ambient scents. The experiments were conducted in collaboration with a major German railway company, in which consumers were exposed to a pleasant, nonconscious processed scent. The results demonstrated the scent effectiveness in the specific service context of train journeys in an olfactory-rich environment. The second experiment lasted for 4 months, whereby regular commuters were examined. This experiment confirmed the positive ambient scent effect. Other consumers were then surveyed in unscented conditions, and this brought about a surprising result, as the effects persisted even when the scent was removed from the services cap.

We can also mention the Paris metro as one of the first forms of public transport to scent its vehicles in 1959, using clove flowers. During the last few decades, it faced quite a large problem due to a very unpleasant scent. Therefore, in 1998, it started another campaign to become the sweetest scented metro. Not every customer liked it, but it was better than the smell globally associated with Paris metro. Accordingly, we can also mention the Metro in Madrid, which has realized several marketing campaigns focused on smell and has implemented scent into its coaches. These campaigns were successful and popular (see more in [71]).

3.5. Telecommunication Companies and IT Industry

Using aroma in the marketing service industry strives to create unique aromas that connect customers directly with their services and brands, with the same main goal as in other segments—to increase turnover and profit. Visiting such spaces is often associated with solving some problems. Therefore, it is necessary to pay attention to the appropriate aroma and its intensity, which can have a significant positive effect on the customer. It can calm them in communication, while it can also have a relaxing effect when waiting in line for a long time; it can increase brand confidence and increase brand awareness, as well as awareness of new products or services, which in turn brings the company's campaigns into a new dimension and makes it easier for customers to remember and identify the brand (see also [85]). For example, the largest telecommunication companies in Slovakia also aromatize their spaces—Telekom and Orange—with the intention of keeping customers in the store for as long as possible, evoking a positive and friendly feeling, making their time in stores more pleasant, encouraging them to buy and spend more, and influencing their emotions and shopping behavior.

An interesting study was focused on challenging the measurement of the effectiveness of scent marketing when applied to products and services that have low olfactory affinity. Findings from the research stemmed from two studies; the first revealed that 17% (after 6 weeks) and 6% (after 12 weeks) of participants recognized a past administered scent (orange scent). Even more interesting was, however, the second study, where ATMs were scented with a sweet orange scent. This study showed that 15% of the interviewees detected the scent flow around the machine at the time of exposure despite significant environmental disturbances (nearby bakery, wintertime face masks). None of the interviewees felt uncomfortable toward the scent, and nearly half of them supported the "scented ATM". The result was that scent can foster customers to create positive attitudes and positively impact purchase intention toward products and services, even in the absence of scent affinity [86].

A relatively unusual sector where aroma marketing also has importance is the IT segment, as discussed by Gosain and Mohit [87]. They presented various dimensions of olfaction in the IT industry, focusing on ongoing research. They showed that smell is somehow used in connection with computers. There has also been some work on smell in virtual reality, albeit to a lesser extent. However, this is quite an underestimated area with great potential. The researchers also perceive the usage of aroma in the field of fire fighter training, where smell gives valuable and potentially life-saving information.

As presented above, telecommunication industries have also found the value of aroma. For this industry, smell has been successfully introduced as a new sensory modality for interactions between human and mobile devices. The first smelling mobile phones were placed on the market in 2008; Sony Ericsson SO701i was scented with an aromatherapy fragrance to support relaxation during phone calls. German inventors later patented a mobile phone with a smell chip, which allows sending and receiving smell messages [87]. Scent has also been integrated into TV screens, which waft smells from a spot on the display when corresponding objects appear. The smell-o-system is used here. However, the authors believe that there is a notable absence of the use of smell in the ambient media literature, which they feel is strange, given that smell is such a perfect ambient medium; it can move easily from our periphery to the center of attention and back out again [87].

3.6. Aromatization in Medical Facilities

Aromatization of space is also widely used in medical facilities of various types, from hospitals to dispensaries and different places providing healthcare. The sterile scent typical of these facilities can be replaced by something more pleasant to distract patients from their health problems, make it more bearable for them to wait before an examination, or calm them down before the procedure itself. Proof was shown, for example, in the study by Lehrner et al. [88], conducted in a dentist's waiting room, which confirmed that patients exposed to the scent (orange or lavender) had lower levels of anxiety, were in a better mood, and were generally calmer. From the methodological point of view, only classical feedback in the form of a self-assessment questionnaire with the Likert scale was used to assess the emotional states researched. Further evidence of the use and impact of aromatization in medical settings was provided in the study by Naja, Bree, and Zaichowsky [89], which focused on whether scents and aroma can influence evaluations of a service experience and perceptions of personal wellness. The testing took place in the hospital's pediatric ward, examining three situations: odorless, with a relaxing scent (exotic fruit), and with a stimulating scent (citrus fruit). From the research methods, traditional methods were used, such as in-depth interviews conducted directly with hospitalized children, with their parents, or with medical staff, along with added insight from observing children in contact with nurses or other patients. Although the study confirmed the importance of aromatizing such spaces, the authors indicated the need for further research in this area due to the current study's limitations, either due to sample size or the possible influence of other factors on the variables studied. Another study was performed in the waiting room environment of a plastic surgeon [90]. The subject of their research was the influence of ambient scent or aroma (lavender) and music (instrumental music) on patient anxiety, evaluation of the waiting environment, and perceived waiting time. From a methodological point of view, patients evaluated the monitored indicators only through a questionnaire. This study concluded that both scent or aroma and music effectively reduce patient anxiety, but only if used separately. When both are active, it is necessary to carefully consider the possible interactions.

3.7. Aromatization in Cultural Facilities

Cinemas, theaters, museums, galleries, casinos, or any other spaces intended for cultural, entertainment, or leisure activities can also be classified as spaces where the use of aroma is essential. The goals of aroma marketing can be different in these cases, depending on the focus of the operation, from eliminating unwanted odors, making the time spent in the facility more pleasant, or enhancing the experience to increasing sales of additional goods, extending time spent in a particular space, and increasing the intention to return. The number of such oriented scientific studies is still relatively low. An example is, e.g., the study [91] carried out in the actual conditions of the González Santana Museum on a sample of 234 visitors, where three different aromas were used: the scent of clean clothes, apple pie, and aftershave. From a methodological point of view, feedback from visitors was collected only at a conscious level through questionnaires using a five-point Likert scale. The study results showed that scent has a significant effect on the perception, evaluation, and the repeated intention to visit the museum. A considerable benefit of this study is in its implementation in the natural conditions of the museum and in offering opportunities for managers of art institutions to differentiate their offer and build the image of their facilities. A similar study [92] was performed in a gallery, even though it was only a virtual exhibition in laboratory conditions. Their study researched the effect of the scent of the environment on the perception of valence, excitement, and memorization of works of art. A total of 86 participants evaluated a series of paintings by two artists while being present in an environment flavored with two scents—citrus and talc. The study confirmed that a pleasant aroma could significantly affect the evaluation and memorization of works of art. However, the research had its limitations, in the form of simulated conditions of a virtual exhibition, testing only two scents, focusing on images by two authors, and testing the scent without interacting with other senses, which opens up opportunities for further research. Another valuable study in natural conditions, this time in a cinema complex, was carried out in Lisbon, Portugal [93]. A sample of 407 spectators aged 14–81 participated in the experiment under aromatization conditions and without any. The findings showed that smell causes significant positive differences in cinema's evaluation, environment, and intention to return. From a methodological perspective, only classical feedback was collected from the participants at a conscious level. Other limitations of the research due to the realization of the study in the natural environment included an unrepresentative sample, as the participants of the experiment were a voluntary audience, and the inability to control all exogenous variables. Another con of the study was the failure to research the effect of scent in combination with other stimuli (music, lighting, colors, etc.) which could be the subject of further research in the future, as consumers perceive their surroundings as a whole. However, despite all the limitations, the study can be considered very beneficial. Another interesting study [94] was carried out in the environment of an aromatized cinema. They tested the effects of olfactory and visual stimuli on remembering information in cinema advertising. A combination of rose and sandalwood scents was chosen for the flavoring following a preselection. Because previous research has suggested that there may be gender differences in fragrance preferences, only 100 women took part in the survey. They found that, while both image and scent improved brand ranking and overall ad memory, they found that scent generated even more positive brand feelings. However, to verify these conclusions, further research will be needed in natural conditions, as this study was conducted in simulated conditions, although it tried to keep a high degree of realism, e.g., by dimming the room. How scents or smells can affect the audience's experience was also the focus of Spence [95] within his research. He claimed that, although the goal of aroma marketing was initially to eliminate unpleasant odors from the audience itself, there has recently been a growing interest in aromatization to make the experience of the performance more enjoyable. Experiential multisensory events are also becoming a trend [96]. In conclusion, we state that the study of aroma marketing in this segment of services has its justification and future.

3.8. Aromatization in Hotels

The intensely competitive environment in the hotel industry or the HORECA segment leads to a constant search for ways to become unique and differentiate oneself from the competition. One of them is sensory marketing, which can get into customers' hearts, minds, and wallets using all five human senses [97]. A pleasant atmosphere is what every successful hotel, guesthouse, restaurant, café, or pastry shop is built on. In a hotel environment, aroma marketing can create an impressive welcome effect, eliminate unpleasant odors, e.g., around the toilets, or create an olfactory logo characteristic only for the hotel, which guests will remember, making them happy to return to the hotel. Smell or aroma has long been neglected in the hotel industry, but today's hoteliers are aware that scents can enhance guest experience or increase the perceived level of service. The choice of a suitable scent for a hotel depends on the focus of the hotel. For example, business hotels are likely to choose universally acceptable scents that create the impression of sophistication, whereas modern hotels will choose a fresh or floral scent. The most frequently flavored areas of hotels include entrance halls, corridors, elevators, and other public areas [98]. This is why most hotel research was carried out in public spaces; however, there was insufficient evidence of the effects of introducing fragrances in private hotel areas such as guest rooms. The study [99] carried out in a four-star hotel in Barcelona aimed to analyze the effect of the scent used in the hotel room on customers' emotions. The authors chose lavender as the scent of the environment for the experiment because it is considered one of the most pleasant scents for humans. In addition, one of the significant benefits of this study lies in the methodological apparatus used, as emotional valence was measured using the FaceReader technology and was not only based on directly asking respondents through questionnaires. This study suggested that the introduction of fragrance into a hotel room can evoke positive emotions in customers. Individuals who experienced a flavored room showed a higher intensity of happiness and emotional valence than individuals who experienced a room without smell or aroma. The author of another study [100] believed that scent can evoke an immediate emotional reaction in hotel guests. He carried out his experiment on a sample of 200 guests at the ITC Sonar Hotel in Kolkata, although he collected feedback only using a classic questionnaire. ITC Sonar operates a whole network of luxury hotels in Kolkata, with its olfactory brand evoking a feeling of luxury. The refreshing scent of white tea welcomes guests as soon as they enter the hotel and contributes to building customer loyalty to the brand itself. The experiment results confirmed that, thanks to the scent, guests felt more relaxed and more pleasant, with more than 85% of customers also expressing their intention to visit the hotel repeatedly. Another study [101] was realized in a hotel in Hong Kong, which also flavors only the entrance public spaces and the reception with a specially created scent, a combination of ginger flower, lily, tuberose, lemongrass, and vanilla. The purpose of their research was to uniformly research the emotional states of guests evoked by the hotel's scent, using a questionnaire technique with a versatile range of scents to measure feelings. The results showed that happiness, pleasure, and sensuality can be included among the most dominant emotions that the scent evoked in the guests. A deeper analysis confirmed that these positive emotions are also associated with motivation to revisit the hotel, overall satisfaction with staying at the hotel, a feeling of loyalty to the brand, or a willingness to buy a scent for home or office.

3.9. Aromatization in Financial Services

Aroma marketing has a specific meaning for financial institutions as well. Banks, insurance companies, leasing companies, or other financial service providers can provide a pleasant scent, e.g., entry welcoming effect, making long queues more pleasant for clients, freeing them from unpleasant duties, or creating a trustworthy and safe atmosphere. Financial services were the subject of a study by [102] who focused on the influence of scent and music. A properly chosen musical background also makes the environment more pleasant and contributes to maintaining a discreet atmosphere. According to the available literature and sources, the authors found fast contemporary music to be the most suitable for testing, along with the scent of lavender mixed with wormwood and nutmeg, as it alleviates anger. Feedback from 607 experiment subjects was obtained via a questionnaire distributed while waiting in line at customer centers during peak hours. The research confirmed that a long wait for the service evoked negative emotions in the clients, which was subsequently reflected in the negative evaluation of the services. Although music had a more significant positive effect on customer reactions in this study, the main advantage of scent is that it is not annoying. In the future, however, the authors suggested testing different musical styles or different intensities of scent. The mentioned study proves that even institutions, in which the visit is not pleasant or expected to be the most pleasant, can be turned into places with a pleasant atmosphere through the correct use of marketing communication tools.

In addition to the mentioned service segments (Table 2), aroma marketing can be applied elsewhere. We did not mention energy service providers, centers for the elderly, entertainment centers, fitness centers, car shops, fashion boutiques, administrative centers, etc. It is possible to create the desired atmosphere and influence consumer behavior almost anywhere; therefore, its further investigation is justified.

Table 2. Studies related to aroma marketing in various segments of services.

Authors/Year	Environment	Scent	Research Techniques	Subjects	Measures
Errajaa et al. (2020)	Restaurants, cafés, hotels	Congruent scent	Traditional	Not reported	Guest satisfaction—brand image
Girard et al. (2019)	Railways	Pleasant ambient scent	Traditional	330 customers—pre-test; 204 customers—1. experiment test and 100 + 74 customers 2. Experiment	Ambient scents' positive long-term and aftereffects on consumers' situational service perception through the survey
Berčík et al. (2016)	Restaurant	Crunchy bread, chicken soup	Traditional	Not reported	Increase in sales of paninis was examined
Spence (2015)	Restaurant/food and beverage sector	Appropriate product aromas	Traditional	Many experiments analyzed	Examining of the various fields of this segment
Kumamoto and Tedjakusuma (2013)	Business	Orange scent	Traditional	2 studies—45 surveyed students, 69 interviewed shoppers	The feasibility of scent as an effective promotional tool for business
Goldkuhl and Styvén (2007)	Services	Not reported	Not reported	Not reported	Examining various fields of this segment
Berčík et al. (2020)	Services	Coffee house	Neuroscience	8 respondents in laboratory and 50 respondents in café	Examining various fields of this segment and the economic impact
Berčík et al. (2020)	Services	Not reported	Traditional	-	Examining various fields of this segment and the economic impact
Randiwela and Alahakoon (2016)	Restaurants	Food aromas	Traditional	Survey—300 respondents and several in-depth interviews	Surveys to examine the impact of sensory marketing elements on perceived quality and brand loyalty in restaurants
Randhir et al. (2016)	Restaurants	KFC food aroma	Traditional	133 respondents	Survey—impact of scent on customers
Hussain (2018)	Fast-food restaurants	Restaurant food aromas	Traditional	300 respondents	Survey—impact of aromas on customers
Hussain and Azeem (2019)	Restaurants	Restaurant food aromas	Traditional	1600 respondents	Survey—impact of aromas on customers—spent time and higher consumption
Camilleri and Mizzi (2020)	Restaurants	Lavender and citrus aromas	Traditional	Observation of customers	Scents' impact on a customer's dining experience in terms of money and length of time spent in mid-range restaurants in Malta
Guéguen and Petr (2005)	Restaurants	Lavender and lemon aromas	Traditional	Observation of customers	Scents' impact on a customer's dining experience in terms of money and length of time spent

Table 2. Cont.

Authors/Year	Environment	Scent	Research Techniques	Subjects	Measures
Isacsson, Alakoski and Bäck (2009)	Tourism	Pinewood resin scent, fresh linen	Traditional	Did not report the exact number of respondents	Exploring the effects of ambient scent in combination with film and sound on sales of excursions
Kuczamer-Kłopotowska (2017)	Tourism	Not reported	Not reported	Not reported	Positive impact of smell and other senses onto the customers
Gosain and Sajwan (2014)	IT industry	Not reported	Not reported	Not reported	Positive usage of the scent in various spheres of the IT industry—digitalization of the smell
Darabi and Mirabi (2018)	Mobile industry	Natural scent	Traditional	150 clients of one of the customer service offices of the mobile operators	The effect of the ambient scent on feelings of comfort, perception of waiting time, loyalty, and charming sensation
Proserpio (2017)	Restaurants	Beef, chocolate, melon, cucumber	Traditional	87 female participants	Investigating food intake, saliva production, and appetite in response to ambient odor
Gaillet et al. (2013)	Restaurants	Melon, pear	Traditional	Two experiments—58 + 70 participants	Examining whether an olfactory food cue could have an impact on food choices
Lehrner et al. (2005)	Dental office	Orange, lavender	Traditional	200 respondents (18–77 years)	Examining whether ambient odors could reduce anxiety and improve mood in patients waiting for dental treatment
Naja, Bree and Zaichowsky (2012)	Pediatric department	Exotic fruit, citrus fruit	Traditional	61 participants (children 8–12 years + parents + staff)	Investigating evaluations of a service experience and perceptions of personal wellness in response to ambient odor
Fenko and Loock (2014)	Plastic surgeon	Lavender	Traditional	117 participants (14–88 years)	The effect of the ambient scent on patient's anxiety, evaluation of the waiting environment, and perceived waiting time
Cirrincione, Estes and Caru (2014)	Virtual exhibition	Talcum, citrus	Traditional	86 participants	Investigating perceived valence, arousal, and remembering of artworks in response to ambient odor
Vega-Gómez et al. (2020)	Museum	Clean clothes scent, scent of apple pie, scent of aftershave	Traditional	234 participants	Investigating influence of scent on perceptions and evaluations, as well as on the intentions to revisit the institution
Verissimo and Pereira (2013)	Cinema complex	Not reported	Traditional	407 participants (14–81 years)	Examining whether scent could produce positive differences in the evaluation of the theater, its environment, and intention to return
Lwin and Morrin (2012)	Simulated movie theater setting	Rose/sandalwood	Traditional	100 female participants	Effects of multisensory cues on brand evaluation and advertising recall

Table 2. Cont.

Authors/Year	Environment	Scent	Research Techniques	Subjects	Measures
Anguera-Torrell et al. (2021)	Hotels' private areas	Lavender	Neuroscience	99 participants	Examining whether ambient scent in a hotel guest room can elicit positive emotions in customers
Chatterjee (2015)	Hotel	White tea	Traditional	230 participants	Investigating influence of scent on attention, experience, and revisiting intention
Denizci Guillet, Kozak and Kucukusta (2019)	Hotel	Combination of ginger flower, peace lily, tuberose, lemongrass, vanilla	Traditional	326 participants	Scents' impact on guests' emotional states
Ali and Ahmed (2019)	Hotel	Not reported	Traditional	400 respondents	The effect of sensory marketing on hotel market share
McDonnell (2007)	Financial services	Lavender, blended with sagebrush and nutmeg	Traditional	607 participants	Examining whether music and scent could increase customer satisfaction among customers kept waiting in a line and reduce queue rage
Yao, Song and Vink (2021)	Aircraft cabin	Lavender, cedar, mandarin	Traditional	276 university students	The effect of scent on the perceived comfort of an environment

We can summarize that the use of aromachology in the service segment has gained significant importance in recent years and has, therefore, been the subject of several scientific studies.

There is substantial research available directly focused on aroma marketing in services such as cafés or restaurants, hotels, medical facilities, financial institutions, cultural facilities, and many more. Table 2 summarizes all 33 studies described by us considering selected indicators (place of experiment, type of aroma used, size of the researched sample of respondents, and researched variables). According to the available resources, we conclude that aromachology is probably the most widely used in the HORECA segment's services [5,25,73–81,97,99–101].

We have described the options of using and researching aromachology in the selected types of services above. Therefore, we conclude that the studies were aimed at researching the impact of aroma in the service segment on selected variables such as customer satisfaction, evaluation of the service, attention, experience, revising intention, and emotional states. Some studies also researched the economic impact of aromatization [5,25,75,76].

The sample size of respondents in individual surveys varied diametrically from tens of respondents [5,73,77,86,89,92,99] to hundreds of respondents [78–81,88,90,91,93,94,97,100–102]. The limitation of certain studies was the omission of these data [72,82,87], the selection of respondents, e.g., involving only women in the survey [73,94], or carrying out the survey on a sample of students [86,103]. Another limitation of several types of research was their implementation only in simulated conditions [92,94,103].

The research of customer behavior due to aroma was, in most cases, researched through explicit feedback through questionnaires [88,90,91,100], in-depth interviews [81,89], or observations [75,76,89]. The use of innovative technologies to research the effect of aroma on consumers' emotions or consumer behavior was relatively limited in particular studies. The benefit of only two up-to-date studies [5,99] was the methodological apparatus used, as emotional valence was measured using the FaceReader technology. Because odors and fragrances have mainly a subconscious effect, we see huge potential in extending explicit testing to implicit feedback research using biometric and neuroimaging tools in consumer neuroscience. In addition to monitoring the effects of aromatization, qualitative air conditions should also be of interest, as they were also taken into account in only a limited number of research studies [5,25].

4. Conclusions

Despite the fact that the relative importance of smell within the human senses is 3.5% [104], it has great importance in marketing. The marketing industry, as well as other sectors, is increasingly confronted with the problem of visual and information overload. This has caused consumers to become increasingly immune to traditional marketing activities and, thus, they register them in a state of so-called perceptual blindness [1–4]. Hence, it is becoming more difficult to attract the customer at the point of sale, which is the last chance to potentially reverse a person's decision to purchase a product. This is the main reason why there is increased interest in influencing several senses at the same time, which could guide shopping behavior. One option is for marketers to focus on the use of smell.

While all other sensory systems represent a long way of transmitting information to the brain, including the transfer and transmission of information, the sense of smell is directly connected to the centers of the brain responsible for emotions and memory. Smell is the most sensitive sense of the human body. Similarly to taste, it uses chemoreceptors to detect the signal, with which we constantly monitor our surroundings.

There are only a limited number of studies in the field of service providers that used neuroscience tools to examine the effect of aromachology on human emotions. Methodological procedures varied widely between each study, making it difficult to compare and extrapolate them. Explicit forms of obtaining feedback through a questionnaire or an in-depth interview were used most commonly. Very often, an olfactometer device was used, which enabled a subjective evaluation of the pleasantness or unpleasantness of odor perception, most often in laboratory conditions. Due to the fact that fragrant compounds and odors mainly have a subconscious effect, it is necessary to extend the methodological apparatus to implicit research using the tools of consumer neuroscience.

In this context, subconscious measurement can be performed using a device that monitors electrical brain activity, e.g., an electroencephalograph, similar to the one used in medicine, but a mobile version. These measurements can also be extended by a biometric method for measuring galvanic skin response (GSR). A less complicated device is for the observation of facial expressions and dilation of eye pupils, where the recorded face video is analyzed by a special software (FaceReader).

Furthermore, new technologies for gaining unconscious feedback are emerging, which work with anonymized data and can monitor the emotional index of a given space through special cameras. The device captures people's emotions when entering and exiting a given space, thus being able to record changes in the feelings of customers or clients. Simultaneously, it can identify whether this change occurred in a positive, neutral, or negative direction. The development of the emotional index can be monitored over time, e.g., at hourly, daily, and monthly intervals.

Given the findings, there is a clear need for research in aromachology in the field of services, not only with the use of consumer neuroscience tools, but also their implementation under real conditions, since environmental factors such as air quality can fundamentally affect overall consumer perception.

Author Contributions: Conceptualization, J.B.; methodology, J.B. and K.N.; software, J.B.; validation, J.B. and K.N.; formal analysis, J.B. and K.N.; investigation, J.B. and K.N.; resources, A.M., J.G. and J.B.; data curation, J.B. and K.N.; writing—original draft preparation, J.B., K.N., J.G. and A.M.; writing—review and editing, K.N.; visualization, J.B.; supervision, J.B.; project administration, J.G.; funding acquisition, J.B. All authors read and agreed to the published version of the manuscript.

Funding: This research was funded by the Erasmus + KA2 Strategic Partnerships grant no. 2018-1-SK01-KA203-046324 "Implementation of Consumer Neuroscience and Smart Research Solutions in Aromachology" (NEUROSMARTOLOGY). The European Commission's support for the production of this publication does not constitute an endorsement of the contents, which reflect the views only of the authors, and the Commission cannot be held responsible for any use which may be made of the information contained therein.

Institutional Review Board Statement: Not applicable.

Informed Consent Statement: Not applicable.

Data Availability Statement: Not applicable.

Conflicts of Interest: The authors declare no conflict of interest.

References

1. Hervet, G.; Guérard, K.; Tremblay, S.; Chtourou, M.S. Is banner blindness genuine? Eye tracking internet text advertising. *Appl. Cogn. Psychol.* **2011**, *25*, 708–716. [CrossRef]
2. Bredemeier, K.; Simons, D.J. Working memory and inattentional blindness. *Psychon. Bull. Rev.* **2012**, *19*, 239–244. [CrossRef] [PubMed]
3. Brinson, N.H.; Eastin, M.S.; Cicchirillo, V.J. Reactance to Personalization: Understanding the Drivers Behind the Growth of Ad Blocking. *J. Interact. Advert.* **2018**, *18*, 136–147. [CrossRef]
4. Dichter, E. A Psychological View of Advertising Effectiveness. *J. Mark.* **1949**, *14*, 61–66. [CrossRef]
5. Berčík, J.; Mravcová, A.; Gálová, J.; Mikláš, M. The use of consumer neuroscience in aroma marketing of a service company. *Potravin. Slovak J. Food Sci.* **2020**, *14*, 1200–1210. [CrossRef]
6. Samuhelová, M.; Šimková, L. Neuromarketing. Úvod do problematiky. *Mark. Sci. Inspir.* **2015**, *10*, 47–55.
7. Falk, E.B.; Berkman, E.T.; Lieberman, M.D. From Neural Responses to Population Behavior: Neural Focus Group Predicts Population-Level Media Effects. *Psychol. Sci.* **2012**, *23*, 439–445. [CrossRef]
8. Ariely, D.; Berns, G.S. Neuromarketing: The hope and hype of neuroimaging in business. *Nat. Rev. Neurosci.* **2010**, *11*, 284–292. [CrossRef]
9. Agarwal, S.; Dutta, T. Neuromarketing and consumer neuroscience: Current understanding and the way forward. *Decision* **2015**, *42*, 457–462. [CrossRef]
10. Bridger, D.; Noble, T. Introduction Business Section. Neuro-Thinking. In *Neuromarketing Year Book*; NMSBA: Utrecht, The Netherlands, 2020.
11. Litt, A.; Shiv, B. Manipulating basic taste perception to explore how product information affects experience. *J. Consum. Psychol.* **2012**, *22*, 55–66. [CrossRef]
12. Milosavljevic, M.; Navalpakkam, V.; Koch, C.; Rangel, A. Relative visual saliency differences induce sizable bias in consumer choice. *J. Consum. Psychol.* **2012**, *22*, 67–74. [CrossRef]
13. Esch, F.R.; Möll, T.; Schmitt, B.; Elger, C.E.; Neuhaus, C.; Weber, B. Brands on the brain: Do consumers use declarative information or experienced emotions to evaluate brands? *J. Consum. Psychol.* **2012**, *22*, 75–85. [CrossRef]
14. Estes, Z.; Gibbert, M.; Guest, D.; Mazursky, D. A dual-process model of brand extension: Taxonomic feature-based and thematic relation-based similarity independently drive brand extension evaluation. *J. Consum. Psychol.* **2012**, *22*, 86–101. [CrossRef]
15. Saad, G.; Stenstrom, E. Calories, beauty, and ovulation: The effects of the menstrual cycle on food and appearance-related consumption. *J. Consum. Psychol.* **2012**, *22*, 102–113. [CrossRef]
16. Reimann, M.; Castaño, R.; Zaichkowsky, J.; Bechara, A. How we relate to brands: Psychological and neurophysiological insights into consumer-brand relationships. *J. Consum. Psychol.* **2012**, *22*, 128–142. [CrossRef]
17. Berčík, J. *Využitie Neuromarketingu vo Vizuálnom Merchandisingu Potravín*; Slovenská Poľnohospodárska Univerzita: Nitra, Slovakia, 2015; 215p.
18. Treleaven-Hassard, S.; Gold, J.; Bellman, S.; Schweda, A.; Ciorciari, J.; Critchley, C.; Varan, D. Using the P3a to gauge automatic attention to interactive television advertising. *J. Econ. Psychol.* **2010**, *31*, 777–784. [CrossRef]
19. Vecchiato, G.; Toppi, J.; Astolfi, L.; De Vico Fallani, F.; Cincotti, F.; Mattia, D.; Bez, F.; Babiloni, F. Spectral EEG frontal asymmetries correlate with the experienced pleasantness of TV commercial advertisements. *Med. Biol. Eng. Comput.* **2011**, *49*, 579–583. [CrossRef]
20. Lin, M. Individual Differences in the Impact of Odorinduced Emotions on Consumer Behaviour. Ph.D. Thesis, Iowa State University, Ames, IA, USA, 2014.
21. Georgiopoulos, C.; Witt, S.T.; Haller, S.; Dizdar, N.; Zachrisson, H.; Engström, M.; Larsson, E.M. Olfactory fMRI: Implications of stimulation length and repetition time. *Chem. Senses* **2018**, *43*, 389–398. [CrossRef]
22. Tomi, K.; Fushiki, T.; Murakami, H.; Matsumura, Y.; Hayashi, T.; Yazawa, S. Relationships between lavender aroma component and aromachology effect. *Acta Hortic.* **2011**, *925*, 299–306. [CrossRef]
23. Wang, C.X.; Chen, S.L. Aromachology and its application in the textile field. *Fibres Text. East. Eur.* **2005**, *13*, 41–44.

24. Mitchell, D.J.; Kahn, B.E.; Knasko, S.C. There's Something in the Air: Effects of Congruent or Incongruent Ambient Odor on Consumer Decision Making. *J. Consum. Res.* **1995**, *22*, 229–238. [CrossRef]
25. Berčík, J.; Paluchová, J.; Vietoris, V.; Horská, E. Placing of aroma compounds by food sales promotion in chosen services business. *Potravinarstvo* **2016**, *10*, 672–679. [CrossRef]
26. Hubert, M.; Kenning, P. A current overview of consumer neuroscience. *J. Consum. Behav.* **2008**, *7*, 272–292. [CrossRef]
27. Genco, S.J.; Pohlmann, A.P.; Steidl, P. *Neuromarketing for Dummies*; John Wiley & Sons: Mississauga, ON, Canada, 2013; 408p.
28. Pinto, R.J.C.; Xavier, I.P.P.P.; Calado, M.D.R.A.; Mariano, S.J.P.S. Analysis of the human reaction to odors using electroencephalography responses. In *Lecture Notes in Engineering and Computer Science*; Newswood Limited: Hong Kong, China, 2014; Volume 1.
29. Warrenburg, S. Effects of fragrance on emotions: Moods and physiology. *Chem. Senses* **2005**, *30* (Suppl. 1), i248–i249. [CrossRef] [PubMed]
30. Herz, R.S. Aromatherapy facts and fictions: A scientific analysis of olfactory effects on mood, physiology and behavior. *Int. J. Neurosci.* **2009**, *119*, 263–290. [CrossRef]
31. Goel, N.; Lao, R.P. Sleep changes vary by odor perception in young adults. *Biol. Psychol.* **2006**, *71*, 341–349. [CrossRef]
32. Martin, G.N. Human electroencephalographic (EEG) response to olfactory stimulation: Two experiments using the aroma of food. *Int. J. Psychophysiol.* **1998**, *30*, 287–302. [CrossRef]
33. McGlone, F.; Österbauer, R.A.; Dematté, L.A.; Spence, C. The Crossmodal Influence of Odor Hedonics on Facial Attractiveness: Behavioural and fMRI Measures. In *Functional Brain Mapping and the Endeavor to Understand the Working Brain*; BoD—Books on Demand: Norderstedt, Germany, 2013; Chapter 11; pp. 209–225.
34. Erenkol, A.D.; Merve, A.K. Sensory marketing. *J. Adm. Sci. Policy Stud.* **2015**, *3*, 1–26. [CrossRef]
35. Lindstrom, M. *Brand Sense: Sensory Secrets Behind the Stuff We Buy*; Free Press: New York, NY, USA, 2010; 175p.
36. Önal-Hartmann, C.; Pauli, P.; Ocklenburg, S.; Güntürkün, O. The motor side of emotions: Investigating the relationship between hemispheres, motor reactions and emotional stimuli. *Psychol. Res.* **2012**, *76*, 311–316. [CrossRef]
37. DeGuzman, P.; Jain, A.; Tabert, M.H.; Parra, L.C. Olfaction Modulates Inter-Subject Correlation of Neural Responses. *Front. Neurosci.* **2020**, *14*, 702. [CrossRef]
38. Moss, M.; Oliver, L. Plasma 1,8-cineole correlates with cognitive performance following exposure to rosemary essential oil aroma. *Ther. Adv. Psychopharmacol.* **2012**, *2*, 103–113. [CrossRef] [PubMed]
39. Kuroda, K.; Inoue, N.; Ito, Y.; Kubota, K.; Sugimoto, A.; Kakuda, T.; Fushiki, T. Sedative effects of the jasmine tea odor and (R)-(-)-linalool, one of its major odor components, on autonomic nerve activity and mood states. *Eur. J. Appl. Physiol.* **2005**, *95*, 107–114. [CrossRef] [PubMed]
40. Höferl, M.; Buchbauer, G.; Jirovetz, L.; Schmidt, E.; Stoyanova, A.; Denkova, Z.; Slavchev, A.; Geissler, M. Correlation of antimicrobial activities of various essential oils and their main aromatic volatile constituents. *J. Essent. Oil Res.* **2009**, *21*, 459–463. [CrossRef]
41. Palokangas, L. *Measuring the Willingness to Purchase Using Methods of Neuromarketing*; Laurea University of Applied Sciences: Vantaa, Finland, 2010; 108p.
42. Berčík, J.; Paluchová, J.; Kleinová, K.; Horská, E.; Nagyová, Ľ. Stimulus, space and hidden customer's reactions: Applying possibilities of neuromarketing. In *Improving Performance of Agriculture and the Economy: Challenges for Management and Policy, Proceedings of the International Scientific Days 2014, Nitra, Slovakia, 21–23 May 2014*; Slovak University of Agriculture: Nitra, Slovakia, 2014.
43. Al-Salman, W.; Li, Y.; Wen, P. Detection of EEG K-complexes using fractal dimension of time frequency images technique coupled with undirected graph features. *Front. Neuroinform.* **2019**, *13*, 45. [CrossRef]
44. Zaiwalla, Z. To EEG or not EEG. *Paediatr. Child. Health* **2018**, *28*, 289–292. [CrossRef]
45. Karunanayaka, P.; Eslinger, P.J.; Wang, J.L.; Weitekamp, C.W.; Molitoris, S.; Gates, K.M.; Molenaar, P.C.M.; Yang, Q.X. Networks involved in olfaction and their dynamics using independent component analysis and unified structural equation modeling. *Hum. Brain Mapp.* **2014**, *35*, 2055–2072. [CrossRef] [PubMed]
46. Bensafi, M.; Iannilli, E.; Schriever, V.A.; Poncelet, J.; Seo, H.S.; Gerber, J.; Rouby, C.; Hummel, T. Cross-modal integration of emotions in the chemical senses. *Front. Hum. Neurosci.* **2013**, *7*, 883. [CrossRef]
47. Zurawicki, L. *Neuromarketing: Exploring the Brain of the Consumer*; Springer: Berlin/Heidelberg, Germany, 2010; 273p.
48. Proust, M. *Swann's Way*; Modern Library: New York, NY, USA, 1928.
49. Laird, D.A. What can you do with your nose? *Sci. Mon.* **1935**, *41*, 126–130.
50. Herz, R.S.; Cupchik, G.C. An experimental characterization of odor-evoked memories in humans. *Chem. Senses* **1992**, *17*, 519–528. [CrossRef]
51. Herz, R.S. An Examination of Objective and Subjective Measures of Experience Associated to Odors, Music, and Paintings. *Empir. Stud. Arts* **1998**, *16*, 137–152. [CrossRef]
52. Herz, R.S.; Schooler, J.W. A naturalistic study of autobiographical memories evoked by olfactory and visual cues: Testing the Proustian hypothesis. *Am. J. Psychol.* **2002**, *115*, 21. [CrossRef]
53. Krbot Skorić, M.; Adamec, I.; Jerbić, A.B.; Gabelić, T.; Hajnšek, S.; Habek, M. Electroencephalographic Response to Different Odors in Healthy Individuals: A Promising Tool for Objective Assessment of Olfactory Disorders. *Clin. EEG Neurosci.* **2015**, *46*, 370–376. [CrossRef]

54. Chovancová, Ľ. Vianočné pozdravy. In *Prvý Čuchový Test Vianočných Vôní. EEG Meranie v Kombinácii s Facereaderom*; Research Agency 2Muse: Bratislava, Slovakia, 2018.
55. ESOMAR. 36 Questions to Help Commission Neuroscience Research. 2012. Available online: https://www.esomar.org/uploads/public/knowledge-and-standards/codes-and-guidelines/ESOMAR_36-Questions-to-help-commission-neuroscience-research.pdf (accessed on 20 May 2020).
56. Madzharov, A.V.; Block, L.G.; Morrin, M. The cool scent of power: Effects of ambient scent on consumer preferences and choice behavior. *J. Mark.* **2015**, *79*, 83–96. [CrossRef]
57. Lawless, H.T.; Heymann, H. *Sensory Evaluation of Food: Principles of Good Practice*; Springer: New York, NY, USA, 2010; 358p.
58. Schiffman, L.G.; Wisenblit, J. *Consumer Behavior*, 12th ed.; Pearson: London, UK, 2019; 512p.
59. Reimann, M.; Bechara, A. The somatic marker framework as a neurological theory of decision-making: Review, conceptual comparisons, and future neuroeconomics research. *J. Econ. Psychol.* **2010**, *31*, 767–776. [CrossRef]
60. Moya, I.; García-Madariaga, J.; Blasco, M.-F. What Can Neuromarketing Tell Us about Food Packaging? *Foods* **2020**, *9*, 1856. [CrossRef]
61. Feinberg, F.M.; Kinnear, T.C.; Taylor, J.R. *Modern Marketing Research: Concepts, Methods, and Cases*, 2nd ed.; South-Western College Pub: Mason, OH, USA, 2013; 720p.
62. Spence, C. Leading the consumer by the nose: On the commercialization of olfactory design for the food and beverage sector. *Flavour* **2015**, *4*, 31. [CrossRef]
63. Fisher, C.E.; Chin, L.; Klitzman, R. Defining neuromarketing: Practices and professional challenges. *Harv. Rev. Psychiatry* **2010**, *18*, 230–237. [CrossRef]
64. Hensel, D.; Iorga, A.; Wolter, L.; Znanewitz, J. Conducting neuromarketing studies ethically-practitioner perspectives. *Cogent Psychol.* **2017**, *4*, 1–13. [CrossRef]
65. Spence, C.; Velasco, C.; Petit, O. The consumer neuroscience of packaging. In *Multisensory Packaging: Designing New Product Experiences*; Springer: Cham, Switzerland, 2019.
66. Newell, B.R.; Shanks, D.R. Unconscious influences on decision making: A critical review. *Behav. Brain Sci.* **2014**, *37*, 1–19. [CrossRef] [PubMed]
67. Domracheva, M.; Kulikova, S. EEG correlates of perceived food product similarity in a cross-modal taste-visual task. *Food Qual. Prefer.* **2020**, *85*, 103980. [CrossRef]
68. Marty, L.; Bentivegna, H.; Nicklaus, S.; Monnery-Patris, S.; Chambaron, S. Non-Conscious Effect of Food Odors on Children's Food Choices Varies by Weight Status. *Front. Nutr.* **2017**, *4*, 16. [CrossRef]
69. Venkatraman, V.; Dimoka, A.; Pavlou, P.A.; Vo, K.; Hampton, W.; Bollinger, B.; Hershfield, H.E.; Ishihara, M.; Winer, R.S. Predicting advertising success beyond traditional measures: New insights from neurophysiological methods and market response modeling. *J. Mark. Res.* **2015**, *52*, 436–452. [CrossRef]
70. Stasi, A.; Songa, G.; Mauri, M.; Ciceri, A.; Diotallevi, F.; Nardone, G.; Russo, V. Neuromarketing empirical approaches and food choice: A systematic review. *Food Res. Int.* **2018**, *108*, 650–664. [CrossRef]
71. Berčík, J.; Gálová, J.; Neomániová, K.; Mravcová, A.; Vietoris, V. *Metodika Skúmania Vplyvu Aromatizácie v Obchode a Službách s Využitím Inovatívnych Nástrojov na Získavanie Spätnej Väzby*; Slovenská Poľnohospodráska Univerzita: Nitra, Slovakia, 2020; 71p.
72. Goldkuhl, L.; Styvén, M. Sensing the scent of service success. *Eur. J. Mark.* **2007**, *41*, 1297–1305. [CrossRef]
73. Proserpio, C.; de Graaf, C.; Laureati, M.; Pagliarini, E.; Boesveldt, S. Impact of ambient odors on food intake, saliva production and appetite ratings. *Physiol. Behav.* **2017**, *174*, 35–41. [CrossRef]
74. Errajaa, K.; Legohérel, P.; Daucé, B.; Bilgihan, A. Scent marketing: Linking the scent congruence with brand image. *Int. J. Contemp. Hosp. Manag.* **2021**, *33*, 402–427. [CrossRef]
75. Guéguen, N.; Petr, C. Odors and consumer behavior in a restaurant. *Int. J. Hosp. Manag.* **2005**, *25*, 335–339. [CrossRef]
76. Camilleri, R.; Mizzi, M. The Effects of Scent on Consumer Behaviour in Maltese Mid-Range Restaurants. *MCAST J. Appl. Res. Pract.* **2020**, *4*, 107–119. [CrossRef]
77. Gaillet, M.; Sulmont-Rossé, C.; Issanchou, S.; Chabanet, C.; Chambaron, S. Priming effects of an olfactory food cue on subsequent food-related behaviour. *Food Qual. Prefer.* **2013**, *30*, 274–281. [CrossRef]
78. Hussain, S. Brand Image and Customer Loyalty Through Sensory Marketing Strategies—A Study on International Fast Food Chain Restaurants. *Int. J. Manag. Stud.* **2018**, *5*, 32–39. [CrossRef]
79. Hussain, S.; Abdul Azeem, M. Sensory Triggers to Drive Sales- Creating Competitive Advantage Through Multisensory Consumption Experience in Restaurants. *Restaur. Bus.* **2019**, *118*, 167–178. [CrossRef]
80. Randhir, R.; Latasha, K.; Tooraiven, P.; Monishan, B. Analyzing the Impact of Sensory Marketing on Consumers: A Case Study of KFC. *J. US China Public Adm.* **2016**, *13*, 278–292. [CrossRef]
81. Randiwela, P.; Alahakoon, S. Sensory marketing is to flourish or perish: Restaurant in Sri Lanka sensory. *Camb. Bus. Econ. Conf.* **2016**, *1*.
82. Isacsson, A.; Alakoski, L.; Bäck, A. Using multiple senses in tourism marketing: The Helsinki expert, Eckerö Line and Linnanmäki amusement park cases. *Tourismos* **2009**, *4*, 167–184.
83. Kuczamer-Kłopotowska, S. Sensory marketing as a new tool of supporting the marketing communication process in tourism services sector. *Handel WEWNĘTRZNY Uniw. Gdański* **2017**, *2*, 226–235.

84. Girard, A.; Lichters, M.; Sarstedt, M.; Biswas, D. Short- and Long-Term Effects of Nonconsciously Processed Ambient Scents in a Servicescape: Findings From Two Field Experiments. *J. Serv. Res.* **2019**, *22*, 440–455. [CrossRef]
85. Darabi, K.; Mirabi, V.R. The effect of ambient scent on consumer experience: Evidence from mobile industry. *Manag. Sci. Lett.* **2018**, *8*, 1199–1206. [CrossRef]
86. Kumamoto, J.; Tedjakusuma, A.P. A study of the impact and effectiveness of scent used for promotion of products and services with low olfactory affinity. In Proceedings of the 5th International Symposium on Management (INSYMA 2018), Chonburi, Thailand, 1 March 2018.
87. Gosain, D.; Mohit, S. Aroma Tells a Thousand Pictures: Digital Scent Technology a New Chapter in IT Industry. *Int. J. Curr. Eng. Technol.* **2014**, *4*, 2804–2812.
88. Lehrner, J.; Marwinski, G.; Lehr, S.; Johren, P.; Deecke, L. Ambient odors of orange and lavender reduce anxiety and improve mood in a dental office. *Physiol. Behav.* **2005**, *86*, 92–95. [CrossRef] [PubMed]
89. Naja, M.; Bree, J.; Zaichowsky, J.L. The use of ambiant scent to improve children's hospital experience. *Int. Congr. Mark. Trends* **2012**, *1*, 77–84.
90. Fenko, A.; Loock, C. The influence of ambient scent and music on patients' anxiety in a waiting room of a plastic surgeon. *Health Environ. Res. Des. J.* **2014**, *7*, 38–59. [CrossRef] [PubMed]
91. Vega-Gómez, F.I.; Miranda-Gonzalez, F.J.; Mayo, J.P.; González-López, Ó.R.; Pascual-Nebreda, L. The scent of art. perception, evaluation, and behaviour in amuseum in response to olfactorymarketing. *Sustainability* **2020**, *12*, 1384. [CrossRef]
92. Cirrincione, A.; Estes, Z.; Carù, A. The Effect of Ambient Scent on the Experience of Art: Not as Good as It Smells. *Psychol. Mark.* **2014**, *31*, 615–627. [CrossRef]
93. Verissimo, J.M.C.; Pereira, R.A. The effect of ambient scent on moviegoers' behavior the effect of ambient scent on moviegoers' behavior. *Port. J. Manag. Stud.* **2013**, *18*, 67–79.
94. Lwin, M.O.; Morrin, M. Scenting movie theatre commercials: The impact of scent and pictures on brand evaluations and ad recall. *J. Consum. Behav.* **2012**, *11*, 264–272. [CrossRef]
95. Spence, C. Scent and the Cinema. *Iperception* **2020**, *11*, 1–26. [CrossRef]
96. Spence, C. Scent in the Context of Live Performance. *Iperception* **2021**, *12*, 1–28. [CrossRef]
97. Ali, M.E.-H.; Ahmed, O.M. Sensory Marketing and its Effect on Hotel Market-Share: Perception of Hotel Customers. *J. Tour. Hosp. Manag.* **2019**, *7*, 116–126. [CrossRef]
98. Peng, S.-Y. Fragrance Marketing: An Innovation in the Hotel Industry. In Proceedings of the 2015 International Conference on Management Science and Management Innovation, Guilin, China, 15–16 August 2015; Volume 6.
99. Anguera-Torrell, O.; León, I.Á.; Cappai, A.; Antolín, G.S. Do ambient scents in hotel guest rooms affect customers' emotions? *Eur. J. Tour. Res.* **2021**, *27*, 1–16.
100. Chatterjee, S. Olfactory branding: A new trend for defining brands through smell—A case of ITC Sonar Hotel in Kolkata, India. *Int. J. Trade Glob. Mark.* **2015**, *8*. [CrossRef]
101. Denizci Guillet, B.; Kozak, M.; Kucukusta, D. It's in the air: Aroma marketing and affective response in the hotel world. *Int. J. Hosp. Tour. Adm.* **2019**, *20*, 1. [CrossRef]
102. McDonnell, J. Music, scent and time preferences for waiting lines. *Int. J. Bank Mark.* **2007**, *25*, 223–237. [CrossRef]
103. Yao, X.; Song, Y.; Vink, P. Effect of scent on comfort of aircraft passengers. *Work* **2021**, *68*, S273–S280. [CrossRef] [PubMed]
104. Horská, E.; Nagyová, Ľ.; Rovný, P. *Merchandising a Event Marketing pre Produkty Pôdohospodárstva*; Slovenská Poľnohospodárska Univerzita: Nitra, Slovakia, 2010; 329p.

Review

The Impact of the Aromatization of Production Environment on Workers: A Systematic Literature Review

Karol Čarnogurský [1], Anna Diačiková [1] and Peter Madzík [2,*]

[1] Department of Management, Catholic University in Ruzomberok, Hrabovská cesta 1A, 034 01 Ruzomberok, Slovakia; karol.carnogursky@ku.sk (K.Č.); anna.diacikova@ku.sk (A.D.)
[2] Department of Business Administration and Management, Technical University of Liberec, Voronezska 13, 460 09 Liberec, Czech Republic
* Correspondence: peter.madzik@gmail.com

Abstract: Literature on aromatization in production environments is very limited. The literature rather describes the impact of aromachology on employees in administrative premises, but published research results on the influence of aromachology in production premises are not available. There are no scientifically based studies and research that analyze and provide at least partial evidence of the impact of fragrances on the productivity and economic performance of companies. For the study of the literature of the area of our scientific interest, we chose the globally most frequently used scientific information database Scopus. In deciding on the selection of keyword combinations and in the search, we relied primarily on our previous experience and the area of research, which is the aromatization of spaces in industrial production, and its impact on the performance of employees, respectively. We also consider the industrial applications of aromachology, and how an indoor environment is important for people's health and comfort.

Keywords: aromachology; scents; smell; behavior; consumer psychology; aroma marketing

Citation: Čarnogurský, K.; Diačiková, A.; Madzík, P. The Impact of the Aromatization of Production Environment on Workers: A Systematic Literature Review. *Appl. Sci.* **2021**, *11*, 5600. https://doi.org/10.3390/app11125600

Academic Editor: Jean-Luc Le Quéré

Received: 30 April 2021
Accepted: 3 June 2021
Published: 17 June 2021

Publisher's Note: MDPI stays neutral with regard to jurisdictional claims in published maps and institutional affiliations.

Copyright: © 2021 by the authors. Licensee MDPI, Basel, Switzerland. This article is an open access article distributed under the terms and conditions of the Creative Commons Attribution (CC BY) license (https://creativecommons.org/licenses/by/4.0/).

1. Introduction

Aromatization of the environment evokes effective or certain emotions. The purpose of aromatizing the internal environment is, of course, to evoke affective emotions with the defined goal of stimulating the perception of the human environment. A scientific view of human perception of flavors has been published by Small et al. [1], who from a medical point of view explain the human perception of aromas by both possible requirements, i.e., nose and mouth. Aromatic molecules contact the olfactory epithelium through the nose, which means that it is the perception of aromas from the outside environment, or through the mouth (retronasal sniffing). Then, the aroma is perceived by the mouth and associated with taste (sweet, sour, salty, spicy and hot). These situations are graphically displayed in Figure 1.

There are two basic principles for the perception of aroma through the human nose, which are named aromatherapy and aromachology. Although these concepts sound very similar, they differ in their principled focus, i.e., the quality of the aroma, its priority purpose, and use, which are summarized in Table 1. However, both support the positive effects of fragrance on a person's mood and emotions. A systematic review of these two different disciplines is published by Čarnogurský et al. [2].

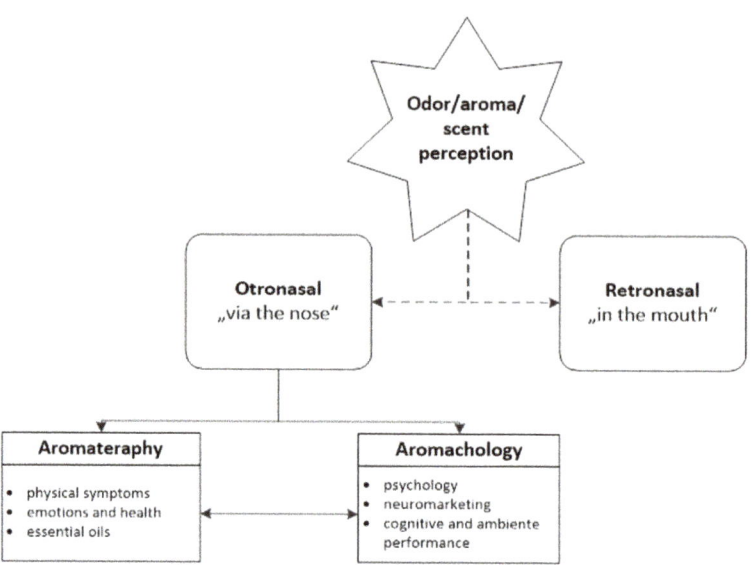

Figure 1. Human perception of aroma.

Table 1. Differences between Aromatherapy and Aromachology.

	Fragrance Quality	Solves Preferentially	Main Purpose	Main Purpose
Aromatherapy	Natural	Launching and causing a specific physiological reaction in humans	Health status of individuals	In medicine
Aromachology	Natural Synthetic	Launching and causing a psychological reaction in humans	Affecting the mood and behavior of people	For commercial purposes-retail, work environment

Aromatherapy is about the therapeutic use of natural scents and about bringing well-being [3–6]. Systematic research has also shown that aromatherapy is one of the popular complementary and alternative drugs, and the beneficial therapeutic effects of aromatherapy on employee psychological health have also been confirmed, including improving work performance and reducing workplace stress [7–10]. Aromachology is based on scientific studies, examines the psychological effects of natural and synthetic scents on humans, and is closely linked to psychology [11–15]. Table 1 shows the basic differences between aromatherapy and aromachology.

In general, the topic of research, analysis, and use of both principles of aromatization, i.e., aromatherapy and aromachology of interior spaces have a different history and depth of research. It strongly depends on the purpose of using these interior spaces.

It can be:

- Production;
- Administrative premises;
- Storage space;
- Grocery store;
- Trade in non-food products;
- Services (travel agencies, real estate agencies, consulting services, banks, financial and insurance institutions);
- Gastronomic establishments (cafes, restaurants, bars);
- Hotels;

- Medical facilities;
- Wellness services, relaxation centers and fitness; and
- Educational institutions, media spaces, households and other unspecified spaces.

Of the above-mentioned internal spaces, aromatization (in the sense of aromatherapy) is commonly used in medical facilities, relaxation centers, fitness, and other areas providing wellness services, respectively. Other services are used in households and administrative premises.

The topic of research into the aromatization (in terms of aromachology) of indoor spaces in which people use retail services, i.e., aromatization in non-food retail environments [16–19] and aromatization in food retail environments [20–22], is also published in the literature. Although ambient scents within retail stores have been shown to influence shoppers, real-world demonstrations of scent effects are infrequent and the existing theoretical explanation for observed effects is limited. Several results demonstrate how emotional processes occurring within stimulus exposure differ across individuals with varying olfactory abilities. Findings reveal an automatic suppression mechanism for an individual's sensitivity to smell.

However, the topic of research and study of aromatization (in terms of aromachology) of interior spaces, in which people work rather manually, is a new area that science is currently beginning to pay attention to [23]. Rather, the literature describes the impact of aromachology on employees in administrative premises, but published research results on the influence of aromachology in production premises are not available. There are no scientifically based studies and research that analyze and provide at least partial evidence of the impact of fragrances on the productivity and economic performance of companies. Nevertheless, the number of companies implementing aromachology is constantly growing, i.e., they flavor their premises or create olfactory traces of various brands, especially in retail, and thus indirectly positively affect the economic performance of their companies. These findings inspired us primarily to study the available scientific literature in the field of aromachology research by focusing on ambient scents of production areas and finding connections between air quality using indoor aromatics and a possible link to work performance.

The article aims to process the most relevant available scientific literature in the field of indoor aromatization with emphasis on application in the production process. However, during the process of processing the available literature, we found that the literature on aromatization in the production environment is very limited, in that it exists, but only very marginally. For this reason, we considered the relevant literature in which information about the existence of aroma/aromatization in production and industry and aroma influence on work performance expressed by a good feeling of employees.

2. Materials and Methods

2.1. Work Performance–Object of the Research

The object of research in the present study is the work environment. The working environment is defined as a set of spatial, material, physical, chemical, microclimatic, physiological, psychological, social, and other conditions in which the production and work process affect the results of production in term of work, motivation, performance, psyche, safety, and health of employees [24]. Good air quality can be defined as "air in which there are no contaminants at damaging concentrations as controlled by aware power and with which an impressive predominant part (80% or more) of the people uncovered do not express disappointment" [25]. The issue of the working environment in the interior (air quality indoor), is mainly addressed by the legislation of individual countries, or the legislation of entire regions, e.g., for the member states of the European Union, it is a set of EU directives on safety and health at work [26]. The mentioned legislation addresses not only the physical demands of work but also the conditions of the working environment in the interior, e.g., temperature, air conditioning, ambient humidity, lighting, noise, air quality, and chemical fumes, which are specific and different for each business entity and its operations. The company is responsible for compliance with the conditions and control by the relevant control body within the competence of the country's government.

The working environment, including air quality, must meet strict standards. This also includes targeted aromatization of premises, which is known in practice and is used mainly in shops, relaxation and wellness centers, administrative premises, or even in households. Air modification in production facilities is not exactly described in the literature [23], rather, questionnaire surveys [27–29] in non-production settings are known.

Only the results of the references of the interior spaces of the objects, which were identified/extracted through the keywords industry and engineering, were included in our subject of research.

We used data from the Scopus indexed database, to obtain data for this article, as Elsevier characterizes it as the largest abstract and citation database of scientific literature and quality web resources in the world. We originally approached the creation of this article as we usually work with literature research, and we have chosen the most frequently used sources for scientific work, Web of Science, Scopus, and Google Scholar. We based this on based on:

- Our many years of experience in scientific work;
- From the experience of the last 3 years devoted to the field of research on aromatization in various environments (including neuromarketing); and
- The achieved very high number and at the same time very low relevance of the obtained links from the mentioned databases, e.g., in the Google Scholar database, when using search strings "aroma" and "industry", "Aromatization" and "industry" we reached 276,000 and 21,600 links, respectively. We selected the largest abstract and citation database of scientific literature, Scopus.

In deciding on the selection of keyword combinations and in the search, we relied primarily on our previous experience and the area of research, which is the aromatization of spaces in industrial production, its impact on the performance of employees, respectively. We also looked at the industrial applications of aromachology. The data were searched in the database by a combination of Article title, Abstract, Keywords. Subsequently, we used frequency analysis and the obtained results were archived in an Excel spreadsheet, which is available on request for potential use.

We entered the following search string into the search engine, which were divided into 4 groups:

- "aroma" and "industry";
- "aroma" and "work performance";
- "aromatization" and "production"; and
- "aromatization" and "industry"

The next step was to define the criteria for which of the available articles will be included in the analysis of the literal revision, and which will be excluded. We found out after reading the title of the article and the abstract, in some cases we also studied the full text, mainly the methods used, the object of research, the main findings, discussion, and implications for further investigation. The selection was made according to the following criteria:

- Articles focused on aroma in industry;
- Articles related to aroma and neuroscience;
- Articles related to work performance and production;
- Articles written in English; and
- Journal and type of scientific article.

Those articles that met our selected selection criteria underwent a detailed analysis. To obtain the required data, we subsequently specified the individual search strings according to the "Subject area", which was "Engineering". We then limited the data by year of publication via "Year" (from 2011 to 2020). Figure 2 (authors own processing) shows the selection process of obtaining expert articles for literature review.

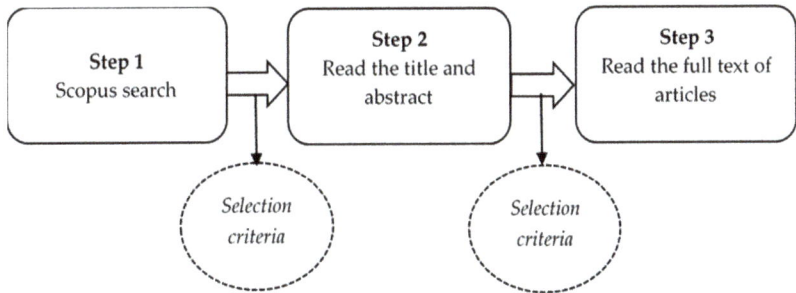

Figure 2. Article selection process.

2.2. Data Extraction

For the study of the literature of the area of our scientific interest, we chose the globally most frequently used scientific information database Scopus.

When creating an information strategy, i.e., in order to find the most relevant links, a method known from marketing research was used, namely market segmentation, where the whole market is divided into segments (market subsets) according to pre-selected criteria (geographical, demographic, psychographic, and behavioral principle of customers), creating the most homogeneous subgroups of consumers that differ as much as possible so that they can be addressed by selected marketing tools. With this approach, 4 groups (segments) of professional papers were created by a combination of keywords, the characteristics of which are in Table 2. In creating a combination of keywords, we used our previous experience in the field of neuromarketing and aromachology [2,23].

3. Results

After entering the keyword "aroma industry", 1805 results have been displayed in the Scopus database since 2011. Figure 3 shows the main subject area and Figure 4 the document type.

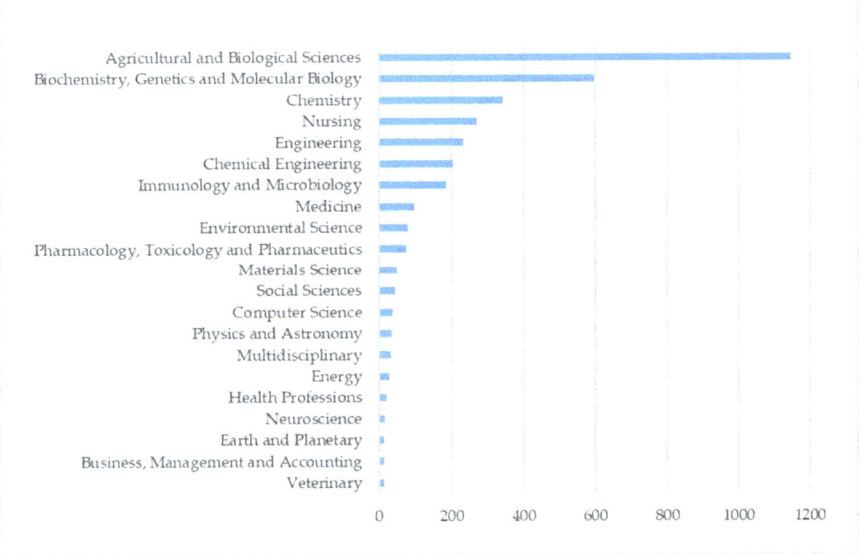

Figure 3. Subject area of the articles.

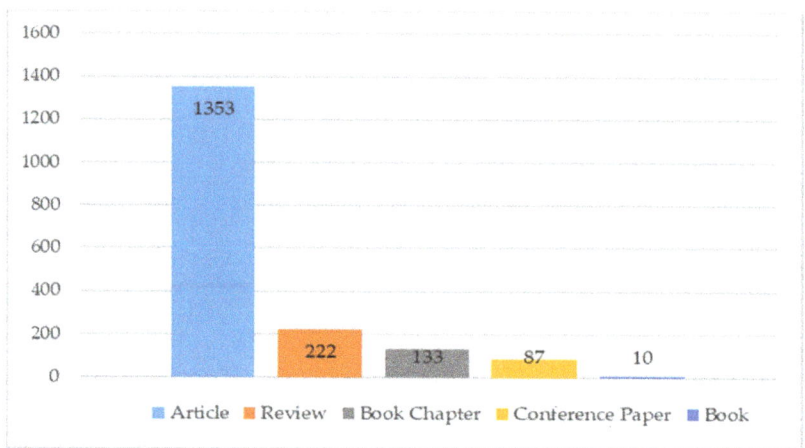

Figure 4. Type of the selected documents.

After studying a large number of scientific articles included in this literature review, we found that most are empirical and deal with the modification of the working environment in connection with cleaning and ventilation air (air quality), thermal, visual, lighting comfort, acoustic environment, building features for designing new buildings and the relationship between acceptability of each environmental parameter. At the time of the pandemic, great attention is paid to the cleaning and flow of air in existing buildings or the design of new buildings. The authors focus on office buildings only, or facilities providing services.

Figure 5 shows the number of articles sorted by year of publication and our search string. The results show in recent years an increase in professional publications in the field, which represents an opportunity to obtain relevant information and the possibility of their use in the future.

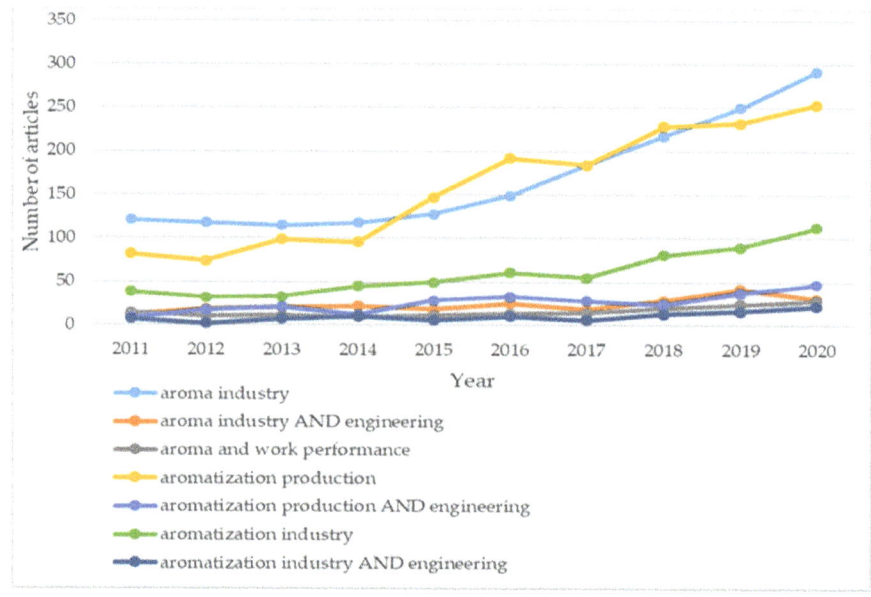

Figure 5. Number of publications per years.

The data in Figure 6 show an overview of the number of words that were relevant to our search topic. In connection with the aromatization of industry, production, respectively work performance, the word chemistry appeared the most, followed by aroma and odors, etc.

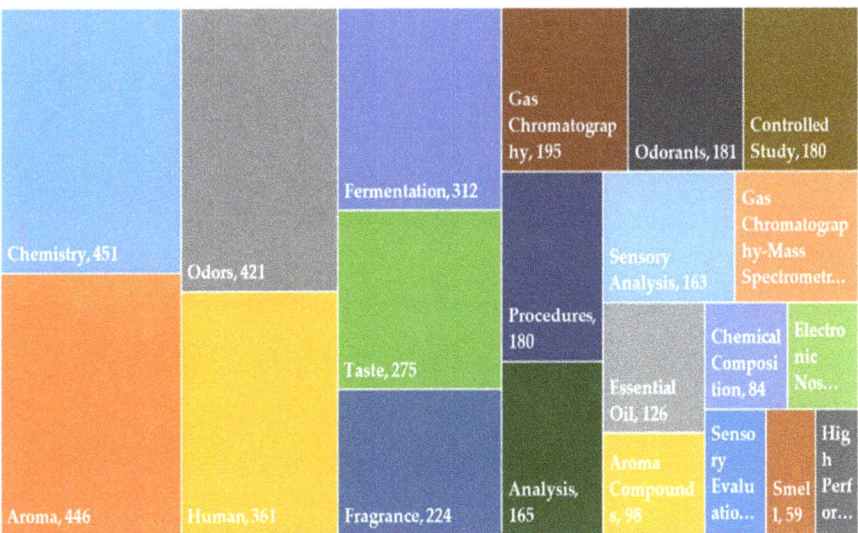

Figure 6. The number of related words.

4. Discussion

- At the beginning of the discussion of the results obtained from the literature review, it is necessary to emphasize that the studied area of aromachology in industry, production environment is not exactly researched and described in contrast to research and publication in the field of neuromarketing and its implications in the retail environment, which are richly represented in indexed but also in non-indexed sources for more than two decades [18,30–43]. If there are published studies, then they are marginal, which is summarized in Table 2. From the many years of experience of the authors of the present article, working in basic and applied research and also in the international holding company of manufacturing companies, this is mainly due to the great diversity of industries;
- The size of industrial premises, the size of which is often incomparable with administrative, business premises and premises for the operation of services;
- The complexity of the aromatization of such spaces, and its control and management;
- Preferential focus of manufacturers on the quality of production, economic results and at the same time; and
- Focusing manufacturers on [24,26] the protection of the health and safety of employees, which is also related to air quality, especially clean air, ventilation, and temperature.

Table 2 is created with as many relevant publications as possible, with tens of hours of study and sorting representing several hundred publications, however, no publications were found directly related to the aromatization of production facilities.

Table 2. Characteristics of the most relevant information sources.

No.	Authors and Reference	Title	Year	Type of Source	Environment	Scent/or Another Factor	Research Subject/Type of Measurement	Practical Implications/Main Conclusion
1.	Wyon, D.P. [40]	Thermal effects on performance	2010	Handbook	indoor administration buildings	heating, cooling, noising; no scent	air quality	Effects on performance and productivity; noise distraction in open offices at 55 dBA has negative effects on the performance of employees.
2.	Wyon D.P. [41]	Enhancing productivity while reducing energy use in buildings	2001	Conference Proceeding	indoor administration building-call-centers	heating, cooling; no scent	air quality	Effects on performance and productivity; field intervention experiments in call-centers demonstrate that the decrement in performance can be larger in practice than it is in realistic laboratory simulation experiments.
3.	Wyon D.P. [42]	The effects of indoor air quality on performance and productivity	2004	Journal	indoor administration buildings-call-centers in northern Europe and the Tropics	Ventilation, temperature; no scent	air quality	It has been shown beyond reasonable doubt that poor indoor air quality in buildings can decrease productivity in addition to causing visitors to express dissatisfaction, the size of the effect is 6–9%.
4.	Seppanen O., Fisk W. [43]	Some Quantitative Relations between Indoor Environmental Quality and Work Performance or Health	2006	Journal	administration environment	ventilation, temperature; no scent	air quality	Quantitative relationships between ventilation rates and short-term sick leave, ventilation rates and work performance, perceived air quality and performance, temperature and performance, and temperature and sick building symptoms (SBS).
5.	Torresin S., Pernigotto G., Cappelletti F., Gasparella A. [44]	Combined effects of environmental factors on human perception and objective performance: A review of experimental laboratory works	2018	Journal (literature review)	non-industrial buildings (Neutral 56%, Office 38%, Aircraft 4%, School 2%)	acoustic, thermal, visual, combined effect; no scent	air quality	A vast literature is available on comfort studies related to the different aspects, aiming at defining quantitative correlations to predict discomfort from the environmental conditions to support design, commissioning, and operation of buildings.

82

Table 2. Cont.

No.	Authors and Reference	Title	Year	Type of Source	Environment	Scent/or Another Factor	Research Subject/Type of Measurement	Practical Implications/Main Conclusion
6.	Baharum F., Zainon M.R., Seng L.Y., Nawi M.N.M. [25]	Analysis of indoor environmental quality influence toward occupants' work performance in Kompleks Eureka, USM	2016	Journal	residential buildings in industrialized areas	acoustic, lighting, temperature, visual; no scent	air quality	Own research via questionnaire survey. Air quality satisfaction is lower than the thermal satisfaction in the buildings.
7.	Fisk, W., Wargocki, P., Zhang, X. [45]	Do Indoor CO_2 Levels Directly Affect Perceived Air Quality, Health, or Work Performance?	2019	Journal	occupied buildings	carbon dioxide; no scent	air quality	Article summarizes the findings of 10 recent studies investigating whether increased carbon dioxide (CO_2) concentrations, with other factors constant, influence perceived air quality, health, or work performance of people.
8.	Niemelä R., Rautio S., Hannula M., Reijula K. [46]	Work environment effects on labor productivity: An intervention study in a storage building.	2002	Journal	harbor storage building	thermal, contamination, lighting, ventilation; no scent	air quality.	As a result of the renovation, thermal conditions, air quality, and lighting conditions improved notably. The employees' subjective evaluations showed the significant decrease in dissatisfaction ratings.
9.	Roskams M., Haynes B. [26]	Predictive analytics in facilities management	2019	Journal	open-plan office	heating, ventilation, air-conditioning, temperature, humidity, illumination, sound pressure; no scent	air quality-own research using wireless sensors	This is the first field study to directly explore the relationship between physical environment data collected using wireless sensors and subjective ratings of environmental comfort building analytics and human analytics, towards the goal of optimizing environmental comfort in the workplace.
10.	Putnam C., Price S. [47]	High-performance facilities engineering: Preparing the team for the sustainable workplace	2004	Journal	green building	energy efficiency; no scent	facilities management department	The green building offers the potential for energy and resource efficiency, lower operating costs for owners and managers, and an indoor environment that enhances worker productivity and comfort.
11.	Barsade S.G., Gibson D.E. [48]	Why Does Affect Matter in Organizations?	2007	Journal	general working environment	no reported; no scent	emotional intelligence	Employees' moods, emotions, and dispositional affect („affect" is another word for "emotion" in organizational behavior studies) influence critical organizational outcomes such as job performance, decision making, creativity, turnover, prosocial behavior, teamwork, negotiation, and leadership.

There are several research studies that publish results on the air quality effects of indoor administration buildings on performance and productivity. The size of this effect may be as high as 6–9% [44,45]. On the other hand, there are only a few expert research studies that would provide information on targeted air modification (other than ventilation) in the internal environment in the production process and the interaction, e.g., that the treated air positively or negatively consciously or unconsciously affects labor productivity, respectively. Published research shows that the indoor environment is important for people's health and comfort [46–49].

Another major research area directly related to the quality of the workspace is the influence of emotions on the workplace [50,51]. The state of the literature shows that affect matters because people are not isolated 'emotional islands.' Rather, they bring all of themselves to work, including their traits, moods, and emotions, and their affective experiences and expressions, which influence others. Emotional intelligence is not a buzz word only familiar in psychology and education, but is now talked about in business circles as well.

From the studied published results of research, partial research, or studies that deal with IAQ (Indoor Air Quality), The IEQ (Indoor Environmental Quality) shows that the authors examined this issue through questionnaire surveys among employees working mostly in administrative buildings [28,39] and open space offices [26], in laboratory conditions and call centers [46], or residential buildings with air pollutants such as Radon, volatile organic compounds (VOCs) and carbonyl compounds [50].

Interesting research was conducted by Mangone et al. [52] in open space offices. They positively evaluated the effect of indoor plants on the thermal comfort of office workers within an office building. Numerous research studies have found that plants have a positive impact on people with respect to a diverse range of performance categories, for example [53–56].

Seppänen and Fisk [43] critically evaluated approximately 100 expert articles on the indoor environmental quality on human health and performance and found that there is a relationship between SBS (sick building symptoms) and work performance. The longer the internal environment is ventilated, the more illness and sickness decrease [56–64]. They also found a direct relationship between ventilation and the work output, but this performance increases only to a certain extent, up to about 30 L/s/person, then the curve acquires a saturated character. All it takes is a lower value of approx. 5 L/s and the performance increases sharply. Although the results are not statistically unambiguous, they nevertheless show that the parameters examined are related to the design of the building and the ventilation of the work areas. In this paper, they have shown that it is possible, with existing data, to estimate quantitative relationships between ventilation rate and illness-caused absence and to quantitatively estimate how work performance is related to ventilation rate, air temperature, and perceived air quality.

Similarly, a paper by S. Torresin et al. [44] looks at 110 literary sources focused on non-industrial buildings. In developed countries, people spend almost 90% of their time inside buildings, where most of their activities take place [62]. Inclusion criteria regarded (acoustic, thermal, visual, and air quality) the investigation of interaction effects between two or more environmental factors in occupant comfort perception and performance and the impact of one environmental factor on the perception of other environmental aspects (crossed effects). The effects of moderate heat stress and open-plan office noise distraction on SBS symptoms and the performance of office workers have been shown by Witterseh et al. [64]. They demonstrated that open office noise distraction, even at the realistic level of 55 dBA, increases fatigue and has many negative effects on the performance of office work, as does a moderately warm air temperature.

The complexity of research on the impact of air quality on the health or work performance of people is also evidenced by the findings by Fisk, Wargocki and Zhang [45]. The published results of the research are not clear and further research is needed to address the discrepancies among the current findings. Experts on workplace air quality assessment have been working for a long time to develop an indoor air quality checklist (IAQ) to introduce the need for workplace air quality control [65]. Four environmental factors—defined by several physical quantities related to acoustical, thermal, visual environments, and Indoor Air Quality (included chemical composition, air velocity), respectively—have been identified as the most important to characterize indoor environments from the American Society of Heating, Refrigeration and Air-conditioning Engineers [66,67]. To control the air from production processes and to eliminate this impact on the study of the effects of flavoring as much as possible, it is possible to use a system called KOALA (Knowing Our Ambient Local Air Quality), which is a low-cost air quality monitor, which was deployed in Sydney (Australia) and was successfully used as air quality monitor data in the internal and external environment via a deep learning technique called long short-term memory (LSTM) [68]. There is also a method of measurement on pollutants and to use health effects on a six-degree scale from good to hazardous. An integrated sensing system is part of a smart building where real-time indoor air quality data are monitored round the clock using sensors and operating in the Internet-of-Things (IoT) environment [69]. It is also useful and extremely necessary to follow the IAQ (Indoor air quality) checklist when planning analyses. This is the newly developed IAQ checklist, which will be one of the key elements in identifying risk elements for the evaluation of indoor air pollutants in indoor environments and this IAQ checklist will highlight the need for IAQ assessment in workplaces [70,71]. Indoor air quality is an important factor for the company, managers and employees because it can affect people's health, comfort, overall well-being and productivity. So the question is, what do businesses have to do if they want to improve the air quality in their operations? There are several options they can realize, from using zero-emission cleaners to installing the latest and greatest air filters to improve indoor air quality. When we think about air quality and benefits for customers, we must not forget the people who spend the most time in the given environment, the employees. Air quality has a big impact on their productivity and safety. This is confirmed by several types of research from renowned institutions and specialized companies. Research is increasingly providing detailed insights into scents and human behavior and offering a range of guidelines on how to succeed in this area.

The results obtained from the study of a systematic literature review on the impact of the aromatization of the production environment on workers were already used in an experiment to examine the impact of aromatization and air quality on the unconscious and conscious perception of employee's satisfaction. The research took place for 7 months in an international company engaged in the production and sale of polypropylene fibers for a wide range of industries. The results of the research were processed and published in professional articles.

5. Conclusions

A large number of scientific articles are devoted to the modification of the working environment in connection with its cleaning and airflow, temperature, or noise. At the time of the pandemic, great attention is paid to the cleaning and flow of air in existing buildings or the design of new buildings. Experts focus on purely administrative buildings or facilities providing services. Attention is paid to the production area for reasons of protection, safety and health at work. There are no known scientific studies on flavoring and the scientific field of aromachology in production facilities. The reasons are discussed in Section 4. From a systematically performed literature review on the modification of the internal environment in buildings, conclusions can be drawn for basic and applied research for use in industry. Although flavoring would not directly affect performance, it is not negligible that workers feel as comfortable as possible in the course of their work. This leads to the conclusion that there is a large research gap for the implication of the scientific discipline on aromachology and subsequently for applied research in manufacturing practice.

Author Contributions: Conceptualization, K.Č. and A.D.; methodology, P.M.; software, K.Č.; validation, A.D., K.Č. and P.M.; formal analysis, P.M.; resources, A.D.; data curation, A.D.; writing—original draft preparation, K.Č. and A.D.; writing—review and editing, P.M.; visualization, P.M. and K.Č.; project administration, K.Č. All authors have read and agreed to the published version of the manuscript.

Funding: This research received no external funding.

Institutional Review Board Statement: Not applicable.

Informed Consent Statement: Not applicable.

Data Availability Statement: Not applicable.

Acknowledgments: This publication has been supported by the Erasmus+ KA2 Strategic Partnerships grant no. 2018-1-SK01-KA203-046324 "Implementation of Consumer Neuroscience and Smart Research Solutions in Aromachology" (NEUROSMARTOLOGY). The European Commission's support for the production of this publication does not constitute an endorsement of the contents, which reflect the views only of the authors, and the Commission cannot be held responsible for any use which may be made of the information contained therein.

Conflicts of Interest: The authors declare no conflict of interest.

References

1. Small, M.D.; Gerber, C.J.; Erica Mak, Y.; Hummel, T. Differential Neural Responses Evoked by Orthonasal versus Retronasal Odorant Perception in Humans. *Neuron* **2005**, *47*, 593–605. [CrossRef]
2. Čarnogurský, K.; Diačiková, A.; Madzík, P. Innovative Research Solutions in Aromachology and Aromatherapy—Literature Review. In Proceedings of the International Scientific Days 2020—"Innovative Approaches for Sustainable Agriculture and Food Systems Development", Nitra, Slovakia, 13–15 May 2020. [CrossRef]
3. Johnson, J.R.; Rivard, R.L.; Griffin, K.H.; Kolste, A.K.; Joswiak, D.; Kinney, M.E.; Dusek, J.A. The effectiveness of nurse-delivered aromatherapy in an acute care setting. *Complement. Ther. Med.* **2016**, *25*, 164–169. [CrossRef]
4. Cooke, B.; Ernst, E. Aromatherapy: A systematic review. *Br. J. Gen. Pract.* **2000**, *50*, 493–496.
5. Price, S.; Price, L. *Aromatherapy for Health Professionals*, 4th ed.; Elsevier Churchill Livingstone: London, UK, 2012; 355p, ISBN 978-0-7020-3564-7.
6. Lis-Balchin, M. *Aromatherapy Science: A Guide for Healthcare Professionals*; Pharmaceutical Press: London, UK, 2006; 451p, ISBN 085369-578-4.
7. Damian, P.; Damian, K. *Aromatherapy: Scent and Psyche: Using Essential Oils for Physical and Emotional Well-Being*; Healing Arts Press: Rochester, VT, USA, 1995; 244p, ISBN 978-089281530-2.
8. Ornelas, S.; Kleiner, B.H. New developments in managing job related stress. *Equal. Oppor. Int.* **2003**, *22*, 64–70. [CrossRef]
9. Huang, L.; Capdevila, L. Aromatherapy Improves Work Performance Through Balancing the Autonomic Nervous System. *J. Altern. Complement. Med.* **2017**, *23*, 214–221. [CrossRef] [PubMed]
10. Andrews, S.E. *The Reduction of Stress Levels in Healthcare Workers Using Aromatherapy*; No 28322828; Brandman University: Irvine, CA, USA; ProQuest Dissertations Publishing: Irvine, CA, USA, 2021.
11. Herz, R.S. Aromatherapy Facts and Fictions: A Scientific Analysis of Olfactory Effects on Mood, Physiology and Behavior. *Int. J. Neurosci.* **2009**, *119*, 263–290. [CrossRef] [PubMed]
12. Van Toller, S.; Dodd, G.H. *Fragrance: The Psychology and Biology on Perfume*; Elsevier Science Publisher Ltd.: Amsterdam, The Netherlands, 1992; 290p, ISBN 1-85166-872-1.
13. Chu, S.; Downes, J.J. Odour-evoked autobiographical memories: Psychological investigations of proustian phenomena. *Chem. Senses* **2000**, *25*, 111–116. [CrossRef] [PubMed]
14. von Kempski, D. The Use of Olfactory Stimulants to Improve Indoor Air Quality. *J. Hum. Environ. Syst.* **2002**, *5*, 61–68. [CrossRef]
15. Sumegi, L.; Ilona, L. *Differential Effects of Lavender and Rosemary on Arousal and Cognitive Performance*; Carleton University: Ottawa, ON, Canada, 2018; 108p, ISBN 978-0-494-79582-8.
16. Morrison, M.; Gan, S.; Dubelaar, C.; Oppewal, H. In-store music and aroma influences on shopper behavior and satisfaction. *J. Bus. Res.* **2011**, *64*, 558–564. [CrossRef]
17. Jacob, C.; Stefan, J.; Guéguen, N. Ambient scent and consumer behavior: A field study in a florist's retail shop. *Int. Rev. Retail. Distrib. Consum. Res.* **2013**, *24*, 116–120. [CrossRef]
18. Ward, P.; Davies, B.J.; Kooijman, D. Olfaction and the retail environment: Examining the influence of ambient scent. *Serv. Bus.* **2007**, *1*, 295–316. [CrossRef]
19. Suthaphot, N.; Chulakup, S.; Chonsakorn, S.; Mongkholrattanasit, R. Application of aromatherapy on cotton fabric by microcapsules. In Proceedings of the RMUTP International Conference, Textiles & Fashion, Bangkok, Thailand, 3–4 July 2012; Available online: http://www.repository.rmutt.ac.th/xmlui/handle/123456789/1739 (accessed on 19 April 2021).

20. Horská, E.; Horská, E.; Sedik, P.; Bercik, J.; Krasnodebski, A.; Witczak, M.; Filipiak-Florkiewicz, A. Aromachology in Food Sector—Aspects of Consumer Food Products Choice. *Nauka. Technol. Jakość* **2018**, *25*, 33–41.
21. Davies, B.J.; Kooijman, D.; Ward, P. The Sweet Smell of Success: Olfaction in Retailing. *J. Mark. Manag.* **2003**, *19*, 611–627. [CrossRef]
22. Chebat, J.C.; Michon, R. Impact of ambient odors on mall shoppers' emotions, cognition, and spending: A test of competi-tive causal theories. *J. Bus. Res.* **2003**, *56*, 529–539. [CrossRef]
23. Čarnogurský, K. Influence of aromatization on the conscious and unconscious perception of work environment. 2021, Under processing.
24. Sundell, J. On the history of indoor air quality and health. *Indoor Air* **2004**, *14*, 51–58. [CrossRef]
25. Zainon, M.R.; Baharum, F.; Seng, L.Y. Analysis of indoor environmental quality influence toward occupants' work performance in Kompleks Eureka, USM. *AIP Conf. Proc.* **2016**. [CrossRef]
26. Roskams, M.; Haynes, B. Predictive analytics in facilities management. *J. Facil. Manag.* **2019**, *17*, 356–370. [CrossRef]
27. Maula, H.; Hongisto, V.; Naatula, V.; Haapakangas, A.; Koskela, H. The effect of low ventilation rate with elevated bioeffluent concentration on work performance, perceived indoor air quality, and health symptoms. *Indoor Air* **2017**, *27*, 1141–1153. [CrossRef] [PubMed]
28. Mitchell, D.J.; Kahn, B.E.; Knasko, S.C. There's Something in the Air: Effects of Congruent or Incongruent Ambient Odor on Consumer Decision Making. *J. Consum. Res.* **1995**, *22*, 229–238. [CrossRef]
29. Bone, P.F.; Pam, S.E. Scents in the Marketplace: Explaining a Fraction of Olfaction. *J. Retail.* **1999**, *75*, 243–262. [CrossRef]
30. Bosmans, A. Scents and Sensibility: When Do (In) congruent Ambient Scents Influence Product Evaluations? *J. Mark.* **2006**, *70*, 32–43. [CrossRef]
31. Zurawicki, L. *Neuromarketing-Exploring the Brain of the Consumer*; Springer: New York, NY, USA, 2010; 271p, ISBN 978-3-540-77828-8.
32. Herrmann, A.; Zidansek, M.; Sprott, D.E.; Spangenberg, E.R. The Power of Simplicity: Processing Fluency and the Effects of Olfactory Cues on Retail Sales. *J. Retail.* **2013**, *89*, 30–43. [CrossRef]
33. Lemke, F.; Clark, M.; Wilson, H. Customer experience quality: An exploration in business and consumer contexts using repertory grid technique. *J. Acad. Mark. Sci.* **2011**, *39*, 846–869. [CrossRef]
34. Ariely, D.; Berns, G.S. Neuromarketing: The hope and hype of neuroimaging in business. *Nat. Rev. Neurosci.* **2010**, *11*, 284–292. [CrossRef]
35. Berčík, J.; Virágh, R.; Kádeková, Z.; Duchoňová, T. Aroma marketing as a tool to increase turnover in a chosen business entity. *Potravin. Slovak J. Food Sci.* **2020**, *14*, 1161–1175. [CrossRef]
36. Berčík, J.; Rybanská, J. Methods used in neuromarketing. *Neuromark. Food Retail.* **2017**, 83–102. [CrossRef]
37. Lwin, M.O.; Morrin, M.; Chong, C.S.T.; Goh, S.X. Odor Semantics and Visual Cues: What We Smell Impacts Where We Look, What We Remember, and What We Want to Buy. *J. Behav. Decis. Mak.* **2015**, *29*, 336–350. [CrossRef]
38. Tomi, K.; Fushiki, T.; Murakami, H.; Matsumura, Y.; Hayashi, T.; Yazawa, S. Relationships between Lavender Aroma Component and Aromachology Effect. *Acta Hortic.* **2011**, 299–306. [CrossRef]
39. Lee, M.S.; Choi, J.; Posadzki, P.; Ernst, E. Aromatherapy for health care: An overview of systematic reviews. *Maturitas* **2012**, *71*, 257–260. [CrossRef] [PubMed]
40. Wyon, D.P. Thermal effects on performance. In *IAQ Handbook*; Spengler, J., Samet, J.M., McCarthy, J.F., Eds.; McGraw-Hill: New York, NY, USA, 2001; Chapter 16.
41. Wyon, D.P. Enhancing productivity while reducing energy use in buildings. In Proceedings of the Conference 'E-Vision 2000' at the Department of Energy, Washington, DC, USA, 11–13 October 2000; RAND Corporation: Washington, DC, USA, 2001.
42. Wyon, D.P. The effects of indoor air quality on performance and productivity. *Indoor Air* **2004**, *14*, 92–101. [CrossRef]
43. Seppänen, O.A.; Fisk, W. Some Quantitative Relations between Indoor Environmental Quality and Work Performance or Health. *HVAC&R Res.* **2006**, *12*, 957–973. [CrossRef]
44. Torresin, S.; Pernigotto, G.; Cappelletti, F.; Gasparella, A. Combined effects of environmental factors on human perception and objective performance: A review of experimental laboratory works. *Indoor Air* **2018**, *28*, 525–538. [CrossRef]
45. Fisk, W.; Wargocki, P.; Zhang, X. Do Indoor CO_2 Levels Directly Affect Perceived Air Quality, Health, or Work Performance? *ASHRAE J.* **2019**, *61*, 70–77.
46. Niemelä, R.; Rautio, S.; Hannula, M.; Reijula, K. Work environment effects on labor productivity: An intervention study in a storage building. *Am. J. Ind. Med.* **2002**, *42*, 328–335. [CrossRef] [PubMed]
47. Putnam, C.; Price, S. High-performance facilities engineering: Preparing the team for the sustainable workplace. *J. Facil. Manag.* **2005**, *3*, 161–172. [CrossRef]
48. Barsade, S.G.; Gibson, D.E. Why Does Affect Matter in Organizations? *Acad. Manag. Perspect.* **2007**, *21*, 36–59. [CrossRef]
49. Amabile, T.M.; Barsade, S.G.; Mueller, J.S.; Staw, B.M. Affect and Creativity at Work. *Adm. Sci. Q.* **2005**, *50*, 367–403. [CrossRef]
50. Madjar, N.; Oldham, G.R.; Pratt, M.G. There's No Place like Home? The Contributions of Work and Nonwork Creativity Support to Employees' Creative Performance. *Acad. Manag. J.* **2002**, *45*, 757–767. [CrossRef]
51. Beldean-Galea, M.S.; Dicu, T.; Cucoș, A.; Burghele, B.-D.; Catalina, T.; Botoș, M.; Țenter, A.; Szacsvai, K.; Lupulescu, A.; Pap, I.; et al. Evaluation of indoor air pollutants in 100 retrofit residential buildings from Romania during cold season. *J. Clean. Prod.* **2020**, *277*, 124098. [CrossRef]

52. Mangone, G.; Kurvers, S.; Luscuere, P. Constructing thermal comfort: Investigating the effect of vegetation on indoor thermal comfort through a four season thermal comfort quasi-experiment. *Build. Environ.* **2014**, *81*, 410–426. [CrossRef]
53. Hartig, T.; Staats, H. The need for psychological restoration as a determinant of environmental preferences. *J. Environ. Psychol.* **2006**, *26*, 215–226. [CrossRef]
54. Qin, J.; Sun, C.; Zhou, X.; Leng, H.; Lian, Z. The effect of indoor plants on human comfort. *Indoor Built Environ.* **2014**, *23*, 709–723. [CrossRef]
55. Lohr, V.I.; Pearson-Mims, C.H.; Goodwin, G.K. Interior Plants May Improve Worker Productivity and Reduce Stress in a Windowless Environment. *J. Environ. Hortic.* **1996**, *14*, 97–100. [CrossRef]
56. White, M.; Smith, A.; Humphryes, K.; Pahl, S.; Snelling, D.; Depledge, M. Blue space: The importance of water for preference, affect, and restorativeness ratings of natural and built scenes. *J. Environ. Psychol.* **2010**, *30*, 482–493. [CrossRef]
57. Fisk, W.J.; Faulkner, D.; Sullivan, D.P. *Accuracy of CO_2 Sensors in Commercial Buildings: A Pilotstudy*; Ernest Orlando Lawrence Berkeley National Laboratory: Berkeley, CA, USA, 2006.
58. Fisk, W.J.; Singer, B.C.; Chan, W.R. Association of residential energy efficiency retrofits with indoor environmental quality, comfort, and health: A review of empirical data. *Build. Environ.* **2020**, *180*, 107067. [CrossRef]
59. Stamatelopoulou, A.; Asimakopoulos, D.; Maggos, T. Effects of PM, TVOCs and comfort parameters on indoor air quality of residences with young children. *Build. Environ.* **2019**, *150*, 233–244. [CrossRef]
60. World Health Organization. *WHO Guidelines for Indoor Air Quality: Selected Pollutants*; WHO: Geneva, Switzerland, 2010.
61. World Health Organization. *Household Air Pollution and Health*; WHO: Geneva, Switzerland, 2016.
62. World Health Organization. *Air Pollution*; WHO: Geneva, Switzerland, 2019.
63. Klepeis, N.E.; Nelson, W.C.; Ott, W.R.; Robinson, J.P.; Tsang, A.M.; Switzer, P.; Behar, J.V.; Hern, S.C.; Engelmann, W.H. The National Human Activity Pattern Survey (NHAPS): A resource for assessing exposure to environmental pollutants. *J. Expo. Sci. Environ. Epidemiol.* **2001**, *11*, 231–252. [CrossRef] [PubMed]
64. Witterseh, T.; Wyon, D.P.; Clausen, G. The effects of moderate heat stress and open-plan office noise distraction on SBS symptoms and on the performance of office work. *Indoor Air* **2004**, *14*, 30–40. [CrossRef]
65. Syazwan, A.; Rafee, B.M.; Shaharuddin, M.; Juahir, H.; Syafiq, M.Y.A.; Ibthisham, A.M.; Nizar, A.; Hanafiah, J.M.; Azhar, M.M.; Anita, A.; et al. Development of an indoor air quality checklist for risk assessment of indoor air pollutants by semiquantitative score in nonindustrial workplaces. *Health Policy* **2012**, *5*, 17–23. [CrossRef]
66. ASHRAE. Interactions affecting the achievement of acceptable indoor environments. In *ASHRAE Guideline*, 10th ed.; ASHRAE: Peachtree Corners, GA, USA, 2011.
67. Frontczak, M.; Wargocki, P. Literature survey on how different factors influence human comfort in indoor environments. *Build. Environ.* **2011**, *46*, 922–937. [CrossRef]
68. Gottschalk, I. Consumer evaluation of ambient scent. *Int. J. Retail. Distrib. Manag.* **2018**, *46*, 530–544. [CrossRef]
69. Lin, M.-H.; Cross, S.N.; Childers, T.L. Understanding olfaction and emotions and the moderating role of individual differences. *Eur. J. Mark.* **2018**, *52*, 811–836. [CrossRef]
70. Liu, N.; Liu, X.; Jayaratne, R.; Morawska, L. A study on extending the use of air quality monitor data via deep learning techniques. *J. Clean. Prod.* **2020**, *274*, 122956. [CrossRef]
71. Ha, Q.P.; Metia, S.; Phung, M.D. Sensing Data Fusion for Enhanced Indoor Air Quality Monitoring. *IEEE Sens. J.* **2020**, *20*, 4430–4441. [CrossRef]

Review

Air Quality as a Key Factor in the Aromatisation of Stores: A Systematic Literature Review

Zdeňka Panovská, Vojtech Ilko and Marek Doležal *

Department of Food Analysis and Nutrition, University of Chemistry and Technology, Technická 5, 166 28 Prague, Czech Republic; zdenka.panovska@vscht.cz (Z.P.); vojtech.ilko@vscht.cz (V.I.)
* Correspondence: marek.dolezal@vscht.cz

Abstract: Scientific literature on indoor air quality is categorised mainly into environmental sciences, construction building technology and environmental and civil engineering. Indoor air is a complex and dynamic mixture of a variety of volatile and particulate matter. Some of the constituents are odorous and originate from various sources, such as construction materials, furniture, cleaning products, goods in stores, humans and many more. The first part of the article summarises the knowledge about the substances that are found in the air inside buildings, especially stores, and have a negative impact on our health. This issue has been monitored for a long time, and so, using a better methodology, it is possible to identify even low concentrations of monitored substances. The second part summarises the possibility of using various aromatic substances to improve people's sense of the air in stores. In recent times, air modification has come to the forefront of researchers' interest in order to create a more pleasant environment and possibly increase sales.

Keywords: indoor air; retail stores; aromachology; volatile compounds; scents

Citation: Panovská, Z.; Ilko, V.; Doležal, M. Air Quality as a Key Factor in the Aromatisation of Stores: A Systematic Literature Review. *Appl. Sci.* **2021**, *11*, 7697. https://doi.org/10.3390/app11167697

Academic Editor: Elza Bontempi

Received: 29 June 2021
Accepted: 19 August 2021
Published: 21 August 2021

Publisher's Note: MDPI stays neutral with regard to jurisdictional claims in published maps and institutional affiliations.

Copyright: © 2021 by the authors. Licensee MDPI, Basel, Switzerland. This article is an open access article distributed under the terms and conditions of the Creative Commons Attribution (CC BY) license (https://creativecommons.org/licenses/by/4.0/).

1. Introduction

Air is the common name for the atmosphere of Earth. Dry air contains, by volume, 78.09% nitrogen, 20.95% oxygen, 0.93% argon, 0.04% carbon dioxide, 0.0018% neon and small amounts of other gases. The concentration of water vapour varies significantly from around 10 ppm by volume in the coldest portions of the atmosphere to as much as 5% by volume in hot, humid air masses [1].

Filtered air includes trace amounts of many other chemical compounds. Many substances of natural origin may be present in, locally and seasonally variable, small amounts as aerosols in an unfiltered air sample, including dust of mineral and organic composition, pollen and spores. Various contaminants, often industrial, may also be present, including chlorine (elemental or in compounds), fluorine compounds and sulphur compounds, such as hydrogen sulphide and sulphur dioxide.

During the last few decades, there has been a growing concern by people and scientists over the quality of the air not only in cities, towns and villages but, also, in buildings where we live, work and shop. Modern homes, offices and shops are insulated much better than they were previously. The methods with which buildings are constructed and operated have changed [2]. New materials are tested, ventilation has improved and the temperature and other parameters are monitored so that the environment and air in buildings does not have a negative impact on our health. In addition to monitoring the air quality and potentially harmful compounds, new possibilities are being developed to improve the purchasing environment of customers. In addition to improving the environment in shops, such as the appropriate temperature, light level, music, decorations and so on, the choice of an appropriate aroma for a shop is becoming increasingly apparent. This article examines the contents of substances the air in shops may contain and then describes the possibilities of how air can be affected in connection with pleasant odours.

2. Materials and Methods

The object of research in the present study was the space of retail stores, where goods and services are sold directly to the consumers who will use them. Commercial properties used for retail purposes include single-tenant stores, grocery stores, restaurants, strip malls and shopping malls. Retail spaces come in a variety of shapes and sizes and may be located in free-standing buildings, enclosed malls, strip shopping centres, downtown shopping districts or mixed-use facilities. Retail spaces are also situated in airports and other transportation facilities, hotel lobbies, sports stadiums and temporary or special event venues.

The second object of this study was the indoor air quality, which has been systematically addressed since the late 1970s. The impact on human health has been discussed several times by the World Health Organization (WHO) [3,4]. In Europe, by demand of the European Commission, the Scientific Committee on Health and Environmental Risks (SCHER) prepared an opinion on the risk assessment on indoor air quality [5]. There is an urgent need for a change that is innovative and takes a systemic, skills-based multidisciplinary approach. At present, the legislation varies from one EU Member State to another, with the absence of standards and control mechanisms. To fill this gap, harmonisation initiatives need to be taken, setting out strategies and parameters at the same time, to control indoor pollutants [6]. The main factors related to indoor air were observed to be:

- Chemicals for intended use or unintentional emissions from different sources [7–12];
- Radon [13,14];
- Particles [15–20];
- Microbes [21];
- Pets and pests [22–29];
- Humidity [30,31];
- Ventilation [32–35];
- Temperature [36–38].

This review is organised as a research paper based on the PRISMA Extension (PRISMA-ScR) approach [39]. A comprehensive literature search from the Scopus and ScienceDirect databases was performed in May 2021 and was limited to articles published in English since 2000. The data was searched in the databases in the fields Article title, Abstract and Keywords. Terms such as indoor, air quality, stores, shops, sensory marketing, scent marketing, aromachology, behaviour and consumer were, among others, used. The most attention was given to studies published in journals included in Journal Citation Reports.

3. Results and Discussion

By entering the term indoor air quality, 13,714 scientific manuscripts (reviews and articles) were found in the ScienceDirect database and 14,863 in the Scopus database since 2000. From this selection, we extracted, using the keyword "shop", 232 results from ScienceDirect and 89 articles from Scopus. The keyword "store" identified 119 and 134 additional results, respectively. The articles that met our selection criteria were subjected to a detailed analysis. As this is a new area of scientific analysis, the number of scientific studies is very limited, with the absence of standardised procedures, as we discuss below.

3.1. Indoor Air Health Risk Substances in Stores

The air quality in buildings is monitored from various perspectives. It is certainly very important to monitor the air quality from a health point of view. There are many works that deal with which substances are found in the air in buildings, why they are found there and how they can affect our health. In 1999, Jones [2] published a review in which he summarised information from more than 200 papers and discussed the current understanding of the relationship between indoor air pollution and health. The article was divided into sections that dealt with the most frequent pollutants, such as carbon dioxide (CO_2), carbon monoxide (CO), total hydrocarbon (THC), formaldehyde (HCHO), respirable particulate matter (PM10) and airborne bacteria. He discussed what kinds of pollutants could influence the quality of indoor air, the range of sources and the measured concentrations of individual substances in the air. Table 1 shows the most observed pollutants, their sources, health effects and some measured concentrations from selected works.

Table 1. Chemical compounds in the air in buildings, their sources and their potential health effects [2].

Chemical Compounds	Sources	Potential Health Effect	Some Finding Concentration
Allergens	House dust, domestic animals, insects	Asthma	
Asbestos	Fire retardant materials, insulation	Asbestos-related lung cancer, mesothelioma, skin irritation	
Benzene	Smoke cigarette, petrol with benzene evaporisation, combustion,	Carcinogenicity and haematotoxicity, genotoxicity	1 µg/m^3 and 5–20 µg/m^3
Carbon dioxide	Metabolic activity, combustion activities, motor vehicles in garages	Asphyxiant, and can also act as a respiratory irritant, headaches, dizziness, and nausea	54,860 mg/m^3
Carbon monoxide	Fuel burning, boilers, stoves, gas or kerosene heaters, tobacco, smoke	Headache, fatigue, dizziness, and nausea	3657 mg/m^3
Formaldehyde	Particleboard, insulation, furnishings	Sneezing, coughing, skin irritation and minor eye irritation	0.08–2.28 mg/m^3
Microorganisms	People, animals, plants, air conditioning systems	Rhinitis (and other upper respiratory symptoms), asthma, atopic dermatitis	
Nitrogen dioxide	Outdoor air, fuel burning, motor vehicles in garages	Potential danger for asthmatics	Outdoor annual mean range of 20–90 µg/m^3 indoor may have 200 µg/m^3
Organic substances	Adhesives, solvents, building materials, volatilisation, combustion, paints, tobacco smoke		
Ozone	Photochemical reactions	Pulmonary function, respiratory diseases, asthmatics	40–300-µg/m^3 concentrations per hour
Particles	Resuspension, tobacco smoke, combustion products		
Polycyclic aromatic hydrocarbons	Fuel combustion, tobacco smoke		
Pollens	Outdoor air, trees, grass, weeds, plants		
Radon Soil	Building construction materials (concrete, stone)	Lung cancer	45.3–150 Bq/m^3
SO$_2$	Burning coal, fuels	Chronic respiratory complaints, respiratory symptoms	(52–78 µg/m^3)
	burning of wood and fossil fuels	Respiratory illness	respirable particles of different sizes
	cigarettes	Eye, nose, and throat irritation	53.2 µg/m^3 in a study of 7 restaurants, whilst a median concentration of 355 µg/m^3
Fungal spores	Soil, plants, foods, internal surfaces	Atopic dermatitis, asthma, rhinitis (and other upper respiratory symptoms)	

Substances known as volatile organic compounds (VOCs) are likely to be very important. They can arise from different sources, including paints, varnishes, solvents and preservatives. The most studied substances are: benzene, toluene, n-decane, limonene, o-xylene, 1,1,1-trichloroethane, p-dichlorobenzene, 1,2,4-trimethylbenzene and p-xylene, undecane, 1,3,5-trimethylbenzene, dichloroethane and trichloroethane [2,5,6,8,11,40,41].

In 2010, the World Health Federation published WHO guidelines for indoor air quality selected pollutants in which the individual substances are discussed in more detail. The substances considered in this review, i.e., benzene, carbon monoxide, formaldehyde, naphthalene, nitrogen dioxide, polycyclic aromatic hydrocarbons (especially benzo[a]pyrene), radon, trichloroethylene and tetrachloroethylene, have indoor sources, are known for their hazardousness to health and are often found indoors in concentrations large enough for health concerns [41]. Fifteen years after the publication of Jones's work, another review was published by Zaatari et al., who focused on the effect of ventilation on the air quality in retail stores [42]. The authors first described the methodology and databases they used for the review. They went through databases such as the ISI Web of science, Compendex and Science Direct and, also, government reports and Google Scholar. They chose the most-known pollutants as keywords and words like retail, mall, shopping, supermarkets, stores and so on. The authors went through more than 110 papers and chose 28 with the most important information connected to measurements in retail spaces. They also discussed some ANSI/ASHRAE Standards, which are the recognised standards for ventilation system design and acceptable indoor air quality (IAQ). The standards specify the minimum ventilation rates and other measures in order to minimise adverse health effects in the occupants. One part of the study was devoted to individual substances (see Table 2). In the second part, they compared the health impact from exposure to VOCs and discussed the individual concentrations found in the works. In another, they discussed substances such as ozone, radon, fungi and bacteria. In the discussion and conclusion of the paper, they summarised their findings: half of the stores exceeded the recommended standards for acrolein, formaldehyde, acetaldehyde, benzene and trichloroethylene. They pointed to acrolein and PM2.5 as potential risks [42].

Table 2. Chemical compounds in the air in buildings, their sources and their concentrations [42].

Chemical Compounds	Sources	Some Finding Concentration
Aromatic compounds Group benzene, toluene, ethlbenzene, xylenes, styreve	Motor vehicle, newspapers in photocopy centers	15 ± 41 ng/g (mean + standard deviation)
Halogenated compounds	Chlorinated cleaning agents, deodorisers	1 ± 1 ng/g
Terpenoids-limonene	Cleaning products	5 ± 5 ng/g
C1–C2 aldehydes Formaldehyde		13 ± 10 ng/g average 26 ng/g maximum
Carbonyls Aceton	Medical, cosmetic products	3 ± 4 ng/g 14 ng/g maximum

Over the past two decades, numerous field studies on indoor air quality and Sick Building Syndrome (SBS) have been conducted. The symptoms of SBS are usually nonspecific and are often somewhat particular to the building being occupied by the workers. In their work, the Chinese authors looked at the link between the temperatures in shops in selected large cities in the west of China in relation to the concentrations of carbon dioxide, formaldehyde and total volatile organic compounds (TVOC). They also did a survey of the employees who worked at the stores to see if there were links between the air quality and SBS. This syndrome has been associated with headaches, tearing and other medical conditions. It turns out that, in large stores such as shopping malls, these symptoms can occur and accumulate. In the summer, the values for some substances are higher and vary between shopping malls. [43].

Li et al. [44] studied the air in Hong Kong, which is said to be one of the most attractive shopping paradises in the world. Good indoor air quality is, therefore, very essential to shoppers. In order to characterise the indoor air quality in shopping malls, nine shopping malls in Hong Kong were selected for the study. The indoor air pollutants included carbon dioxide (CO_2), carbon monoxide (CO), total hydrocarbons (THC), formaldehyde (HCHO), respirable particulate matter (PM10) and the total bacteria count (TBC). The results showed that more than 40% of the shopping malls had 1-h average CO_2 levels above the 1000 ppm of the ASHRAE standard on both weekdays and weekends. Additionally, they had average weekday PM10 concentrations that exceeded the Hong Kong Indoor Air Quality Objective (HKIAQO). The highest indoor PM10 level at a mall was 380 µg/m^3. Of the malls surveyed, 30% had indoor airborne bacteria levels above the 1000 cfu/m^3 set by the HKIAQO. The elevated indoor CO_2 and bacteria levels could result from high occupancy combined with insufficient ventilation. The increased PM10 levels could probably be attributed to illegal smoking inside these establishments. In comparison, the shopping malls that contained internal public transport drop-off areas, where vehicles were parked with idling engines, and had their major entry doors closed to heavy traffic roads had higher CO and PM10 indoor levels. In addition, the extensive use of cooking stoves without adequate ventilation inside food courts could increase the indoor CO_2, CO and PM10 levels [44].

Li et al. [44] also described the methodology in their paper in detail. They used an air bag sampling method to sample the CO and THC. The CO was analysed with a Thermo Electron (model 48) Gas Filter Correlation CO Ambient Analyser. A methane (MHC) and nonmethane hydrocarbon (NMHC) analyser (model Thermo-Electron 55C) analysed the THC. The measurement results from air bag sampling at the sampling locations at the selected levels in a shopping mall were averaged to obtain the final concentrations.

In their work, the authors Lei et al. [45] designed and described a method for assessing the air quality based on the use of a wavelet neural network. The model can be applied to the evaluation of indoor air quality in large shopping malls.

Du et al. [46] compared the indoor environment quality of green and conventional shopping mall buildings based on customers' perceptions, but they especially paid more attention to the temperature conditions. Differences were found in the indoor environmental quality objective (IEQ) and in the customers' subjective satisfaction between the two buildings. The measurement results showed that a green shopping mall building is superior to a conventional one in terms of the indoor thermal environment, indoor illumination, relative humidity, carbon dioxide concentration and noise level. Moreover, the results of the questionnaire found that customers showed a higher tolerance toward the IEQ when they recognised that a building was green and that their age and/or duration of time spent in the building also affect evaluations of environmental satisfaction [46].

3.2. The Smell in the Stores

Another aspect is how we can affect the air quality and the types of smells and how they affect our mental state. Research in this area is still in its infancy. In the area of trade, there has been great development in recent decades. There was a shift from small shops to large supermarkets. The competition is great, and therefore, the effort to attract the customers lies in the environment. The air quality and smell in a store also play a role here. Nowadays, people spend more time indoors in shopping centres than in outdoor markets. Therefore, the air is a very essential part of the shopping experience. Belgian authors described in their introduction a lot of environmental effects on the pleasantness of the shopping experience for customers, but they focused on the relationship with a distinct and particularly negative emotion—namely, irritation [47].

There has been a growth of literature on perceptions of places through smells in the last decade. Smells are inevitable in people's everyday experiences in cities, variously sourced from human activities to building materials and the landscape, forming an invisible world around us [48].

One of the first summary articles on this theme was published in 2012. The aim of the authors was to discuss the findings from the literature regarding the effects of odours on shopping behaviour and the methodology of individual studies and comments on the results related to perception [49].

A year later, another review of authors Roxana et al. on that topic was published [50]. The main purpose of their paper was to present an extended literature review of the relevant empirical studies that examined the effect of ambient scent on consumers' perceptions, consumers' emotions and consumers' behavioural responses in the context of retailing. The paper also concentrated on identifying the principal dimensions of ambient scents (presence versus absence, congruity versus incongruity and pleasantness versus unpleasantness) and examined the impact of these dimensions of ambient scents on the evaluation of a product, of a store or of a shopping mall and their impact on the shopping behaviour within a store [50].

A perceptual model of smell pleasantness was introduced by Chinese authors in 2018 [51]. Their paper, taking pleasantness as a perceptual quality dimension, aimed to explore indicators influencing people's pleasantness of smell in a selected case. A grounded theory was used as a methodological approach in their study in the selected case. Nineteen participants were recruited for smell walking with semi-structured interviews. Overall, nine indicators emerged from participants' descriptions that contributed to their smell pleasantness: cleanliness, preference, appropriateness, naturalness, freshness, familiarity, calmness, intensity and purity. The perceptual model, in line with the smell concept, also provides a communicational tool among urban planners and designers to describe and assess the qualities of a smell [51].

In 2012, Guéguen [52] published an article about the effects of pleasant ambient fragrances on women. In his work, he also mentioned other studies that were done in the nineties. Baron [53] discussed the influence of fragrance and willingness to help in the longer term. His preliminary study already showed that people are more responsive to partners' needs in the presence of pleasant scents. In his work, he showed the positive influence of fragrance on certain activities, e.g., Grimes [54] found that students volunteered to spend more time on work when they were exposed to a vanilla or lavender odour before the request. Other authors also showed that participants exposed to a pleasant odour during a learning task were more willing to comply with the experimenter's request for help at the end of the task. Similarly, it was also found that undergraduate students who answered a questionnaire that had been saturated with a lavender or peppermint aroma were more likely to take part in a telephone survey [52]. All of the mentioned studies observed that pleasant smells can help improve behaviour and the willingness to help. [52–54]. For a majority of these authors, this effect could be explained by mood. Pleasant ambient odours could have activated a positive mood, which, in turn, led the participants to respond more favourably. The activation of a positive effect linked to the presence of a pleasant odour has been confirmed by mood measurements. Daily associations with smells, such as the smell of fresh bread from a bakery on the way to bus station in the morning and the smell of breweries and cigarettes from pubs on the way back home after work, enrich our experiences and make us know better the places we live [52]. Recently, new works have been published. In 2019, Lenders assessed consumer behaviours in real trade. The conclusions of his work showed that the most important factor is the intensity of the scent. Only above the thresholds did they affect the behaviours of the customer. For one thing, he was willing to spend more time in the store, and some unscheduled purchasing behaviour also applied [55]. Lenders also discussed the papers of other authors [55]. He summarised that the studies were usually conducted in diverse settings, such as laboratories, malls, clothing stores and clubs, and used different reasonings for selecting a specific scent. Scents such as lemon, orange, grapefruit, bergamot, basil, tea, lemon, chocolate, vanilla, cinnamon, seawater, peppermint, ginger, food-based lavender, rosemary, liquorice, coffee and, additionally, some aromas such as faint mint, flora and wood were all studied [54].

The authors from Monash University in Australia [56] looked at the possibility of better competitiveness through the application of music in conjunction with fragrance. Through experimental testing in a fashion store, it turned out that young people can be influenced and that it is necessary to choose the right level of music and fragrance. In their case, vanilla was chosen [56].

Authors from Switzerland published a paper about perceptions induced by coffee. Coffee is one of the most popular beverages in the world. People like to spend time in cafes. The smell of coffee is mostly associated with breakfast, relaxation and sitting with friends. The aroma of coffee is often observed in studies, because it belongs to typical aromas. The aim of the Swiss scientists was to study not only the hedonic motivation but, also, the so-called functional motivation. They looked at the impact of both the motivations on customer responses, as well as performances in terms of satisfying other senses [57]. Another very nice smell for people is chocolate. The scent of chocolate, for instance, can evoke pleasure and arousal for most consumers. The aroma of chocolate, compared to the smells of other foods, changes the activity in the human central nervous system, and the scent of chocolate can also reduce consumers' attention, perhaps implying that, during their shopping trip, consumers evolve from shopping for a specific product to enjoying the whole shopping experience [58]. Belgium authors combined these findings with the prediction of the Stimulus–Organism–Response paradigm and assumed that the scent of chocolate would lead to approach behaviour. They selected a chocolate scent to be diffused in the store. A first pre-test was conducted to verify the affective and arousing quality of the chocolate scent used in the study. Twenty participants (10 men and 10 women) were asked to sniff the scent (which was put on a cotton-tipped stick in a dark glass bottle) and to evaluate its pleasantness and its level of arousal on a 7-point semantic differential scale (i.e., unpleasant/pleasant and unaroused/aroused). Before the other experiment, the chocolate scent was dispersed in the bookstore at different levels of intensity and for several durations. Forty-eight customers replied to two questions: Did you notice something special in the store atmosphere? Now that we have mentioned the presence of a scent, do you detect the scent? A field study with 201 participants showed that a chocolate scent positively influenced the general approach behaviour and negatively influenced the goal-directed behaviour in a bookstore [58].

Another study examined whether diffusing pleasant scents could overcome consumers' negative responses to a messy store. They investigated the effect of pleasant scents (un)related to neatness on consumer evaluations of a tidy versus a messy store. An experiment with 198 respondents revealed that a pleasant scent not associated with neatness functions as a positively valanced prime, causing consumers to evaluate the products in the tidy store more positively than the products in the messy store. Additionally, when diffused in a messy store, a pleasant ambient scent has a negative effect on consumers' product evaluations because of the mismatch between the pleasant scent and the unpleasant messy layout. However, this negative effect can be cancelled out by diffusing a pleasant scent that is associated with neatness [59].

One of the latest articles on olfactory marketing was published by Spanish authors in 2020 [60]. The aim of their work was to get answers about the influence of smell on the evaluation and behaviour of museum consumers. Three rooms in two different floors of the museum were filled with scents. They used a cloth scent for the historical dressing room, the scent of apple pie for the kitchen and the scent of aftershave for the barber shop. For five days, they tested the suitable concentrations. The authors described the experiment in detail, including the selection of concentrations, a questionnaire and the scale. The museum was visited by 3960 people during the study, and the authors received 234 observations. The obtained results were statistically processed with the help of MANCOVA and showed that the scents had a direct effect on the perception of the environment and on the individual evaluations. The people who visited the museum and its rooms with scents evaluated the museum more positively [60].

This study [60] was also valuable because the literary overview of the subject was very well-presented (a total of 100 links). The individual sections were devoted to the olfaction of marketing and perception, marketing and evaluation and marketing in relation to gender. Out of 100 references, one part was devoted to the functioning of the senses, especially smell and another part to marketing, and of the works published after the year 2000, about 40 were directly devoted to the relationship between odour and consumer emotions in shops [60]. Concerning shops, the studies focused on medical facilities (dentists and hospitals), bookstores, malls, cafes, museums, fashion stores, etc.

A particularly interesting article was printed in 2020 [61]. The authors introduced a new device for measuring odours that can be used also for marketing studies. qPODs (Portable Olfactive Devices, Curion) are novel olfactory delivery systems that allow the sampling of a wide variety of stimulus types. Participants evaluate odours by opening a port at the top of the qPOD and sampling a controlled air stream. Thirty-one participants in this study smelled and evaluated the pleasantness and intensity of citral, citronellol, geraniol, PEA, nonalactone and vanillin delivered via qPODs and by traditional sniff jars. The hedonic and emotional responses were compared. Their emotional reactions to the odours were captured with the PANAS (Positive and Negative Affect Schedule) at the beginning of each testing session and then again after exposure to each odour. They also completed the newly developed Mood Signature Questionnaire, which asks participants to assign a mood to each odour rather than reporting how it makes them feel. Though the odours presented in the sniff jars were rated as significantly more intense ($p < 0.001$), there were no differences between the presentation types for perceived pleasantness, changes in positive or negative mood following odour exposure or the emotional descriptors (mood signatures) participants assigned to the odours [61].

3.3. Possibilities for Improving Indoor Air Quality

New technologies need to be developed in the industry so that less and less health-threatening substances are released into the air. Industrial plants must use new technologies for air purification. They can use mechanical methods of air cleaning (centrifugal cleaning, water cleaning and wet cleaning) or physicochemical methods of air purification (condensation, filtration and precipitation). The main technologies for the prevention of air pollution include, for example, gravity settling chambers and separators of various types, such as electrostatic and cyclone. Selective catalytic reduction systems and various types of filters, including biofilters and washing machines, are also used.

There are three approaches to improving the air quality; it is necessary to reduce emission sources, develop new technologies for air purification and pay close attention to ventilation systems. Due to the wide range of substances that pollute the air, scientists are focusing on the possibilities of effectively cleaning the air, especially in buildings, but usually, there is not only one possibility. The air purification technologies are constantly being improved. Firstly, adsorption filters are used for air purification, which differ in the material used, the amount and the combination of layers and size of pores. For example, different ones used are as nylon, cotton, polyester nonwoven fabric filter, flax and hemp filters, a multi-layered structure of cellulose fibre and particles of perlite. Combinations of the materials were described in an Indian work [62].

The methods used vary, of course, depending on which substances need to be removed from the air. For example, polypropylene and polystyrene are used to remove particles, but there are also new materials, such as a porous material named SUNSPACE ("SUstaiNable materials Synthesized from by-Products and Alginates for Clean air and better Environment") and silica fume (SF), which are tested for cleaning the air [63].

In their review, Chinese authors described different materials that are used as adsorbents, such as carbon, zeolite and metal–organic framework materials (MOFs). The authors described, in great detail, the advantages and disadvantages of materials, paying close attention to the power and development of other new structures and their potential uses [64].

Another work described using a porous membrane consisting of birnessite-type MnO_2 that was filled in with polystyrene porous nanofibers (MnO_2/PS HPNM) fabricated by a versatile electrospinning method [65].

In 2020, a review was published concerning indoor air pollution also relating human diseases and summarising the current trends and possibilities for air control and air quality improvement. The review was divided into corresponding sections and summarised the findings from 211 works [66]. In addition to the use of filters, attention was also focused on new technologies such as oxidation processes (AOPs), of which it appears that photocatalysis will have the greatest use, during which indoor air pollutants are distributed due to the exposure of semiconductor photocatalysts under sufficiently energetic exposure. The advantage of this method is the direct degradation of gaseous pollutants (especially volatile organic compounds) into CO_2 and water and the applicability of removing low-concentration pollutants. The semiconductors used as photocatalysts in this technology include titanium dioxide (TiO_2), polymer (or graphite), tungsten oxide (WO_3), carbon dioxide (CN), bisexual Ag, cadmium sulphide (CdS) and other MO_x metal oxides (M = Fe and Zn) [66,67].

4. Conclusions

People are spending more leisure time in indoor shopping centres than in the past, so creating a positive environment for them can be a big advantage for retailers. A pleasant smell seems to be one of these circumstances. Our findings may contribute to a better understanding of shoppers' emotions and their behaviours in response to in-store scents. We need to study what can influence people, as it is known that shoppers differ in their sensitivities to smell and the emotions evoked due to, for example, gender, age, mood at the time of shopping or length of time spent shopping.

Author Contributions: Conceptualisation, Z.P. and M.D.; methodology, V.I.; software, V.I.; validation, Z.P., V.I. and M.D.; formal analysis, V.I.; resources, Z.P., V.I. and M.D.; data curation, V.I.; writing—original draft preparation, Z.P. and M.D.; writing—review and editing, V.I. and M.D.; visualisation, V.I. and M.D.; supervision, M.D. and project administration, M.D. All authors have read and agreed to the published version of the manuscript.

Funding: This research was funded by the Erasmus+ KA2 Strategic Partnerships grant no. 2018-1-SK01-KA203-046324 "Implementation of Consumer Neuroscience and Smart Research Solutions in Aromachology" (NEUROSMARTOLOGY).

Institutional Review Board Statement: Not applicable.

Informed Consent Statement: Not applicable.

Data Availability Statement: The data used to support the findings of this study are available from the corresponding author upon request.

Acknowledgments: The European Commission's support for the production of this publication does not constitute an endorsement of the contents, which reflect the views only of the authors, and the Commission cannot be held responsible for any use which may be made of the information contained therein.

Conflicts of Interest: The authors declare no conflict of interest.

References

1. Gerald Schubert, G.; Walterscheid, R.L. Earth. In *Astrophysical Quantities*, 4th ed.; Cox, A.N., Ed.; AIP Press: New York, NY, USA, 2000; pp. 258–259.
2. Jones, A.P. Indoor air quality and health. *Atmos. Environ.* **1999**, *33*, 4535–4564. [CrossRef]
3. Suess, M.J. The Indoor Air Quality programme of the WHO regional office for Europe. *Indoor Air* **1992**, *2*, 180–193. [CrossRef]
4. Mølhave, L.; Krzyzanowski, M. The right to healthy indoor air: Status by 2002. *Indoor Air* **2003**, *13*, 50–53. [CrossRef] [PubMed]
5. Scientific Committee on Health and Environmental Risks (SCHER). Preliminary Report on Risk Assessment on Indoor Air Quality. Available online: https://ec.europa.eu/health/archive/ph_risk/committees/04_scher/docs/scher_o_048.pdf (accessed on 26 April 2021).
6. Settimo, G.; Manigrasso, M.; Avino, P. Indoor Air Quality: A Focus on the European Legislation and State-of-the-Art Research in Italy. *Atmosphere* **2020**, *11*, 370. [CrossRef]
7. Alarie, Y. Sensory irritation by airborne chemicals. *Crit. Rev. Toxicol.* **1973**, *2*, 299–363. [CrossRef] [PubMed]

8. Alarie, Y.; Schaper, M.; Nielsen, G.D.; Abraham, M.H. Structure-activity relationships of volatile organic chemicals as sensory irritants. *Arch. Toxicol.* **1998**, *72*, 125–140. [CrossRef] [PubMed]
9. Nielsen, G.D. Mechanisms of activation of the sensory irritant receptor by airborne chemicals. *Crit. Rev. Toxicol.* **1991**, *21*, 183–208. [CrossRef] [PubMed]
10. Doty, R.L.; Cometto-Muñiz, J.E.; Jalowayski, A.A.; Dalton, P.; Kendal-Reed, M.; Hodgson, M. Assessment of upper respiratory react and ocular irritative effects of volatile chemicals in humans. *Crit. Rev. Toxicol* **2004**, *34*, 85–142. [CrossRef]
11. Wolkoff, P.; Wilkins, C.K.; Clausen, P.A.; Nielsen, G.D. Organic compounds in office environments—Sensory irritation, odor, measurements and the role of reactive chemistry. *Indoor Air* **2006**, *16*, 7–19. [CrossRef]
12. Shusterman, D. Review of upper airway, including olfaction, as mediator of symptoms. *Environ. Health Perspect.* **2002**, *110* (Suppl. 4), 649–653. [CrossRef]
13. International Agency for Research of Cancer. *Man-Made Mineral Fibres and Radon. IARC Monographs on the Evaluation of Carcinogenic Risks to Humans*; International Agency for Research of Cancer: Lyon, France, 1998; Volume 43.
14. Darby, S.; Hill, D.; Auvinen, A.; Barros-Dios, J.M.; Baysson, H.; Bochicchio, F.; Deo, H.; Falk, R.; Forastiere, F.; Hakama, M.; et al. Radon in homes and risk of lung cancer: Collaborative analysis of individual data from 13 European case-control studies. *BMJ* **2005**, *330*, 1–6. [CrossRef] [PubMed]
15. World Health Organization, Regional Office for Europe. *Health Aspects of Air Pollution with Particulate Matter, Ozone and Nitrogen Dioxide: Report on a WHO Working Group, Bonn, Germany, 13–15 January 2003*; WHO Regional Office for Europe: Copenhagen, Denmark, 2003. Available online: https://apps.who.int/iris/handle/10665/107478 (accessed on 26 April 2021).
16. World Health Organization, Regional Office for Europe & European Centre for Environment and Health. *Effects of Air Pol-lution on Children's Health and Development: A Review of the Evidence*; WHO Regional Office for Europe: Copenhagen, Denmark, 2005. Available online: https://apps.who.int/iris/handle/10665/107652 (accessed on 26 April 2021).
17. Lam, C.-W.; James, J.T.; McCluskey, R.; Arepalli, S.; Hunter, R.L. A review of carbon nanotube toxicity and assessment of potential occupational and environmental health risks. *Crit. Rev. Toxicol.* **2006**, *36*, 189–217. [CrossRef] [PubMed]
18. Wainman, T.; Zhang, J.; Weschler, C.J.; Lioy, P. Ozone and limonene in indoor air: A source of submicron particle exposure. *Environ. Health Perspect.* **2000**, *108*, 1139–1145. [CrossRef]
19. Sarwar, G.; Olson, D.A.; Corsi, R.L. Indoor particles: The role of terpene emission from consumer products. *J. Air Waste Manag. Assoc.* **2004**, *54*, 367–377. [CrossRef] [PubMed]
20. Afsari, A.; Matson, U.; Ekberg, L.E. Characterization of indoor sources of fine and ultrafine particles: A study conducted in a full-scale chamber. *Indoor Air* **2005**, *15*, 141–150. [CrossRef] [PubMed]
21. Schaub, B.; Lauener, R.; von Mutius, E. The many faces of the hygiene hypothesis. *J. Allergy Clin. Immunol.* **2006**, *117*, 969–977. [CrossRef] [PubMed]
22. D'Amato, G.; Spieksma, F.T.M.; Liccardi, G.; Jäger, S.; Russo, M.; Kontou-Fili, K.; Nikkels, H.; Wüthrich, B.; Bonini, S. Pollen-related allergy in Europe. *Allergy* **1998**, *53*, 567–578. [CrossRef] [PubMed]
23. Platts-Mills, T.A.E.; Rakes, G.; Heyman, P.W. The relevance of allergen exposure to the development of asthma in children. *J. Allergy Clin. Immunol.* **2000**, *105*, S503–S508. [CrossRef]
24. Nielsen, G.D.; Hansen, J.S.; Lund, R.M.; Bergqvist, M.; Larsen, S.T.; Clausen, S.K.; Thygesen, P.; Poulsen, O.P. IgE-mediated asthma and rhinitis I: A role of allergen exposure? *Pharmacol. Toxicol.* **2002**, *90*, 231–242. [CrossRef]
25. Eggleston, P.A. Ecology and elimination of cockroaches and allergens in the home. *J. Allergy Clin. Immunol.* **2001**, *1007*, S422–S429. [CrossRef]
26. Phipatanakul, W.; Eggleston, P.A.; Wright, E.C.; Wood, P.A.; The National Cooperative Inner-City Asthma Study. Mouse allergen. I. The prevalence of mouse allergen in inner-city homes. *J. Allergy Clin. Immunol.* **2000**, *106*, 1070–1074. [CrossRef] [PubMed]
27. Phipatanakul, W.; Eggleston, P.A.; Wright, E.C.; Wood, P.A.; The National Cooperative Inner-City Asthma Study. Mouse allergen. II. The relationship of mouse allergen exposure to mouse sensitization and asthma morbidity in inner-city children with asthma. *J. Allergy Clin. Immunol.* **2000**, *106*, 1075–1080. [CrossRef] [PubMed]
28. Beasley, R.; Crane, J.; Lai, C.K.W.; Pearce, N. Prevalence and etiology of asthma. *J. Allergy Clin. Immunol.* **2000**, *105*, S466–S472. [CrossRef]
29. Chan-Yeung, M.; Becker, A. Primary prevention of childhood asthma and allergic disorders. *Curr. Opin. Allergy Clin. Immunol.* **2006**, *6*, 146–151. [CrossRef]
30. Reinikainen, L.; Jaakkola, J.J.K. Significance of humidity and temperature on skin and upper airway symptoms. *Indoor Air* **2003**, *13*, 344–352. [CrossRef]
31. Wolkoff, P.; Nøjgaard, J.K.; Franck, C.; Skov, P. The modern office desiccates the eyes? *Indoor Air* **2006**, *16*, 258–265. [CrossRef]
32. Seppänen, O.A.; Fisk, W.J.; Mendell, M.J. Association of ventilation rates and CO_2 concentrations with health and other responses in commercial and institutional buildings. *Indoor Air* **1999**, *9*, 226–252. [CrossRef] [PubMed]
33. Seppänen, O.A.; Fisk, W.J.; Lei, Q.H. Ventilation and performance in office work. *Indoor Air* **2005**, *16*, 28–36. [CrossRef]
34. Shaughnessy, R.J.; Haverinen-Shaughnessy, U.; Nevalainen, A.; Moschandreas, D. The effects of classroom air temperature and outdoor air supply rate on the performance of school work by children. *Indoor Air* **2006**, *16*, 465–468. [CrossRef] [PubMed]
35. Wargocki, P.; Wyon, D.P. The effects of outdoor air supply rate and supply air filter condition in classrooms on the performance of schoolwork by children. *HVAC&R Res.* **2007**, *13*, 165–191.

36. Healy, J.D. Excess winter mortality in Europe: A cross country analysis identifying key risk factors. *J. Epidemiol. Community Health* **2003**, *57*, 784–789. [CrossRef]
37. Kosatsky, T. The 2003 European heat waves. *Eurosurveillance* **2005**, *10*, 148–149. [CrossRef]
38. Reinikainen, L.; Jaakkola, J.J.K. Effects of temperature and humidification in the office environment. *Arch. Environ. Health* **2001**, *56*, 365–368. [CrossRef] [PubMed]
39. Page, M.J.; McKenzie, J.E.; Bossuyt, P.M.; Boutron, I.; Hoffmann, T.C.; Mulrow, C.D.; Shamseer, L.; Tetzlaff, J.M.; Akl, E.A.; Brennan, S.E.; et al. The prisma 2020 statement: An updated guideline for reporting systematic reviews. *BMJ Clin. Res. Ed.* **2021**, *372*, n71.
40. Burdack-Freitag, A.; Heinlein, A.; Florian Mayer, F. Material Odor Emissions and Indoor Air Quality. In *Springer Handbook of Odor*, 1st ed.; Buettner, A., Ed.; Springer International Publishing: Freising, Germany, 2017; pp. 563–585.
41. WHO. *Guidelines for Indoor Air Quality: Selected Pollutants*; WHO Regional Office for Europe: Copenhagen, Denmark, 2010. Available online: http://www.who.int/iris/handle/10665/260127 (accessed on 7 June 2021).
42. Zaatari, M.; Nirlo, E.; Jareemit, D.; Crain, N.; Srebric, J.; Siegel, J. Ventilation and indoor air quality in retail stores: A critical review (RP-1596). *HVAC&R Res.* **2014**, *20*, 276–294.
43. Shang, Y.; Li, B.; Baldwin, A.N.; Ding, Y.; Yu, W.; Cheng, L. Investigation of indoor air quality in shopping malls during summer in Western China using subjective survey and field measurement. *Build. Environ.* **2016**, *108*, 1–11. [CrossRef]
44. Li, W.M.; Lee, S.C.; Chan, L.Y. Indoor air quality at nine shopping malls in Hong Kong. *Sci. Total Environ.* **2001**, *273*, 27–40. [CrossRef]
45. Lei, L.; Chen, W.; Xue, Y.; Liu, W. A comprehensive evaluation method for indoor air quality of buildings based on rough sets and a wavelet neural network. *Build. Environ.* **2019**, *162*, 106296. [CrossRef]
46. Du, X.; Zhang, Y.; Lv, Z. Investigations and analysis of indoor environment quality of green and common shopping mall buildings based on customers' perception. *Build. Environ.* **2020**, *177*, 106985. [CrossRef]
47. Demoulin, N.; Willems, K. Service scape irritants and customer satisfaction: The moderating role of shopping motives and involvement. *J. Bus. Res.* **2019**, *104*, 295–306. [CrossRef]
48. Zardini, M. Toward a sensorial urbanism. In *Sense of the City: An Alternate Approach to Urbanism*; Zardini, M., Ed.; Lars Muller Publications: Montreal, QC, Canada, 2005; pp. 17–27.
49. Teller, C.; Dennis, C. The effect of ambient scent on consumers' perception, emotions and behaviour: A critical review. *J. Mark. Manag.* **2012**, *28*, 14–36. [CrossRef]
50. Roxana, O.M.; Ioan, P. The effects of ambient scent on consumer behavior: A review of the literature. *Ann. Univ. Oradea Econ. Sci. Ser.* **2013**, *22*, 1797–1806.
51. Xiao, J.; Tait, M.; Kang, J. A perceptual model of smellscape pleasantness. *Cities* **2018**, *76*, 105–115. [CrossRef]
52. Guéguen, N. The sweet smell of . . . courtship: Effects of pleasant ambient fragrance on women's receptivity to a man's courtship request. *J. Soc. Psychol.* **2012**, *32*, 123–125. [CrossRef]
53. Baron, R.A. The sweet smell of . . . helping: Effects of pleasant ambient fragrance on prosocial behavior in shopping mall. *Pers. Soc. Psychol. Bull.* **1997**, *23*, 498–503. [CrossRef]
54. Grimes, M. Helping behavior commitments in the presence of odors: Vanilla, lavender, and no odor. In *National Undergraduate Research Cleaning House*; 1999; Volume 2. Available online: http://www.webclearinghouse.net (accessed on 28 June 2021).
55. Leenders, M.A.A.M.; Smidts, A.; Haji, A.E. Ambient scent as a mood inducer in supermarkets: The role of scent intensity and time-pressure of shoppers. *J. Retail. Consum. Serv.* **2019**, *48*, 270–280. [CrossRef]
56. Gan, S.; Morrison, M.; Dubelaar, C.; Oppewal, H. In-store music and aroma influences on shopper behavior and satisfaction. *J. Bus. Res.* **2011**, *64*, 558–564.
57. Labbe, D.; Ferrage, A.; Rytz, A.; Pace, J.; Martin, N. Pleasantness, emotions and perceptions induced by coffee beverage experience depend on the consumption motivation (hedonic or utilitarian). *Food Qual. Prefer.* **2015**, *44*, 56–61. [CrossRef]
58. Doucé, L.; Poels, K.; Janssens, W.; De Backer, C. Smelling the books: The effect of chocolate scent on purchase-related behavior in a bookstore. *J. Environ. Psychol.* **2013**, *36*, 65–69. [CrossRef]
59. Doucé, L.; Janssens, W.; Swinnen, G.; Van Cleempoel, K. Influencing consumer reactions towards a tidy versus a messy store using pleasant ambient scents. *J. Environ. Psychol.* **2014**, *40*, 351–358. [CrossRef]
60. Vega-Gómez, F.I.; Miranda-Gonzalez, F.J.; Pérez Mayo, J.; González-López, Ó.R.; Pascual-Nebreda, L. The Scent of Art. Perception, Evaluation, and Behaviour in a Museum in Response to Olfactory Marketing. *Sustainability* **2020**, *12*, 1384. [CrossRef]
61. Gaby, M.J.; Tepper, J.B. A comparison of hedonic and emotional responses to common odors delivered by qPODs (Portable Olfactive Devices) and traditional sniff jars. *Food Qual. Prefer.* **2020**, *80*, 13804. [CrossRef]
62. Sowjanya, M.; Aditya, K.; Adeeb Hussain, S. Effect of combination of fabric material layers in reducing air pollution. *Mater. Today* **2021**, *38*, 3424–3428.
63. Zanoletti, A.; lBilo, F.; Borgese, L.; Depero, L.E.; Fahimi, A.; Ponti, J.; Valsesia, A.; La Spina, R.; Montini, T.; Bontempi, E. SUNSPACE, A Porous Material to Reduce Air Particulate Matter (PM). *Environ. Int.* **2021**, *6*, 534. [CrossRef] [PubMed]
64. Yue, X.; Ling Ma, N.; Sonne, C.; Guan, R.; Shiung Lam, S.; Van Le, Q.; Chen, X.; Yang, Y.; Gu, H.; Rinklebe, J.; et al. Mitigation of indoor air pollution: A review of recent advances in adsorption materials and catalytic oxidation. *J. Hazard. Mater.* **2021**, *405*, 124138. [CrossRef] [PubMed]

65. Hu, M.; Yin, L.; Zhou, H.; Wu, L.; Yuan, K.; Pan, B.; Zhong, Z.; Xing, W. Manganese dioxide-filled hierarchical porous nanofiber membrane for indoor air cleaning at room temperature. *J. Membr. Sci.* **2020**, *605*, 118094. [CrossRef]
66. Huang, Y.; Sai Hang Ho, S.; Lu, Y.; Niu, R.; Xu, L.; Cao, J.; Lee, S. Removal of Indoor Volatile Organic Compounds via Photocatalytic Oxidation: A Short Review and Prospect. *Molecules* **2016**, *21*, 56. [CrossRef] [PubMed]
67. Van Tran, V.; ParkYoung, D.; Lee, C. Indoor Air Pollution, Related Human Diseases, and Recent Trends in the Control and Improvement of Indoor Air Quality. *Int. J. Environ. Res. Public Health* **2020**, *17*, 2927. [CrossRef] [PubMed]

Communication

Screening of the Honey Aroma as a Potential Essence for the Aromachology

Jana Štefániková [1], Patrícia Martišová [1,*], Marek Šnirc [2], Peter Šedík [3,*] and Vladimír Vietoris [4]

1. AgroBioTech Research Centre, Slovak University of Agriculture in Nitra, Tr. A. Hlinku 2, 94976 Nitra, Slovakia; jana.stefanikova@uniag.sk
2. Department of Chemistry, Faculty of Biotechnology and Food Sciences, Slovak University of Agriculture, Trieda A. Hlinku 2, 94976 Nitra, Slovakia; marek.snirc@uniag.sk
3. Center for Research and Educational Projects, Faculty of Economics and Management, Slovak University of Agriculture in Nitra, Tr. A. Hlinku 2, 94976 Nitra, Slovakia
4. Department of Technology and Quality of Plant Products, Faculty of Biotechnology and Food Sciences, Slovak University of Agriculture, Trieda A. Hlinku 2, 94976 Nitra, Slovakia; vladimir.vietoris@uniag.sk
* Correspondence: patricia.martisova@uniag.sk (P.M.); sedik.peter@gmail.com (P.Š.)

Abstract: The aim of the study was to determine the aroma profiles of four kinds of Slovak honey (sunflower, honeydew, acacia, and linden) by a qualitative and quantitative screening of their volatile compounds and by gas chromatography for the potential use in the aromachology and the business sphere. The results showed that several unique volatiles were identified in one kind of honey, while they were not identified in the remaining ones. The acacia honey had the unique volatile linalool oxide (1.13–3.9%); linden honey had the unique volatiles nerol oxide (0.6–1.6%), ethyl esters (0.41–8.78%), lilac aldehyde D (6.6%), and acetophenone (0.37%). The honeydew honey had the unique volatiles santene (0.28%) and cyclofenchene (0.59–1.39%), whereas 2-bornene (0.43–0.81%) was typical for sunflower honey. While linden honey was characterized by fruity ethyl esters, honeydew honey had more monoterpenoid compounds. In the principal component analysis model, the four kinds of honey could not be differentiated by aroma volatiles. However, it was possible to classify the linden and sunflower honey using the LDA. In conclusion, the current study provided experimental evidence that the marker compounds from different kinds of honey might be promising candidates for production of inhaling aromas.

Keywords: volatile organic compounds; scents; aromatization; bee product; gas chromatography

1. Introduction

An aroma represents an effective marketing tool and is considered to be a new way of in-store communication with customers [1]. According to Horská et al. [2], nowadays the usage of fragrance compounds and essential oils in many business sectors is increasing. Many companies are using their own branded aromas in their shops, offices, or even during some marketing events or campaigns. More and more companies are creating aroma logos or corporate scents to be used indoors. Even retailers apply specific aromas to create comfortable environment where customers would spend more time and money by purchasing more products [3].

In general, these odors and aromas are distributed by installing aromatizers or diffusers in certain areas [4]. Moreover, aromatization may attract new customers; however, at first it is necessary to conduct aroma testing in order to select appropriate aromas prior to their implementation. For example, application of cappuccino aroma at store in Slovakia increased the volume of sales in confectionery category (desserts, chocolate bars, chocolates, and waffles) [5]. Furthermore; Berčík et al. [6] indicates that implementing aromatization in business spaces has positive impact on economic indicators, including the sector of services.

Aroma, as a marketing stimulus plays, an important role even in the food industry and gastronomy [7]. Honey, as a food product, has (besides health benefits and nutritional values) very specific characteristics from an organoleptic point of view. It is used not only in the food sector, but also in the cosmetic and pharmaceutical industries [8,9]. Healing properties of honey are used for massages, therapy wraps, or for production of scented candles. Honey contains compounds with antioxidant [10], antibacterial, antifungal, anticancer [11], and anti-inflammatory effects [8,9,11]. Compounds with such properties are mainly polyphenols [8,11]. However, these effects were confirmed also for some volatile organic compounds (VOCs), particularly terpenes [12,13]. VOCs from honey were previously determined by GC-MC analysis of simultaneous extraction and distillation extracts [14,15], HS-SPME/GC-MS [16–21], HS-GC-MS [22], and HS-SPME/GC×GC-TOF-MS [23,24] analyses. Even though honey diffusers are available on the market, there are no studies evaluating their impact on the business sphere.

The aim of this study was to characterize the aroma profiles of Slovak honey samples, in order to (i) find differences between four kinds of monofloral honey, and (ii) to determine promising volatile candidates for production of inhaling aromas.

2. Materials and Methods

2.1. Samples

In this study, a set of four kinds of honey (sunflower $n = 5$, acacia $n = 5$, honeydew $n = 5$, and linden $n = 5$) were analyzed (Table 1). The honey samples (300 g) were sourced from local Slovak small-scale beekeepers and were harvested in 2020. All the honey samples were stored at 20 °C and analyzed within six months after being harvested. Content of sugar was determined by refractometer designed to make corrections based on temperature using automatic temperature compensation (HR901, Krüss GmbH, Hamburg, Germany). A total of 20 samples (4×5) were analyzed in triplicate.

Table 1. Basic characterization of Slovak honey samples, including kind of honey, location, and sugar content.

Kind of Honey	Sample No.	Location (City)	Content of Sugar (°Brix [1] ± SD [2])
Honeydew	1	Kremnica	81.0 ± 0.0
	2	Sabinov	80.6 ± 0.0
	3	Nitra	80.8 ± 0.0
	4	Senec	81.6 ± 0.0
	5	Levoča	81.0 ± 0.0
Acacia	6	Choča	80.0 ± 0.0
	7	Oponice	81.2 ± 0.0
	8	Šala	79.0 ± 0.0
	9	Levice	80.2 ± 0.0
	10	Krupina	82.2 ± 0.0
Linden	11	Nitra	80.0 ± 0.0
	12	Zvolen	77.0 ± 0.0
	13	Krupina	78.2 ± 0.0
	14	Senica	78.8 ± 0.0
	15	Komárno	80.2 ± 0.0
Sunflower	16	Hlohovec	79.0 ± 0.0
	17	Oponice	79.0 ± 0.0
	18	Šala	78.6 ± 0.0
	19	Levice	81.8 ± 0.0
	20	Komárno	80.2 ± 0.0

[1] °Brix—Sugar content of an aqueous solution, where °Brix represents 1 g of sucrose in 100 g of solution. [2] SD, Standard Deviation ($n = 3$).

2.2. Determination of Volatile Organic Compounds

Sample preparation and isolation of VOCs were chosen based on a previous study by Kružík et al. [16]. VOCs were extracted from the honey samples using SPME fiber (DVB/CAR/PDMS 50/30 µm; Supelco, Bellefonte, PA, USA) with CombiPAL automated sample injector 120 (CTC Analytics AG, Zwingen, Switzerland). Each of the honey samples (2 g) was dissolved in a 20 mL glass vial using 2 mL NaCl solution in distilled water (200 g/L). The gas chromatography (Agilent GC7890B) with mass spectrometry (Agilent MSD 5977A) (Agilent Technologies Inc., Santa Clara, CA, USA) method equipped with the column HP-5ms (30 m × 0.25 mm × 0.25 µm; Agilent Technologies) previously described by Kružík et al. [16] was used for determination of VOCs in a modified version. A modified temperature program 40 °C (1 min), 5 °C/min, 250 °C (1 min) was used. Individual compounds were identified based on the comparison of the mass spectra with the commercial database of the National Institute of Standards and Technology (NIST, Gaithersburg, MD, USA) mass spectral library (NIST17), and on the assessment of retention times with the literature [16,17]. The relative content (expressed in percentage) of determined compounds was calculated by dividing individual peak area by the total area of all peaks. Each sample was measured in triplicate.

2.3. Statistical Analysis

All of the data obtained were analyzed by descriptive statistics arithmetic average and standard deviation. To determine the aroma differences (>5% content) between the honey samples, descriptive statistics, normality tests, LDA (Linear Discriminant Analysis) and the PCA (Principal Component Analysis) were performed using the MS Excel and XLSTAT package program [25].

3. Results

By analyzing the saline solution of honey by GC-MS analysis, in total, ninety-four VOCs were identified, including alkanes, alcohols, alkenes, nitriles, acids, esters, monoterpenes, monoterpenoids, aldehydes, and ketones (Table S1). Several volatiles, that were present in one kind of honey and not in the other ones, can be marked as markers. The values shown in the Table 2 for each unique VOC are means of triplicate determinations with the standard deviation, retention time, and previous identification by the literature. As an example, the chromatograms of each kind of honey sample are shown in Figures S1–S4.

Table 2. Identified unique VOCs in four kinds of honey with percentage content [1] ± SD [2] and previous identification in literature [3].

Kind of Honey	Sample No.	Rretention Time (min)	Compound	Percentage Content (%)	SD	Literature
Acacia	9	10.5	Linalool oxide	1.13	0.15	[16–20,23,24,26–29]
	8		Linalool oxide	3.90	0.25	
	8	3.1	3-methyl-2-Butenal	0.86	0.08	[26,27]
	8	8.6	5,6-dimethylene-Cyclooctene	0.42	0.00	–
	6	23.9	2,6,10-Trimethyltridecane	0.48	0.14	–
Linden	13	13.4	Nerol oxide	0.60	0.07	[19,20,22,27]
	11		Nerol oxide	1.60	0.07	
	15	11.4	Linalyl acetate	0.56	0.23	–
	14	18.4	ethyl Nonanoate	0.57	0.24	[18,24,27]
	12		ethyl Nonanoate	1.30	0.25	
	15	13.8	Lilac aldehyde D	6.60	0.65	[14,16,21,23,26,30]
	12	19.6	ethyl Citronellate	5.17	0.37	–
	12	21.8	ethyl Decanoate	0.55	0.20	[15,19,20,22,24,27]
	12	20.2	ethyl Benzenepropanoate	0.41	0.07	[24]

Table 2. Cont.

Kind of Honey	Sample No.	Rretention Time (min)	Compound	Percentage Content (%)	SD	Literature
	14	13.9	ethyl Benzoate	7.63	2.48	[16,18–20,22,26–28,31,32]
	13		ethyl Benzoate	1.76	0.65	
	12	23.6	ethyl 4-isopropylbenzoate	0.43	0.13	–
	12	1.8	Ethyl acetate	8.78	3.40	[19,20,24,26,29–31,33,34]
	14		ethyl Benzeneacetate	1.70	0.29	
	13	16.6	ethyl Benzeneacetate	0.43	0.04	[22,24]
	12		ethyl Benzeneacetate	1.18	0.34	
	12	17.0	2-phenylethyl Acetate	0.55	0.08	[16,19,20,26,27]
	13	20.0	3,5-Dimethyl-2-octanone	0.71	0.16	[26]
	12	2.9	3-methyl-1-Pentanal	1.70	0.77	[24]
	13	4.0	3-methyl-1-Pentanol	0.59	0.11	–
	12		3-methyl-1-Pentanol	4.57	0.43	
	15	6.2	3-methyl-Pentanoic acid	1.16	0.31	[16,23,35]
	15	3.9	4,4-Dimethyl-3-oxopentanenitrile	3.76	0.54	–
	11	8.64	7-exo-ethenyl-Bicyclo[4.2.0]oct-1-ene	0.85	0.05	–
	13	10.2	Acetophenone	0.37	0.08	[15,24,27,28,36,37]
	15	1.6	Dimethyl sulfide	5.36	1.51	[17,24,29,32,37]
Honeydew	3	9.3	trans-beta-Ocimene	0.53	0.10	[19,20,23,27]
	2	21.9	Tetradecane	2.42	0.28	[23]
	4	4.9	Santene	0.28	0.12	–
	1	13.82	p-Mentha-1,5-dien-8-ol	0.59	0.05	–
	1		p-Mentha-1,5-dien-8-ol	4.80	0.48	
	2	15.0	Dodecane	1.99	0.29	[23,24,27]
	1	14.9	2-Propylphenol, methyl ether	0.52	0.08	–
	3	9.6	3-Carene	0.55	0.10	[20]
	3	2.0	3-methyl-Butanal	0.94	0.02	[17,24,29–35]
	4	16.4	4-(1-methylethyl)-Benzaldehyde	0.23	0.00	–
	1	8.58	alpha-Terpinene	0.57	0.04	[18–20,22,23,27,31]
	3	7.8	beta-Myrcene	0.92	0.20	[22,23]
	1	9.0	beta-Phellandrene	0.45	0.02	[30]
	1	7.82	Carveol	0.77	0.01	[23]
	1	20.5	Cosmene	0.84	0.09	[20]
	3	8.9	D-Limonene	1.67	0.36	[17–20,23,24,27,29,32]
	2	19.0	2-Methoxy-4-vinylphenol	0.21	0.02	[24,35]
	1		2-Methoxy-4-vinylphenol	0.41	0.00	
	1	6.7	2,4-Thujadiene	0.42	0.04	[22,23]
	3	4.3	3-Furanmethanol	0.79	0.28	–
	3	3.1	2,3-Butanediol	0.69	0.07	[19,23,32]
	3	7.4	1-Octen-3-ol	0.86	0.18	[21,31,32]
Sunflower	18	23.1	β-Calarene	2.75	0.90	–
	20		Cyclofenchene	1.20	0.37	
	19		Cyclofenchene	0.64	0.04	
	18	16.1	Cyclofenchene	1.39	0.18	–
	17		Cyclofenchene	0.59	0.09	
	16		Cyclofenchene	0.89	0.11	
	20		2-Bornene	0.68	0.42	
	19	16.0	2-Bornene	0.43	0.12	–
	18		2-Bornene	0.44	0.10	
	16		2-Bornene	0.81	0.27	

[1] The relative content (expressed in percentage) of determined compounds. [2] SD, Standard Deviation (n = 3). [3] Previously identified as VOCs in honey.

The PCA for four kinds of honey (Figure 1) revealed that 46.42% of the total variation embodied in 15 variables could be effectively condensed into, and explained, by the first two principal components (PCs), with eigenvalues of 4.3 and 2.7, respectively. The results show that the various kinds of honey contain characteristic volatile substances. On the other hand, there were no differences between the tested kinds of honey. The compounds as 3-methyl-1-pentanol, dimethyl ether, p-cymen-8-ol, lilac aldehyde D, and dimethyl sulfide are characteristic for linden honey. The acacia, sunflower, and honeydew honey samples were characterized by lilac aldehyde B, benzaldehyde, furfural, trans-linalool oxide, linalool, acetic acid, and hotrienol.

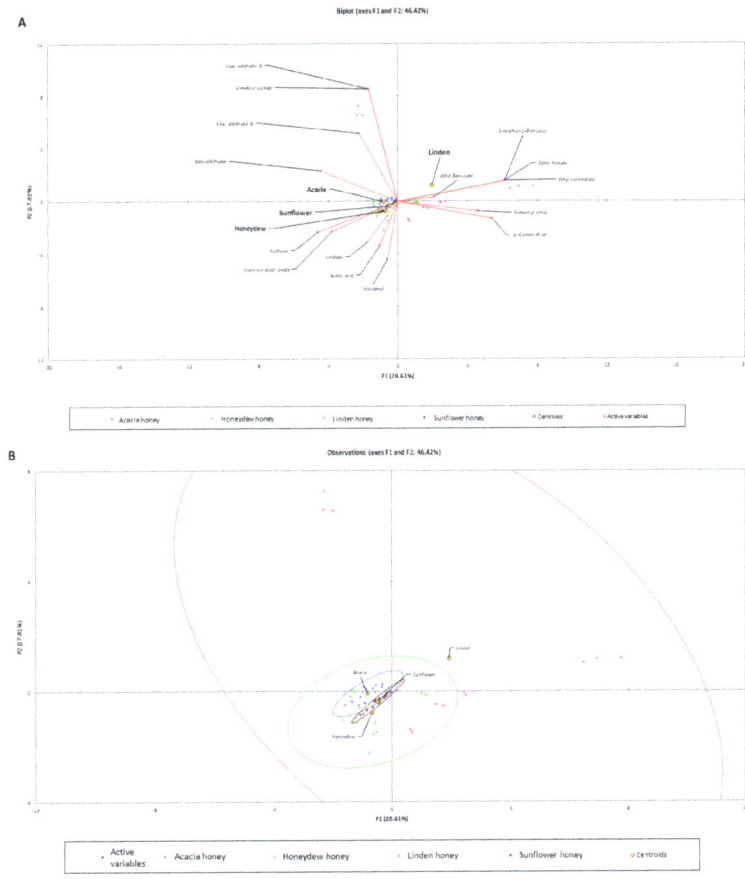

Figure 1. PCA evaluation of four kinds of honey (honeydew, acacia, linden, and sunflower); (**A**)—significant (>5%) aroma profile of samples with corresponding aromas; (**B**)—categorization of samples.

Discriminant analysis was used to classify the tested kinds of honey samples. The Wilks' Lambda test showed that the difference between the means vectors of the samples were significant ($p < 0.0001$). The first two eigen vectors explains 97.26% of variance (Figure 2). The confusion matrix calculated for the four tested samples was equal to 94.74% (data not shown). The Cross-validation: prior and posterior classification was performed to calculate the membership probabilities for unknown samples. The total accuracy of the cross-validation model was 85.96% (Table 3). Discriminant analysis can be used to classify the linden and sunflower kinds of honey but the acacia and honeydew kinds of honey were misclassified.

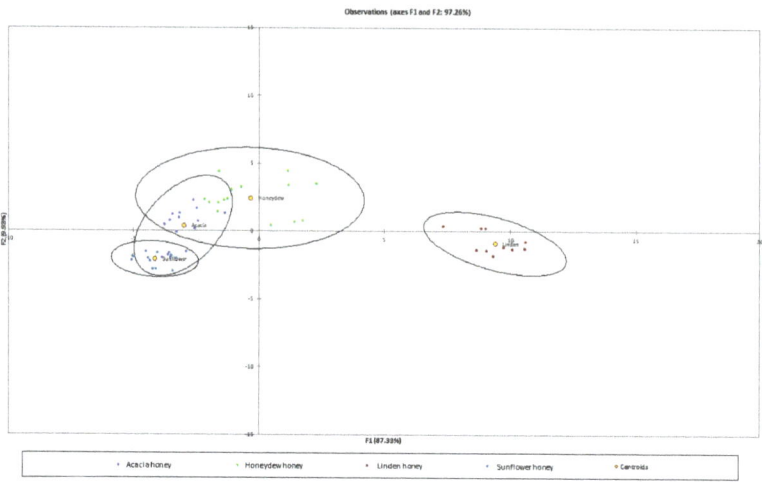

Figure 2. LDA map of kind of honey based on VOCs content.

Table 3. Confusion matrix for the cross-validation results.

from\to	Acacia	Honeydew	Linden	Sunflower	Total	% Correct
Acacia	10	1	0	4	15	66.67%
Honeydew	3	12	0	0	15	80.00%
Linden	0	0	12	0	12	100.00%
Sunflower	0	0	0	15	15	100.00%
Total	13	13	12	19	57	85.96%

4. Discussion

In total, 94 VOCs were detected in sunflower, acacia, honeydew, and linden honey samples. Some of these compounds have been previously reported by Plutowska et al. [26] in Polish linden, honeydew, and acacia honey. Sunflower and acacia honey samples from different countries were characterized by Radovic et al. [31]. The linalool oxide, as marker for acacia honey, is consistent with our results. The sunflower honey markers were α-pinene and 3-methyl-2-butanol according to Radovic et al. [31].

In this study, sunflower honey was characterized by β-calarene, cyclofenchene, and 2-bornene. Linden and honeydew had the most marker compounds. While tested linden honey was characterized by fruity ethyl esters [33], honeydew honey samples had more monoterpenoid compounds originated from aromatic plants [38]. The identified compounds in the tested honey samples were previously reported also in different kinds of honey [14–24,26–37], except linalyl acetate, which was previously tested for the fumigation of beehives to control the honey bee parasites [39]. Altogether, 16 volatiles have not been previously identified in honey samples.

According to The International Fragrance Association [40], 53 volatiles are recommended as honey fragrances. On the other hand, we identified honey volatile markers, which are not recommended as honey fragrances in the Fragrance Ingredient Glossary [40], but they are used in, for example, perfumery. The linden and honeydew samples contained anisyl alcohol (2-(para-anisyl) alcohol) (0.73%, and 0.80%, respectively), characterized as mild-floral, very sweet odor, reminiscent of lilac and vanilla with a faint, delicate, balsamic background used in perfumery [40].

The acetophenone is formed during the phenylpropane metabolism [37], and it was previously reported in chestnut honey [36,37]. However, this volatile was not previously considered by the research teams as a specific marker for the floral honey. It is characterized as a "floral" aroma fragrance described as: almond, orange, cherry, honeysuckle, jasmine, and strawberry [40]. In the present work, the acetophenone was found in linden honey (0.38%).

Each tested sample had hotrienol which is known as probably being formed during the honey's ripening [41]. It was previously found in rapeseed honey from Czech beekeepers [16], leatherwood honey from Tasmania [41], and Greek citrus honey [42]. It could be the next honey fragrance, which is missing in the Fragrance Ingredient Glossary [40]. It can be used in many flavors, such as elderflower, grape, berry, and honey [43].

5. Conclusions

We confirmed that each kind of honey had its own unique volatiles, but the aroma differences by PCA in the tested monofloral honey samples were not confirmed. It is possible to classify linden and sunflower kinds of honey by using LDA. On the other hand, the LDA cannot clearly classify acacia and honeydew honey based on the selected VOCs. The reason may also be that the linden and honeydew honey samples have rich aromatic profiles and cover less aromatic honey samples. Studies evaluating their impact in the marketing or aromachology respectively were not published yet. According to our results, the anisyl alcohol, hotrienol, and acetophenone may be used as the honey fragrance.

In conclusion, the question arises as to whether customers would be able to recognize individual kinds of honey scents, and how this would affect their behavior.

Supplementary Materials: The following are available online at https://www.mdpi.com/article/10.3390/app11178177/s1. Table S1: Content of VOCs in four kinds of honey samples determined by HS-SPME GC-MS; Figure S1: Chromatogram of sunflower honey; Figure S2: Chromatogram of acacia honey; Figure S3: Chromatogram of honeydew honey; Figure S4: Chromatogram of linden honey.

Author Contributions: Conceptualization, J.Š., P.M. and P.Š.; methodology, J.Š. and P.M.; formal analysis, J.Š. and P.M.; resources, P.Š. and P.M.; data curation, M.Š.; writing—original draft preparation, J.Š., P.M., M.Š., P.Š. and V.V.; writing—review and editing, J.Š., P.M., M.Š., P.Š. and V.V.; visualization, J.Š., P.M. and M.Š.; project administration, V.V.; funding acquisition, V.V. All authors have read and agreed to the published version of the manuscript.

Funding: This research was funded by the Slovak Research and Development Agency based on Contract no. APVV-17-0564 "The Use of Consumer Neuroscience and Innovative Research Solutions in Aromachology and its Application in Production, Business and Services" and the Grant Agency of The Slovak University of Agriculture in Nitra, grant number 14-GASPU-2021 "Analysis of consumer behavior towards honeys enriched with health-promoting substances".

Institutional Review Board Statement: Not applicable.

Informed Consent Statement: Not applicable.

Acknowledgments: We thank to the Operational Program Integrated Infrastructure within the project: Demand-driven research for the sustainable and innovative food, Drive4SIFood 313011V336, co-financed by the European Regional Development Fund (0.9) and the Operational Program Research and Innovation: "Support of research activities in the ABT RC", 313011T465, co-financed by the European Regional Development Fund (0.1).

Conflicts of Interest: The authors declare no conflict of interest. The funders had no role in the design of the study; in the collection, analyses, or interpretation of data; in the writing of the manuscript; or in the decision to publish the results.

References

1. Rimkute, J.; Moraes, C.; Ferreira, C. The Effects of Scent on Consumer Behaviour. *Int. J. Consum. Stud.* **2016**, *40*, 24–34. [CrossRef]
2. Horská, E.; Šedík, P.; Berčík, J.; Krasnodębski, A.; Witczak, M.; Filipiak-Florkiewicz, A. Aromachology in food sector-aspects of consumer food products choice. *Żywność Nauka Technologia Jakość* **2018**, *25*, 33–41. Available online: https://wydawnictwo.pttz.org/wp-content/uploads/2019/02/03_Horska.pdf (accessed on 28 July 2021).
3. American Marketing Association. Good Smells Are Good Marketing: How to Use Scent to Your Advantage. 2020. Available online: https://www.ama.org/marketing-news-home (accessed on 15 June 2021).
4. Jurášková, O.; Horňák, P. *Large Dictionary of Marketing Communications*; Grada Publishing: Praha, Czech Republic, 2012; 272p.

5. Berčík, J.; Virágh, R.; Kádeková, Z.; Duchoňová, T. Aroma marketing as a tool to increase turnover in a chosen business entity. *Potravin. Slovak J. Food Sci.* **2020**, *14*, 1161–1175. [CrossRef]
6. Berčík, J.; Mravcová, A.; Gálová, J.; Mikláš, M. The use of consumer neuroscience in aroma marketing of a service company. *Potravin. Slovak J. Food Sci.* **2020**, *14*, 1200–1210. [CrossRef]
7. Berčík, J.; Paluchová, J.; Neomániová, K. Neurogastronomy as a Tool for Evaluating Emotions and Visual Preferences of Selected Food Served in Different Ways. *Foods* **2021**, *10*, 354. [CrossRef]
8. Machado De-Melo, A.A.; de Almeida-Muradian, L.B.; Sancho, M.T.; Pascual-Maté, A. Composition and properties of *Apis mellifera* honey: A review. *J. Apic. Res.* **2017**, *57*, 5–37. [CrossRef]
9. Bogdanov, S.; Jurendic, T.; Sieber, R.; Gallmann, P. Honey for Nutrition and Health: A Review. *J. Am. Coll. Nutr.* **2008**, *27*, 677–689. [CrossRef]
10. Grassmann, J. Terpenoids as plant antioxidants. In *Vitamins and Hormones*, 1st ed.; Litwack, G., Ed.; Academic Press: Cambridge, MA, USA, 2005; Volume 72, pp. 505–535. [CrossRef]
11. Mărgăoan, R.; Topal, E.; Balkanska, R.; Yücel, B.; Oravecz, T.; Cornea-Cipcigan, M.; Vodnar, D.C. Monofloral Honeys as a Potential Source of Natural Antioxidants, Minerals and Medicine. *Antioxidants* **2021**, *10*, 1023. [CrossRef]
12. Kopaczyk, J.M.; Warguła, J.; Jelonek, T. The variability of terpenes in conifers under developmental and environmental stimuli. *Environ. Exp. Bot.* **2020**, *180*, 1–11. [CrossRef]
13. Porres-Martínez, M.; Gonzáles-Burgos, E.; Carretero, M.E.; Gómez-Serranillos, M.P. In vitro neuroprotective potential of the monoterpenes α-pinene and 1,8-cineole against H_2O_2-induced oxidative stress in PC12 cells. *Z. Naturforsch.* **2016**, *71*, 191–199. [CrossRef] [PubMed]
14. Castro-Vázquez, L.; Diáz-Maroto, M.C.; Pérez-Coello, M.S. Aroma composition and new chemical markers of Spanish citrus honeys. *Food Chem.* **2007**, *103*, 601–606. [CrossRef]
15. Serra Bonvehí, J.; Ventura Coll, F. Flavour index and aroma profiles of fresh and processed honeys. *J. Sci. Food Agric.* **2003**, *83*, 275–282. [CrossRef]
16. Kružík, V.; Grégrová, A.; Ziková, A.; Čižková, H. Rape honey: Determination of botanical origin based on volatile compound profiles. *J. Food Nutr. Res.* **2019**, *58*, 339–348.
17. Kružík, V.; Grégrová, A.; Rajchl, A.; Čížková, H. Study on honey quality evaluation and detection of adulteration by analysis of volatile compounds. *J. Apic. Sci.* **2017**, *16*, 17–27. [CrossRef]
18. Acevedo, F.; Torres, P.; Oomah, B.D.; de Alencar, S.M.; Massarioli, A.P.; Marín-Venegas, R.; Albarral-Ávila, V.; Burgos-Díaz, C.; Ferrer, R.; Rubilar, M. Volatile and non-volatile/semi-volatile compounds and in vitro bioactive properties of Chilean Ulmo (*Eucryphia cordifolia* Cav.) honey. *Food Res. Int.* **2017**, *94*, 20–28. [CrossRef] [PubMed]
19. da Costa, A.C.V.; Sousa, J.M.B.; da Silva, M.A.A.P.; Garruti, D.D.S.; Madruga, M.S. Sensory and volatile profiles of monofloral honeys produced by native stingless bees of the Brazilian semiarid region. *Food Res. Int.* **2018**, *105*, 110–120. [CrossRef] [PubMed]
20. da Costa, A.C.V.; Sousa, J.M.B.; Bezerra, T.K.A.; da Silva, F.L.H.; Pastore, G.M.; da Silva, M.A.A.P.; Madruga, M.S. Volatile profile of monofloral honeys produced in Brazilian semiarid region by stingless bees and key volatile compounds. *LWT* **2018**, *94*, 198–207. [CrossRef]
21. Bianchi, F.; Mangia, A.; Mattarozzi, M.; Musci, M. Characterization of the volatile profile of thistle honey using headspace solid-phase microextraction and gas chromatography-mass spectrometry. *Food Chem.* **2011**, *129*, 1030–1036. [CrossRef]
22. de Lima Morais da Silva, P.; de Lima, L.S.; Caetano, Í.K.; Torres, Y.R. Comparative analysis of the volatile composition of honeys from Brazilian stingless bees by static headspace GC-MS. *Food Res. Int.* **2017**, *102*, 536–543. [CrossRef]
23. Špánik, I.; Janáčová, A.; Šusterová, Z.; Jakubík, T.; Jánošková, N.; Novák, P.; Chlebo, R. Characterization of VOC composition of Slovak monofloral honeys by GCxGC-TOF-MS. *Chem. Pap.* **2012**, *67*, 127–134. [CrossRef]
24. Dymerski, T.; Chmiel, T.; Mostafa, A.; Sliwinska, M.; Wisniewska, P.; Wardencki, W.; Namiesnik, J.; Gorecki, T. Botanical and Geographical Origin Characterization of Polish Honeys by Headspace SPME-GC×GC-TOFMS. *Curr. Org. Chem.* **2013**, *17*, 1–19. [CrossRef]
25. XLSTAT (Addinsoft). *Analyse de Données et Statistique avec MS Excel*; Addinsoft: New York, NY, USA, 2014.
26. Plutowska, B.; Chmiel, T.; Dymerski, T.; Wardencki, W. A headspace solid-phase microextraction method development and its application in the determination of volatiles in honeys by gas chromatography. *Food Chem.* **2011**, *126*, 1288–1298. [CrossRef]
27. Patrignami, M.; Fagúndez, G.A.; Tananaki, C.; Thrasyvoulou, A.; Lupano, C.E. Volatile compounds of Argentinean honeys: Correlation with floral and geographical origin. *Food Chem.* **2018**, *246*, 32–40. [CrossRef] [PubMed]
28. Seisonen, S.; Kivima, E.; Ven, K. Characterization of the aroma profiles of different honeys and corresponding flowers using solid-phase microextraction and gas chromatography-mass spectrometry/olfactometry. *Food Chem.* **2015**, *169*, 34–40. [CrossRef] [PubMed]
29. Tanleque-Alberto, F.; Juan-Borrás, M.; Escriche, I. Quality parameters, pollen and volatile profiles of honey from North and Central Mozambique. *Food Chem.* **2019**, *277*, 543–553. [CrossRef]
30. Kaškonienė, V.; Venskutonis, P.R.; Čeksterytė, V. Composition of volatile compounds of honey of various floral origin and beebread collected in Lithuania. *Food Chem.* **2008**, *111*, 988–997. [CrossRef]
31. Radovic, B.S.; Careri, M.; Mangia, A.; Musci, M.; Gerboles, M.; Anklam, E. Contribution of dynamic headspace GC-MS analysis of aroma compounds to authenticity testing of honey. *Food Chem.* **2001**, *72*, 511–520. [CrossRef]

32. Kortesniemi, M.; Rosenvald, S.; Laaksonen, O.; Vanag, A.; Ollikka, T.; Vene, K.; Yang, B. Sensory and chemical profiles of Finnish honeys of different botanical origins and consumer preferences. *Food Chem.* **2018**, *246*, 351–359. [CrossRef]
33. Leng, P.; Hu, H.-W.; Cui, A.-H.; Tang, H.-J.; Liu, Y.-G. HS-GC-IMS with PCA to analyze volatile flavor compounds of honey peach packaged with different preservation methods during storage. *LWT* **2021**, *149*, 1–9. [CrossRef]
34. Escriche, I.; Sobrino-Gregorio, L.; Conchado, A.; Juan-Borrás, M. Volatile profile in the accurate labelling of monofloral honey. The case of lavender and thyme honey. *Food Chem.* **2017**, *226*, 61–68. [CrossRef]
35. Ruisinger, B.; Schieberle, P. Characterization of the Key Aroma Compounds in Rape Honey by Means of the Molecular Sensory Science Concept. *J. Agric. Food Chem.* **2012**, *60*, 4186–4194. [CrossRef] [PubMed]
36. Bonaga, G.; Giumanini, A.G. The Volatile Fraction of Chestnut Honey. *J. Apic. Res.* **1986**, *25*, 113–120. [CrossRef]
37. Guyot, C.; Bouseta, A.; Scheirman, V.; Collin, S. Floral Origin Markers of Chestnut and Lime Tree Honeys. *J. Agric. Food Chem.* **1998**, *46*, 625–633. [CrossRef]
38. Jerković, I.; Kuś, P.M. Terpenes in honey: Occurrence, origin and their role as chemical biomarkers. *RSC Adv.* **2014**, *4*, 31710–31728. [CrossRef]
39. Gonzales-Coloma, A.; Reina, M.; Diaz, C.E.; Fraga, B.M.; Santana-Meridas, O. Natural Product-Based Biopesticides for Insect Control. *Ref. Modul. Chem. Mol. Sci. Chem. Eng.* **2013**, 1–55. [CrossRef]
40. The International Fragrance Association. Fragrance Ingredient Glossary. 2020. Available online: https://ifrafragrance.org/docs/default-source/glossary/ifra-fragrance-ingredient-glossary---april-2020.pdf?sfvrsn=dc0e87ff_2&fbclid=IwAR0zezEAAkz2xTt7G2w-DIpJg6-gjBkYn4sbM8jx7kO1uXc04rsvx5_gw1A (accessed on 20 June 2021).
41. Rowland, C.Y.; Blackman, A.J.; D'Arcy, B.R.; Rintoul, G.B. Comparison of organic extractives found in leatherwood (*Eucryphia lucida*) honey and leatherwood flowers and leaves. *J. Agric. Food Chem.* **1995**, *43*, 753–763. [CrossRef]
42. Alissandrakis, E.; Tarantilis, P.A.; Harizanis, P.C.; Polissiou, M. Aroma investigation of unifloral Greek citrus honey using solid-phase microextraction coupled to gas chromatographic-mass spectrometric analysis. *Food Chem.* **2017**, *100*, 396–404. [CrossRef]
43. Berger, R.G. (Ed.) *Flavours and Fragrances. Chemistry, Bioprocessing and Sustainability*; Springer: Hannover, Germany, 2007; Volume 648, ISBN 978-3-540-49338-9. [CrossRef]

Article

Aromatic Profile of Hydroponically and Conventionally Grown Tomatoes

Melina Korčok [1], Nikola Vietorisová [1], Patrícia Martišová [2], Jana Štefániková [2], Anna Mravcová [3] and Vladimír Vietoris [1,*]

[1] Department of Technology and Quality of Plant Products, Faculty of Biotechnology and Food Sciences, Slovak University of Agriculture in Nitra, Trieda A. Hlinku 2, 949 76 Nitra, Slovakia; xkorcok@uniag.sk (M.K.); vietoris@uniag.sk (N.V.)
[2] AgroBioTech Research Centre, Slovak University of Agriculture in Nitra, Trieda A. Hlinku 2, 949 76 Nitra, Slovakia; patricia.martisova@uniag.sk (P.M.); jana.stefanikova@uniag.sk (J.Š.)
[3] Department of Social Sciences, Faculty of Economics and Management, Slovak University of Agriculture in Nitra, Trieda A. Hlinku 2, 949 76 Nitra, Slovakia; anna.mravcova@uniag.sk
* Correspondence: vladimir.vietoris@uniag.sk

Abstract: Hydroponics is a more environmentally friendly and economical way of growing crops that allows crops to be grown all year round, regardless of soil and climate conditions. Hydroponic cultivation of various fruits, vegetables, flowers, etc., is well known and used today. Tomatoes also play an important role in hydroponic cultivation. Tomatoes grown in this way should have a more pronounced aroma and flavor, and the fact that they are harvested at the ripe stage should also be reflected in the fresh red color and appropriate organoleptic characteristics of the fruit. This study was concerned with the sensory analysis of hydroponically grown tomatoes (*Solanum lycopersicum*) compared with conventionally grown tomatoes of the same species. Samples were evaluated by instrumental sensory analysis using an electronic nose as well as a sensory panel. In this study, the difference between hydroponically and conventionally grown tomatoes was demonstrated. These differences were also captured by the consumers (sensory panel). When analyzing the odor profile of the samples, we found that hydroponic tomatoes are characterized by the presence of chemical organic compounds, namely: 2-methylpropanol, 2,3-pentanedione, and (Z)-3-hexen-1-ol or 1-hexanol, which cause the fruity aroma of the fruit. These substances are very likely to characterize the differences between the tested samples. The electronic nose has shown to be a potentially suitable tool for detecting differences and identifying typical product markers, which may suggest its further use in food authentication detection. It is also interesting to find almost no correlation between the two methods studied.

Keywords: aromachology; scents; behavior; aroma; hydroponics; conventional cultivation; tomato; sensory analysis; sensory panel; electronic nose

1. Introduction

Today's market offers us a wide choice of fruit and vegetables throughout the whole year. Consumers are increasingly paying attention to the quality of their food and sensory quality is becoming more and more important for consumer decision making when choosing a product. It is certainly an important factor when purchasing the same product again, where consumers mainly consider whether the product was of the required aroma and taste characteristics for them [1].

The flavor is a combined sensation of taste and aroma; sugars, acids, and volatile compounds are their main determinants [1]. A large number of volatile compounds have been identified and the volatile profile of tomato has been investigated closely in many studies [2–5]. The resulting flavor characteristic of tomato is the result of complex interactions between organic acids, sugars, and more than 400 volatile compounds. Of the volatile compounds identified, less than 10% are present at significant concentrations and at thresholds that are likely to affect the odor and taste of tomatoes. Several studies have shown that only 16 of the total aromatic volatiles are present in sufficient quantities to be detected by the olfactory system. Therefore, the following selected descriptors are recognized as carriers of tomato taste and are present in significant quantities in the fruit. However, minor volatiles with negative odor units should not be neglected as they may still contribute to the overall aroma as adjuvants [6,7]. The individual interactions between volatiles, also those involving the gustatory and olfactory systems are significant. These complicate the aroma because specific volatile aromas perceived by the retronasal olfactory system can influence the perception of sweetness or sourness and vice versa [8,9]. Tomato fruit aroma is important in determining consumer perception and acceptability of fruit products [1]. The aroma of fresh ripe tomato is mainly attributable to cis-3-hexenal, cis-3-hexenol, hexanal, 1-penten-3-one, methyl salicylate, 2-isobutylthiazole and ß-ionone in appropriate concentrations. These compounds are biosynthetically derived from the degradation of compounds such as fatty acids, amino acids, carotenoids, and are also formed by other biosynthetic pathways [10].

In recent decades, the selection of tomato cultivars has emphasized parameters such as yield, fruit size, firmness, product flawlessness, disease resistance, ease of handling and longer shelf life, rather than sensory aspects of fruit quality. As a result, consumers started to complain about the poor tomato flavor [11–13]. Tomato flavor is now commonly referred to as "classic tomato flavor" or "old-fashioned tomato flavor", which indicate the deterioration of the sensory quality of commercial tomato fruits. However, it is unclear how, why and whether the quality of the fruit has actually changed, but consumers associate recent varieties with a lack of aroma, although such an association has not been scientifically proven. The fact is that there is now an increasing number of consumers who demand freshly grown products with a higher quality of aroma, flavor, and taste [1]. It is this recent problem, but also the demand for higher quality products, and the need of the market for year-round availability of tomatoes that stimulates the search for new ways of their growing.

Hydroponic growing systems offer an opportunity to at least augment the traditional in global food production. The advantages of hydroponic growing systems include the reduction of water wastage (recirculation), the ability to manipulate conditions to maximize production (according to [14], NaCl treatment which increases sweetness, sourness, umami (i.e., flavor deliciousness) and overall preference) in a limited space (vertical gardens), and the fact that crops are grown in a controlled environment (control of pests, nutrients, and attributes necessary for optimal plant growth). Hydroponics is becoming an increasingly popular way of growing crops, as it has several advantages compared to the traditional way of growing tomatoes [15].

In agriculture, hydroponic cultivation is a common cultivation method in greenhouses, or more precisely in hydroponic environments, where plants are grown in an inert substrate (such as perlite or rockwool) using crop fertilization (irrigation with a nutrient solution) [16]. In a hydroponic system and in soil cultivation, before the elements are bioavailable to the plant, the inorganic and organic parts must be dissolved and decomposed in water. In soil-grown plants, the elements stick to the soil particles and pass into the soil solution where they can be absorbed by the roots of the plant. In hydroponically grown plants, the nutrient solution containing the elements comes into contact with the plant roots, where the roots can then take up the minerals and water [15].

According to some data, tomatoes represent the largest share of hydroponically grown crops, as this method of cultivation can produce red and juicy tomato fruits with a variety of flavors, colors and can contain health-promoting ingredients such as lycopene, which helps maintain a healthy cardiovascular system and provides a wide range of other health benefits. Verdoliva et al. [17] stated that hydroponically grown tomatoes had higher lycopene and β-carotene content compared to conventionally grown tomatoes. It is from these substances that the volatile compounds that contribute to the typical tomato aroma are produced metabolically. These authors report that they have been able to produce crops of similar or better quality in the hydroponic way compared to food grown in soil, using significantly less water. It is clear that hydroponic tomatoes can taste as good as tomatoes grown in rich soil outdoors, or even better [18,19]. Tomatoes grown in this way should have a more pronounced aroma and flavor, and the fact that they are harvested at the ripe stage should be reflected in the fresh red color and adequate sensory characteristics of the fruit. Although the hydroponic system has many advantages, it does not automatically guarantee a high-quality product. As the technology advances, it is important to consider the sensory characteristics of the hydroponic product [20].

The aroma of tomato has been the subject of research, and the two main techniques have been the most commonly used for aroma assessment—sensory analysis and conventional gas chromatography-mass spectrometry (GC-MS). These methods are generally time consuming and difficult. A good application of these methods is important to obtain adequate results. In recent years, electronic nose systems (e-nose) have been designed to address the need for routine quality testing in the food industry. Electronic nose devices are designed to simulate the human olfactory system and are devices that can detect and recognize odors and flavors using an array of sensors. The use of the e-nose consists in the analysis of volatile organic compounds and single emerging odors that are released as gases or vapors from solids or liquids. Since the day the first prototype was developed, the e-nose has become a useful device in several applications in solving urgent problem situations, finding relevance in various industrial fields such as healthcare, automotive, food industry, environmental monitoring, food storage, and even military industry. Especially in the food industry and medicine, traditional methods of object recognition are too slow, expensive, and mostly subjective, which can result in fatal mistakes. Instead, e-nose technology offers a fast, sensitive, low-cost, and objective alternative. Moreover, the potential of this new sensing method continues to grow rapidly with new developments in sensor and computer learning technologies [21–23].

There are many different types of tomatoes to choose from on the shelves of supermarket chains. There are different varieties, sizes, shapes, colors, different ways of growing tomatoes, whether conventional, organic, hydroponic or many others. Can consumers identify the difference between the offered tomatoes? Could hydroponically grown tomatoes really taste and smell differently from conventional ones? If so, what accounts for these differences? From these questions, the main objectives of the present study emerge, in which we focused on the characterization of the aromatic profile of hydroponically grown tomatoes. For this purpose, a sensory analysis of hydroponically grown tomatoes compared to conventionally grown fruits of the same species was designed and carried out. The evaluated hydroponically grown samples came from Slovakia and Czechia, while the conventionally grown samples came from abroad. Structurally, this study was divided into two parts. The first part dealt with the instrumental sensory analysis of tomato odor profiles using e-nose and the second part dealt with the determination of differences with a more detailed focus on flavor profiles between hydroponic and conventionally grown tomatoes through the sensory panel using profile methods. The study also focused on the determination of odorants typical for hydroponically grown tomato species.

2. Materials and Methods

2.1. Sampling

Ten types of cherry tomatoes grown either hydroponically or conventionally were sampled on the basis of a food market survey targeting wholesale chains. All samples were purchased at the same time and used Slovak and Czech hydroponically grown tomatoes compared to foreign conventional tomatoes. These samples came from the Netherlands, Belgium and Italy. The samples were labeled with a three-digit numerical code, and only code marking was used at all times. All the tomato samples evaluated were of first-class quality. In this case, we experimented on the basis of the products available on the market, so the samples differed in variety or were not described on the packaging.

A summary of the samples evaluated was given in the form of Table 1.

Table 1. Overview of sensory evaluated samples.

Hydroponically Grown Tomatoes		
Sample Number	Country of Origin	Variety
V269	Slovak Republic	Unreported
V801	Slovak Republic	Unreported
V153	Czech Republic	Unreported
V512	Czech Republic	Unreported
V931	Slovak Republic	Tramezzino
V740	Slovak Republic	Mc Dreamy
Conventionally Grown Tomatoes		
Sample Number	Country of Origin	Variety
V297	Belgium	Axiana
V102	Netherlands	Sweetele
V188	Netherlands	Dulcita
V826	Italy	Dulcita

2.2. Sample Preparation

The study consisted of two parts. The first part used an electronic nose, which is a tool for analyzing organoleptic features using artificial perception. The second part focused on the evaluation of sensory properties using a sensory panel. After purchase, the samples to be evaluated using the electronic nose were allowed to rest and cure overnight at constant room temperature. These samples were scrape-free, washed and cut into small pieces, and 5 g of each sample was transferred into the appropriate vials according to the three-digit code. The filled vials were allowed to stand sealed for 2 h at room temperature in the laboratory and after this time, the samples were subjected to e-nose analysis. The samples for evaluation by the sensory panel were given in quantities of approximately 15 g and corresponded to the characteristics evaluated and the requirements for assessing the taste of the fruit, and therefore, each sample consisted of approximately one whole fruit and one half tomato fruit. During preparation, emphasis was placed on ensuring the homogeneity of the samples and compliance with the hygiene and sampling principles of ISO 8589. Similar to the preparation of samples for e-nose evaluation, samples were labeled with the same three-digit code.

2.3. Methods

2.3.1. Electronic Nose

Ten tomato samples were analyzed using a Heracles II electronic nose (Alpha MOS, Toulouse, France), with three constant replicates taken from each species. The sample preparation procedure was described above and represented an average sample according to standard sampling procedures. Samples were mixed in a balanced random order in the tray and analysis was performed automatically using an autosampler. Data were processed with the native AlphaSoft 14.2 program.

2.3.2. Sensory Panel Assessment

In the second part of the study, sensory evaluation of tomato samples was carried out by a sensory panel in the sensory laboratory of the Slovak University of Agriculture in Nitra, Department of Hygiene and Food Safety. The sensory panel consisted of 12 evaluators in two sessions, which, in our case, represented a group of selected persons (according to ISO 8586:2007 standard). Suitable environmental conditions were ensured (average ambient temperature of 20 °C at a relative humidity of approximately 65%), as well as all appropriate environmental conditions relating to the room, lighting and avoidance of other objective factors that could influence the evaluation process. The samples were distributed to the evaluator in a random, balanced order. The evaluators were provided with a taste neutralizer and a five-minute rest interval.

In the first part, the evaluators assessed the tomatoes from a more comprehensive point of view using a scoring test (including visual characteristics and texture).

The second part of the questionnaire consisted of evaluating the sensory profiles by observing what values the raters assigned to the samples on a 15 cm scale in the attributes of aroma and flavor and their subcategories. The basic flavor attributes evaluated were sour taste, sweet taste, and variations of ripe-overripe taste, metallic taste, spicy/sharp taste, and off-taste. Specific values were obtained by measuring the position of each sample on a given axis.

2.4. Statistical Analysis

Principal component analysis (PCA) was used to process the electronic nose results, where features with the greatest discriminatory power between samples were selected. For visualization, the native electronic nose program AlphaSOFT version 14.1 was used. For the purpose of predicting the growing patterns, we used the machine learning (ML) technique of the Caret of statistical software package R 4.0.2. Several algorithms (KNN, SVM, RF and LDA) were used; the results are available below. We used canonical correlation analysis (CCA) of the statistical software CCA package R version 4.0.2 to find the relationship between the sensory data and the electronic nose data.

The results obtained through the sensory panel were evaluated in RStudio version 3.6.3 using the PCA method and the SensoMiner package. The results are represented by standard descriptive indices (shown by boxplots). Pairwise comparison tables indicate the *p*-value after calculation by the non-parametric Friedman test.

3. Results and Discussion

3.1. Electronic Nose

The distribution of the samples based on the total odor profile is shown in Figure 1. This distribution was based on the volatile organic compounds released during the analysis process. We selected 12 major odorants based on discriminant strength relative to all observed samples. From this figure, we can see that samples V740 (SR), V102 (NL) and V269 (SR) have a volatile profile as they form a large triangle during the measurement time. We consider samples V297 (BE) and V512 (CZ) to be stable and least variable in the change of the odor profile. The other samples have an approximately constant odor spectrum, which means that they are almost equally extractive. The position of samples V102 (NL) and V269 (SR) suggests to us that these samples are similar. These two samples are also characterized by high odor content. Interestingly, these samples represent hydroponically (V269) and conventionally (V102) grown samples. The Slovak sample of hydroponically grown tomatoes (V801) also shows similarities with these two samples.

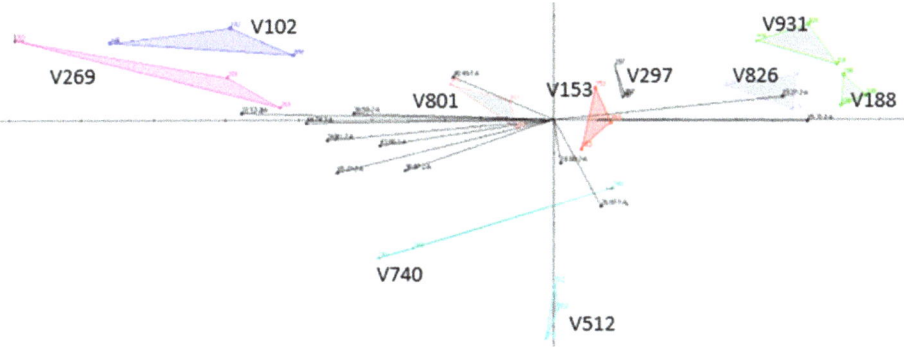

Figure 1. Total odor profile of samples with corresponding odors.

Samples (V826, V931, V188) that are in the same quadrant are similar. These samples represent tomatoes that have been stripped of their top leaves in the processing and packaging process.

This figure also shows the odors captured by the e-nose during the analysis of the samples. Specific odorous substances produced by volatile organic compounds are represented by lines in the figure and their direction indicates the products that contain the most of them. At the ends of the lines are numbers used to identify the compounds that were present in the samples. We can confirm that samples V102 (NL), V269 (SR) and V740 (SR) are more extractive even though they contain fewer types of odorous compounds compared to the others. Odor compounds 26.07-1-A and 15.31.1-A (listed in Table 1) are typical of most hydroponically grown samples with strong discrimination power.

In the following procedure, we discussed the most basic identifiers that occurred in significant amounts in tomato samples grown hydroponically. From the total odor profile that was detected and generated from the electronic nose database, we selected the first five basic odor markers that occurred in the greatest amount in the samples through the program. Based on this, the localization and odor spectrum of the samples were changed. This is illustrated in Figure 2. Since 98% of the 100% results obtained were evaluated, we assess that the results obtained are reliable as well as quantitatively and qualitatively adequate.

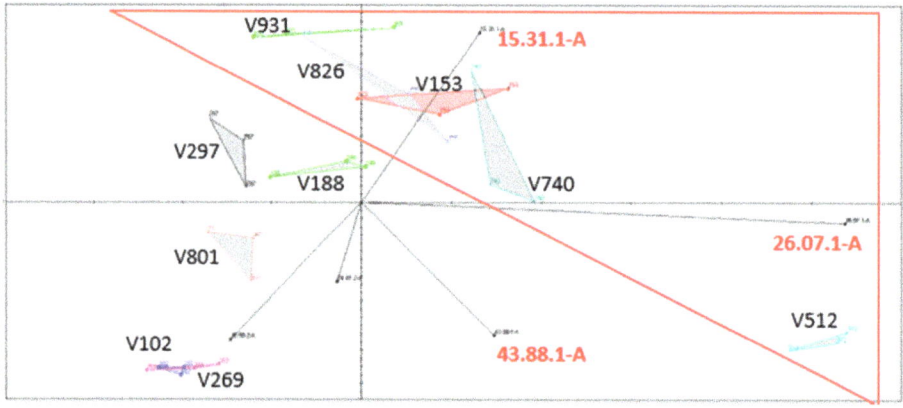

Figure 2. Categorization of samples with selection of main markers.

E-nose was able to identify differences between the evaluated samples and classify them into two groups: hydroponically and conventionally grown tomatoes. The device assessed the hydroponic tomatoes as demonstrably similar and placed them side by side on the graph. For better clarity, we marked all these samples in the form of a triangle. Bottom left quadrant represents the samples that the device assessed as conventionally grown. This includes sample V102 (NL), but also samples V801 (SR) and V269 (SR), which are incorrectly classified in this category as they are hydroponically grown tomatoes. The erroneous categorization of these two samples can be explained by the fact that these samples represent stemless tomatoes. The device also included sample V826, which represents conventionally grown tomatoes, in the triangle representing hydroponically grown tomatoes. This sample appears to contain a similar odor spectrum to hydroponically grown tomatoes. After discounting this one sample, our study indicates that e-nose has potential to be a suitable instrumental sensory analysis tool that can be used to detect hydroponically and conventionally grown crops. Similar study indicates that there is potential for the use of the e-nose to complement routine sensory analysis of tomatoes [24]. A similar view is shared by the authors [25], who state that e-nose is a fast and effective technique that does not require special sample preparation to determine the aroma of the product and it is therefore widely used for the detection of food adulteration. They further suggest that in the case of some foods, the aroma of the product is specific enough to distinguish the original product from its counterfeit or adulterated product. Several studies have used this fact and thus e-nose has also been used in the context of authentication and adulteration of fresh juices made from cherry tomatoes. Other authors [26] confirmed the possibility of using this device to detect adulterated food. Our results may indicate the possibility of using e-nose in the process of food authentication and in estimating food adulteration, specifically hydroponically grown tomatoes. To confirm this, we recommend working with a larger number of samples in future research.

In the past, much research has led to the development of extraction and analytical techniques useful for obtaining a detailed profile of volatiles from tomatoes. A large number of volatiles have been identified and the volatile profile of tomato has been investigated in detail in many studies. Already in 1998 [4], relationships between chemical compounds and sensory properties of tomatoes were established. (Z)-3-hexenal, hexanal, 1-octen-3-one, methional, 1-penten-3-one, and 3-methylbutanal were among the most odor-active aromatic volatiles in fresh tomatoes. The aroma, taste and aftertaste of different tomato varieties were evaluated by quantitative descriptive analysis. Using PCA analysis, they found that the first three components presented 70% of the total variance. According to [5], volatiles characteristic of tomatoes include acyclic, cyclic and heterocyclic hydrocarbons, alcohols, phenols, ethers, aldehydes, ketones, carboxylic acids, esters and lactones, as well as compounds containing nitrogen, sulfur and halogens. Of these, molecules such as 1-penten-3-one, hexanal, cis-3-hexenal, trans-2-hexenal, 1-penten-3-ol, 3-methylbutanol, cis-3-hexen-1-ol, 2-isobutylthiazole, trans-2 heptanal, 6-methyl-5-hepten-2-one, 6-methyl-5-hepten-2-ol, methyl salicylate, geranyl acetone, and phenyl ethanol are important.

As mentioned earlier, in this study, we focused on the five basic odors that were present in the samples in the highest amount. After the electronic nose divided the odor profile of the evaluated samples into hydroponic (inside the triangle) and conventionally grown, we were able to identify three main odor cues characteristic for hydroponically grown tomatoes (Figure 2). These are substances listed as 15.31.1-A, 26.07.1-A and, marginally, 43.88.1-A. Under the label 15.31.1-A, we are most likely to recognize the chemical organic compound 2-methylpropanol. This substance is responsible for the typical fruity flavor and the green, unripe notes of the fruit. It is highly likely that the compound dimethyl sulphide, presenting fruity and vegetal notes, also completes this set of odors. The odor substance labeled 26.07.1-A is the chemical compound 2,3-pentanedione representing a fruity flavor. This substance also promotes the freshness feeling of the fruit and participates in the formation of the sweet character. The last compound associated with the sensory character of hydroponically grown tomatoes is (Z)-3-hexen-1-ol or 1-hexanol, causing a fruity, grassy, fresh, and unripe flavor or aroma to the fruit. Correlation between (Z)-3-hexen-1-ol and flavor intensity was also proven in the study of contribution of C6 volatiles to taste and aroma [9]. Other authors report that C6 compounds are the most widespread volatiles in tomato fruit and contribute to tomato flavor in various ways. Similar to our study, the presence of (Z)-3-hexen-1-ol in hydroponically grown tomatoes was also detected by those authors [1]. In some studies, this substance is associated with consumer acceptability [27].

Therefore, our study has shown that presence of substances: 2-methylpropanol, 2,3-pentanedione, (Z)-3-hexen-1-ol or 1-hexanol is potentially the difference between hydroponically and conventionally grown tomatoes. All four volatiles were also identified in a review of proven volatiles in tomatoes and tomato products in 1986 [2]. To confirm this, in future research, we recommend to upgrade research design with larger number of tested samples. In the case of machine learning analysis, we used the original electronic language dataset, whose most discriminative odorants/retention index is shown in Table 2. The dataset was then divided into 80% training data and 20% data for validation.

Using various algorithms, we found that LDA (0.879) was the most suitable, followed by Random Forrest (0.78) and SVM (0.684) using the Caret statistical package from R 4.0.2;

KNN (0.578) were not suitable to predict hydroponic or conventional cultivation. The results including Kappa parameter are shown in Figure 3.

Table 2. Overview of retention index, sensors, and its discrimination powers (AlphaSoft 14.2 database).

Index	Sensors	Discrimination Power
6	15.31-1-A	0.958
16	26.07-1-A	0.951
60	38.50-2-A	0.949
53	24.41-2-A	0.945
24	43.86-1-A	0.945
52	23.27-2-A	0.942
62	44.74-2-A	0.939
23	40.49-1-A	0.935
48	18.87-2-A	0.923
51	22.12-2-A	0.915

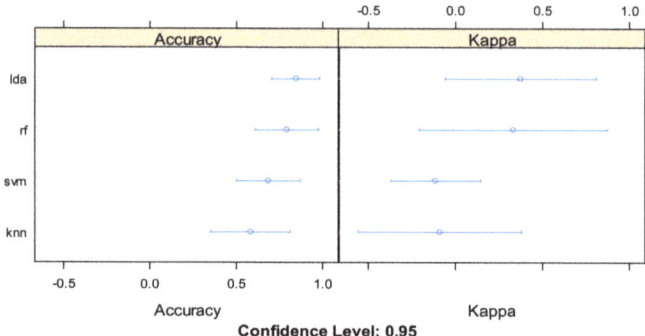

Figure 3. Machine learning applied algorithms (Caret Package, R 4.0.2).

3.2. Sensory Analysis Carried Out by the Evaluators

Sensory analysis can be affected by various factors. Compared to production methods, variety had greater influence on sensory attributes of tomatoes [28]. Similarly, Treftz et al. [20] reported that sensory evaluation can be influenced by several factors such as genetic composition, pre-harvest factors (light, temperature, humidity, and wind) and post-harvest factors. Other influences include price, brand, and consumer mood, which affect the sensory evaluation of the product. These authors suggest that these are all important factors to consider when evaluating the hydroponically grown product for sensory attributes. Other authors have shown that the inner tissues of tomato fruit contained higher concentrations of 3-methylbutanol, 2-methylbutanol, 3-methylbutanol, and 2-methylbutanol than pericarp [6]. The composition and types of contents in tomato were studied by some authors and they concluded that the concentration of alcohol in tomato seeds was higher than that in other tissues. This finding was focused on higher amounts of 2-methylpropanol, 3-methylbutanol, and 2-methylbutanol [29]. There is a consistent relationship between color and taste, especially in red cultivars, but according to study by Oluk et al. [30], brown cultivars were appreciated as much as their red counterparts. The brown variety had the highest sweetness, typical aroma and hardness scores, while the yellow variety had the lowest typical aroma sweetness score. In terms of sensory parameters, the red and brown varieties scored higher than the yellow and orange varieties. This means that during sensory analysis, it is important to evaluate same-color samples.

In our study, sensory panel evaluated homogenic-looking samples and the evaluation was divided into two parts. In the first part of the sensory evaluation, a 5-level scoring test was used, which focused on the more complex agricultural character of tomatoes. The results obtained were analyzed in SensoMiner software, based on which we obtained a graphical representation of the different attributes and the results obtained are shown in the form of Figure 4. From this graphical representation, we can see that in the odor attribute, samples V102 (NL) and V153 (CZ) were judged as the least intense and they achieved worse evaluation. Medium values were assigned by the evaluators to samples representing conventionally grown tomatoes: V188 (NL), V297 (BE), and V826 (IT). Of all the samples evaluated, no sample proved to be dominantly more intense in the odor attribute compared to the other samples. Samples representing hydroponically grown tomatoes: V269 (SR), V512 (CZ), V740 (SR), and V931 (SR) were ranked with the highest values obtained, which means that they showed a more intense odor. These results correspond with those obtained using e-nose.

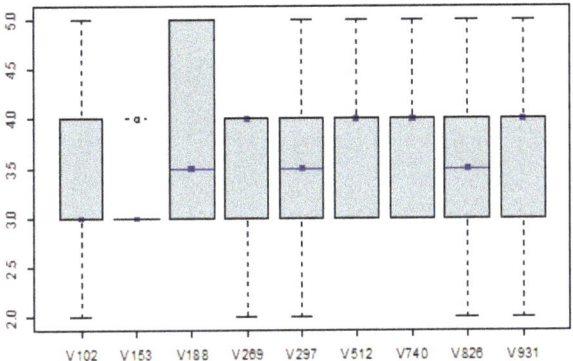

Figure 4. Sensory analysis of tomato fruit odor.

Another attribute evaluated by the sensory panel was the smell of the tomato fruit on the cut. From the data shown in the form of Figure 5, we can see that there were no clear worse or better results between the samples. Samples V188 (NL), V269 (SR), V512 (Strabena, CZ), V740 (SR), and V931 (SR) were evaluated as more satisfactory by the sensory panel in terms of odor on the cut. In contrast, samples V102 (NL), V153 (CZ), and V826 (IT) were characterized by a less intense aroma profile. In terms of the attribute evaluated, sample V297, which represents conventionally grown Belgian tomatoes, was rated as the most pleasant. The graphical distribution of samples V512 (CZ) and V826 (IT) tells us that these samples had a wide odor spectrum.

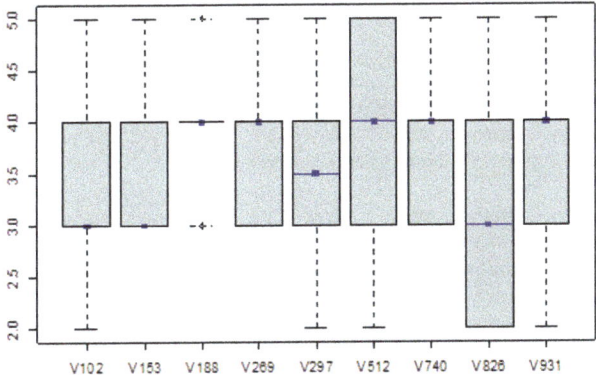

Figure 5. Sensory analysis of the smell of fruit on the cut.

The human perception of tomato flavor lies in the integration of taste and aroma. Tomato aroma is a balance of acid and sugar recognized by the tongue and the effect of volatile compounds in the fruit that cause the aroma is recognized by the nose, therefore, we considered important the results obtained by sensory evaluation of tomato flavor, which are graphically represented in the form of Figure 6. For the flavor attribute, the sample V153 (CZ) stood out as more intense. This sample received, on average, the highest possible score and it is the sample that represents hydroponically grown tomatoes. Compared to this sample, samples V188 (NL), V512 (CZ), and V931 (SR) were rated as less intensive. These samples represent the tomatoes of both groups. The sample that was rated lowest by the sensory panel and rated as less suitable for this attribute was sample V269 (SR). The other samples were at the level of average taste acceptable by consumers.

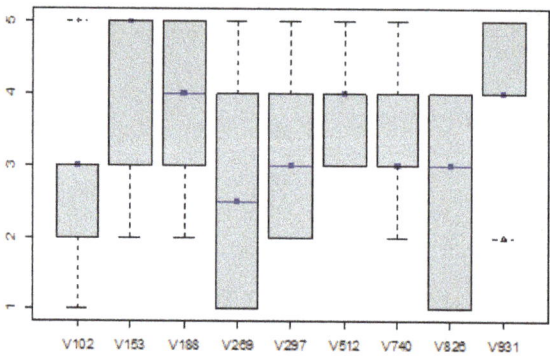

Figure 6. Sensory analysis of the flavor of the fruit.

The results obtained by the scoring test were subjected to PCA analysis and Figure 7 was constructed. The first part of Figure 7a shows the distribution of the samples within the summary scores of all the attributes evaluated, namely: appearance, smell, smell of the fruit on the cut, texture, taste, and overall impression. Based on the data obtained from the sensory analysis, we can rank samples V269 (SR) and V297 (BE), as well as samples V102 (NL) and V826 (IT) as statistically significantly similar. The remaining evaluated samples scored similarly, meaning that these samples show similar sensory characteristics. Based on the samples' position within the graph, we can conclude that the sensory evaluators were also able to detect differences between hydroponic and conventional tomatoes. This means that also through the panelists' evaluation with the simple scoring test and subsequent PCA analysis, it is possible to show differences between tomatoes grown in two different ways. Other authors have compared hydroponically and conventionally grown crops from sensory point of view. For example, in one study, the authors compared hydroponically and conventionally grown strawberries. The study found that consumers did not have strong preference between hydroponic and soil-grown strawberries, but indicated that of the 13 attributes examined, overall aroma and aroma intensity were the only attributes that reached statistical significance ($p < 0.05$). Hydroponically grown strawberries showed higher mean ratings for these two categories. Consequently, they reported that due to the environmental benefits of hydroponic production combined with the favorable ratings of descriptive sensory analysis, it may be desirable for the consumer and beneficial for the environment to grow strawberry varieties in infertile areas to provide fresh fruit [20]. In 2011, a study was conducted to compare hydroponically, conventionally, and organically grown lettuces. A significant difference was found between either hydroponically and conventionally grown lettuces ($p = 0.03$) or between organically and conventionally grown lettuces ($p = 0.009$), but not between hydroponically and organically grown lettuces ($p = 0.6956$). In the opinion of the sensory panel, hydroponically and organically grown lettuces had more intense smell (odor) [31]. Similarly, in our study, consumers rated hydroponically grown tomatoes with the highest scores, meaning that they demonstrated a more intense odor. These results were confirmed by e-nose.

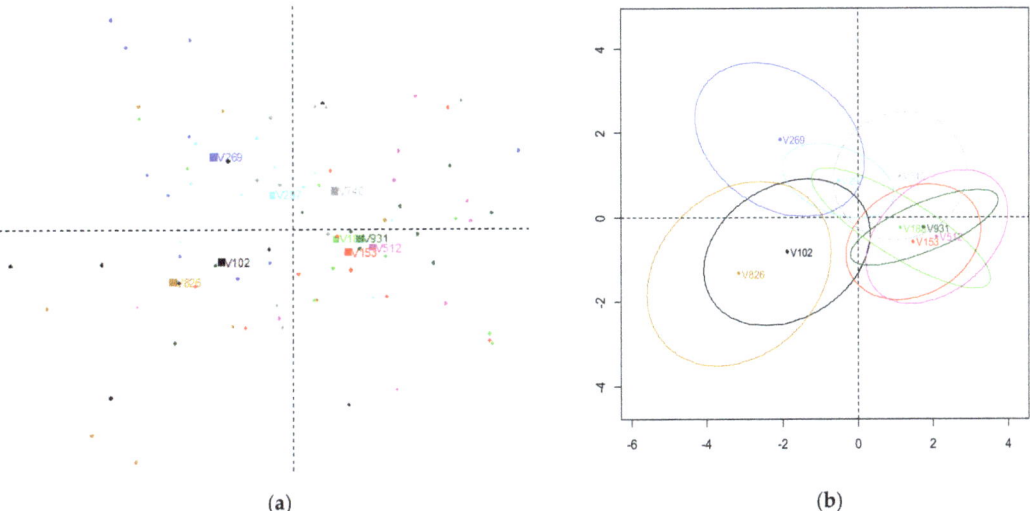

Figure 7. (a) PCA analysis of the overall character of the samples (point test); (b) PCA analysis of the complex profile of the samples (point test)—output by Sensominer software.

Within the second part of Figure 7b, the ellipses shown represent the variance of the values given in the sensory evaluation of each attribute. We can say that the samples V297 (BE) and V931 (SR) have the narrowest variance of the values obtained. A very wide variance is visible for samples V826 (IT), V102 (NL), and V269 (SR).

Table 3 was subsequently generated from the results of the scoring test, showing the demonstrability of differences between the tested samples. The resulting values, which are highlighted in yellow in the table, indicate that there is a difference between them at the alpha level of significance = 0.05. For us, the most important results are indicated in bold. Sample V826 (IT), which belongs to conventionally grown tomatoes, was marked as statistically significantly different. Its dissimilarity was not proven for samples V102 (NL) and V269 (SR). This means that these samples had similar sensory characteristics to the tomatoes that were stemless. The Slovak hydroponically grown tomatoes V931 were statistically significantly different from other samples, namely samples V102 (NL), V297 (BE), and V826 (IT). Similarly, to the Slovak sample, the Czech tomato (V512) differed from the samples that were grown conventionally (V102, V297, and V826).

Table 3. Demonstrability of differences between samples (sensory evaluation) (yellow label statistical difference $p < 0.05$).

	V102	V153	V188	V269	V297	V512	V740	V826	V931
V102	1	0.0549	0.0985	0.0804	0.1240	0.0279	0.0550	0.6970	0.0481
V153		1	0.9235	0.00833	0.0350	0.8637	0.2268	0.0115	0.8957
V188			1	0.0718	0.3100	0.7846	0.3827	0.0207	0.8946
V269				1	0.3465	0.0050	0.0666	0.0550	0.0057
V297					1	0.0206	0.3057	0.0406	0.0144
V512						1	0.2068	0.0063	0.8747
V740							1	0.0127	0.2043
V826								1	0.0106
V931									1

The second part of the sensory analysis performed by the sensory panel consisted of assessing the sensory profiles through the hedonic scale. Our evaluators assessed the odor-flavor profile of the tomato, i.e., the flavor. Flavor refers to the sensory impression of the food or other substance, which is determined mainly by chemical combinations of taste and smell. To obtain the results, we used a similar program to the scoring test, namely SensoMiner, and we provide the results by visualizing them in the table evaluating the treated averages of the measured values. From a statistical point of view, we used Friedman's non-parametric test. The provable differences between the samples are demonstrated to us by the values shown in Table 4. Statistically demonstrably stronger, more pronounced attributes are shown in blue. Attributes in which specific samples were rated as statistically demonstrably weaker are shown in yellow. From the values shown, we can see that in terms of sweet flavor, tomato sample with stem V931, hydroponically grown in Slovakia, dominates. The evaluators identified the foreign, conventionally grown samples V297 (BE) and V826 (IT) as statistically significantly less sweet. In this context, lower fruit ripeness was also associated with sample V826 and a demonstrably more acidic flavor with sample V297. Sample V740 (SR) was also found to be sour. Sample V269 (SR) was less acidic than the other samples. In terms of the other evaluated flavors, there was no clear difference between the samples. This means that there were no spicy, peppery, hot, metallic, or other foreign odors or flavors present in the samples that would significantly affect the character of the tomatoes. As a result, it can be said that samples V297 (BE) and V826 (IT), which represented foreign conventionally grown tomato varieties, were marked as less ripe or underripe by this method of evaluation and were therefore less sweet but more acidic to the evaluators compared to other samples. These results can be explained with the findings from previous studies that have shown that tomato volatiles which affect odor and taste of the tomato are formed during the ripening process in the intact tomato and during maceration of the tomato, for example, when slicing, chewing or blending. A reasonable amount of cis-3-hexenal also exists in the ripe green tomato, but its concentration increased more than 20 times in the ripe form [11]. These samples were from abroad and had to be shipped to Slovakia; they may be chilled during the transportation and as a result of that, their volatile content may have been reduced as shown in the study by Tieman et al. [9] where refrigeration of tomatoes have previously been found to reduce the volatile content of fresh tomato fruit. It has been reported that chilling injury results in membrane damage, which can disrupt the lipoxygenase enzymatic pathway that results in C-6 aldehydes (hexanal, hexanol, cis-3-hexenal, cis-3-hexenol, trans-2-hexenal, etc.) from membrane lipids [8]. On the other hand, Yilmaz [32] gave a list of volatiles whose amount increases after disruption of tissues (cis-2-hexenal, trans-2-hexenal, hexanal, trans-2-heptenal, 1-penten-3-one, 1-penten-3-ol, and geranyl acetone).

Table 4. PCA analysis of sensory profiles (blue label statistically better, yellow label vice versa).

	Sweet Flavor	Ripe/Overripe	Sour Flavor	Peppery/Hot/Spicy Flavor	Metallic Flavor	Other Foreign Flavor
V931	7.52	6.17	4.46	1.58	1.15	0.59
V102	5.56	6.14	3.33	1.39	1.74	1.43
V512	5.48	5.20	4.35	2.30	0.91	0.89
V153	6.02	5.21	3.99	1.62	2.14	0.92
V188	6.17	5.80	3.68	2.21	1.73	1.41
V740	4.46	5.42	6.22	2.15	1.02	0.85
V269	4.48	6.67	2.63	1.55	2.28	2.00
V297	2.36	4.85	6.55	2.16	2.32	1.64
V826	3.10	2.46	4.11	1.98	2.20	2.00

The demonstrability of the differences from the results of the sensory profile evaluations at alpha level = 0.05% is shown in Table 5. The sample V826 (IT) was also the most different according to this analysis. This sample is statistically significantly different from all samples except the Dutch stemless tomatoes. Tomato sample V740 (SR) was significantly different from sample V153 (CZ) and from V269 (SR).

Table 5. Demonstrability of differences between samples (sensory profiles) (yellow label statistical difference $p < 0.05$).

	V102	V153	V188	V269	V297	V512	V740	V826	V931
V102	1	0.9121	0.9857	0.9211	0.0379	0.6828	0.1126	0.0504	0.6559
V153		1	0.9365	0.6461	0.0658	0.8984	0.0470	0.0078	0.3164
V188			1	0.7963	0.0737	0.8130	0.0917	0.0176	0.5927
V269				1	0.0049	0.2519	0.0181	0.0234	0.4146
V297					1	0.0749	0.3593	0.0106	0.0042
V512						1	0.1121	0.0114	0.1929
V740							1	0.0000	0.0374
V826								1	0.0008
V931									1

The similarity between the samples was then also analyzed using PCA method and a similarity map of the samples was constructed (Figure 8). An extract from Figure 8a shows the individual description and distribution of the samples through a complex odor profile by combining the individual flavors assessed. The resulting position of the samples in the graph indicates that samples V740 (SR) and V297 (BE) are rated as statistically demonstrably similar, meaning that these samples are similar in their odor profile composition. Since sample V826 (IT) is located in a separate quarter, we can conclude that this sample is statistically significantly different from the other samples. In the graph, the other samples are placed close to each other, indicating that these samples are very similar.

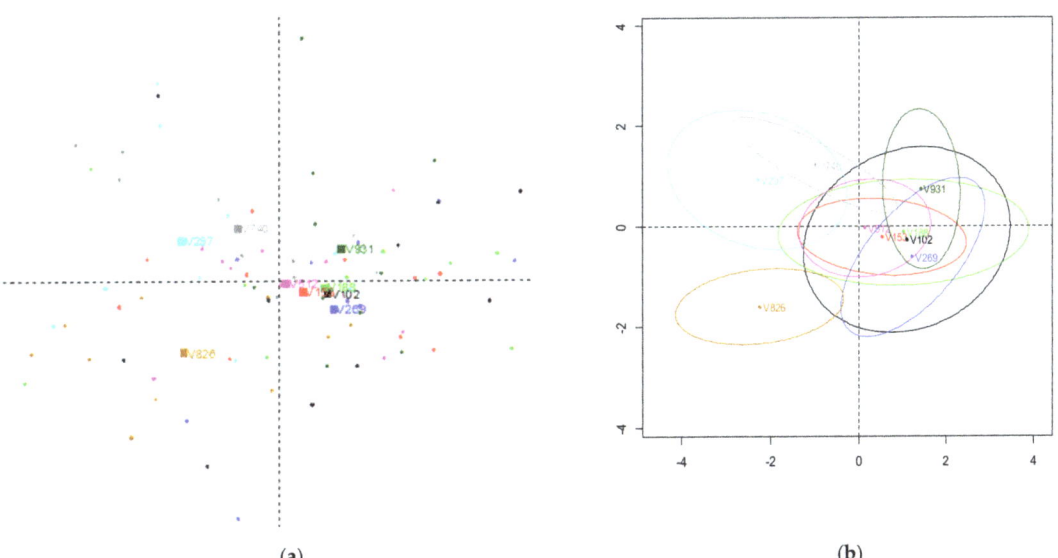

Figure 8. (a) PCA analysis of the flavor assessment of samples (sensory profiles); (b) PCA analysis of the complex profile of samples (sensory profiles).

A PCA similarity map was also constructed (Figure 8b), which shows the variances obtained from the results of the sensory profile evaluations. In this case, each ellipse represents values from minimum to maximum. Sample V826 (IT) also emerged as statistically demonstrably different from the other samples in this case, which does not have such a large variance, but apparently quite different sensory properties, as we have confirmed in the previous results. We observe a similar flavor in samples V740 (SR) and V297 (BE). Among the group of samples with related characteristics, the conventionally grown samples from the Netherlands (V102 and V188) have a broad profile.

In the analysis of the relationship between the two types of measurements, we can conclude that there is no relationship between the data from the electronic nose to the data from the sensory evaluation. The odor profile is complex in both types of tomato grown and the two methods do not correlate with each other at all (R = 0.07). The results are demonstrated in Figure 9.

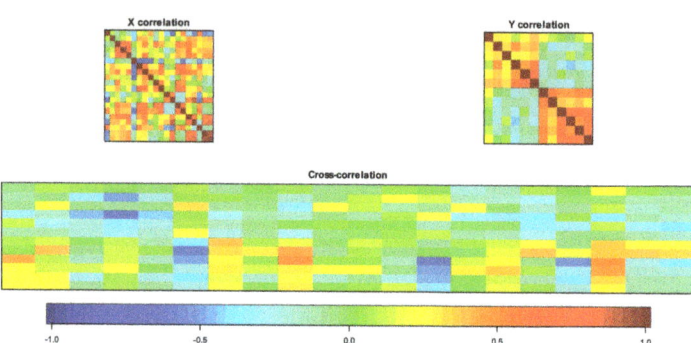

Figure 9. Canonical correlation analysis X matrix (electronic nose data, R = 0.34), Y matrix (sensory analysis data, R = 0.22), bottom XY (cross-correlation matrix of XY data, R = 0.07).

4. Conclusions

Sensory analysis of hydroponically and conventionally grown tomatoes was carried out using e-nose and sensory panel. In both cases, there were demonstrable differences between the two groups and the study proved that there is the difference between tomatoes grown with nutrient solution and those grown conventionally in soil. Based on the obtained results, we can conclude that we can potentially use the electronic nose to detect the difference between the samples. E-nose device was able to divide the analyzed samples into two groups, namely hydroponically and conventionally grown tomatoes. This fact shows us that we could potentially use e-nose for detecting food adulteration, namely, conventionally grown tomatoes declared as hydroponically grown tomatoes and vice versa. For future research, to obtain more accurate results, we recommend testing a larger number of samples and purchasing samples from one location or country.

In our research, we were also able to identify three main odor traces characteristic for hydroponically grown tomatoes: 2-methylpropanol, 2,3-pentanedione, (Z)-3-hexen-1-ol or 1-hexanol (substances registered as 15.31.1-A, 26.07.1-A and, marginally, 43.88.1-A). It is very likely that these substances characterize the difference between tested samples. Sensory panel was also able to detect the difference between hydroponically and conventionally grown tomatoes, which tells us that even consumers themselves are able to recognize the differences between the two groups. For the prediction of hydroponically and convectively grown tomatoes, we used a machine learning technique (ML), with the linear LDA algorithm performing best. There was no relationship between the sensory evaluation data and the artificial perception evaluation.

Author Contributions: Conceptualization, N.V., V.V. and J.Š.; methodology, N.V., V.V., P.M. and J.Š.; software, V.V. and A.M.; validation, V.V. and M.K.; formal analysis, N.V., J.Š. and P.M.; investigation, M.K., V.V. and N.V.; resources, M.K., V.V., N.V. and A.M.; data curation, J.Š., P.M. and V.V.; writing—original draft preparation, M.K., V.V. and A.M.; writing—review and editing, M.K., A.M. and V.V.; visualization, V.V., A.M., J.Š. and N.V.; supervision, J.Š. and V.V. All authors have read and agreed to the published version of the manuscript.

Funding: The research was also funded by the research grant APVV-17-0564 "The Use of Consumer Neuroscience and Innovative Research Solutions in Aromachology and its Application in Production, Business and Services".

Institutional Review Board Statement: Not applicable.

Informed Consent Statement: Not applicable.

Data Availability Statement: Not applicable.

Conflicts of Interest: The authors declare no conflict of interest.

References

1. Jukić Špika, M.; Dumičić, G.; Brkić Bubola, K.; Soldo, B.; Goreta Ban, S.; Vuletin Selak, G.; Ljubenkov, I.; Mandušić, M.; Žanić, K. Modification of the Sensory Profile and Volatile Aroma Compounds of Tomato Fruits by the Scion × Rootstock Interactive Effect. *Front. Plant Sci.* **2021**, *11*, 616431. [CrossRef] [PubMed]
2. Petro-Turza, M. Flavor of tomato and tomato products. *Food Rev. Int.* **1986**, *2*, 309–351. [CrossRef]
3. Buttery, R.G.; Teranishi, R.; Ling, L.C. Fresh tomato aroma volatiles: A quantitative study. *J. Agric. Food Chem.* **1987**, *35*, 540–544. [CrossRef]
4. Krumbein, A.; Auerswald, H. Characterization of aroma volatiles in tomatoes by sensory analyses. *Food Nahr.* **1998**, *42*, 395–399. [CrossRef]
5. Paolo, D.; Bianchi, G.; Lo Scalzo, R.; Morelli, C.F.; Rabuffetti, M.; Speranza, G. The Chemistry behind Tomato Quality. *Nat. Prod. Commun.* **2018**, *13*, 1225–1232. [CrossRef]
6. Wang, L.; Qian, C.; Bai, J.; Luo, W.; Jin, C.; Yu, Z. Difference in volatile composition between the pericarp tissue and inner tissue of tomato (*Solanum lycopersicum*) fruit. *J. Food Process Preserv.* **2017**, *42*, e13387. [CrossRef]
7. Wu, Q.; Tao, X.Y.; Ai, X.Z.; Luo, Z.S.; Mao, L.C.; Ying, T.J.; Li, L. Effect of exogenous auxin on aroma volatiles of cherry tomato (*Solanum lycopersicum* L.) fruit during postharvest ripening. *Postharvest Biol. Technol.* **2018**, *146*, 108–116. [CrossRef]
8. Baldwin, E.A.; Goodner, K.; Plotto, A. Interaction of Volatiles, Sugars, and Acids on Perception of Tomato Aroma and Flavor Descriptors. *J. Food Sci.* **2008**, *73*, 294–307. [CrossRef]
9. Tieman, D.; Bliss, P.; McIntyre, L.M.; Blandon-Ubeda, A.; Bies, D.; Odabasi, A.Z.; Rodríguez, G.R.; der Knaap, E.; Taylor, M.G.; Goulet, C.H.; et al. The Chemical Interactions Underlying Tomato Flavor Preferences. *Curr. Biol.* **2012**, *22*, 1035–1039. [CrossRef]
10. Davidovich-Rikanati, R.; Sitrit, Y.; Tadmor, Y.; Pichersky, E.; Dudareva, N.; Lewinsohn, E. Tomato Aroma: Biochemistry and Biotechnology. In *Biotechnology in Flavor Production*, 2nd ed.; Havkin-Frenkel, D., Dudai, N., Eds.; Wiley-Blackwell: Hoboken, NJ, USA, 2016; pp. 243–263.
11. Carbonell-Barrachina, A.A.; Agustí, A.; Ruiz, J.J. Analysis of flavor volatile compounds by dynamic headspace in traditional and hybrid cultivars of Spanish tomatoes. *Eur. Food Res. Technol.* **2006**, *222*, 536–542. [CrossRef]
12. Causse, M.; Saliba-Colombani, V.; Lesschaeve, I.; Buret, M. Genetic analysis of organoleptic quality in fresh market tomato. 2. Mapping QTLs for sensory attributes. *Theor. Appl. Genet.* **2001**, *102*, 273–283. [CrossRef]
13. Baldwin, E.; Plotto, A.; Narciso, J.; Bai, J. Effect of 1-methylcyclopropene on tomato flavour components, shelf life and decay as influenced by harvest maturity and storage temperature. *J. Sci. Food Agric.* **2011**, *91*, 969–980. [CrossRef]
14. Sato, S.; Sakaguchi, S.; Furukawa, H.; Ikeda, H. Effects of NaCl application to hydroponic nutrient solution on fruit characteristics of tomato (*Lycopersicon esculentum* Mill.). *Sci. Hortic.* **2006**, *109*, 248–253. [CrossRef]
15. Treftz, C.; Omaye, S.T. Hydroponics: Potential for augmenting sustainable food production in non-arable regions. *Nutr. Food Sci.* **2016**, *46*, 672–684. [CrossRef]
16. Sanjuan-Delmás, D.; Josa, A.; Muñoz, P.; Gassó, S.; Rieradevall, J.; Gabarrell, X. Applying nutrient dynamics to adjust the nutrient-water balance in hydroponic crops. A case study with open hydroponic tomato crops from Barcelona. *Sci. Hortic.* **2020**, *261*, 108908. [CrossRef]
17. Verdoliva, S.G.; Gwyn-Jones, D.; Detheridge, A.; Robson, P. Controlled comparisons between soil and hydroponic systems reveal increased water use efficiency and higher lycopene and β-carotene contents in hydroponically grown tomatoes. *Sci. Hortic.* **2021**, *279*, 109896. [CrossRef]
18. Schmautz, Z.; Loeu, F.; Liebisch, F.; Graber, A.; Mathis, A.; Griessler Bulc, T.; Junge, R. Tomato Productivity and Quality in Aquaponics: Comparison of Three Hydroponic Methods. *Water* **2016**, *8*, 533. [CrossRef]
19. Morgan, L. Hydroponic Tomatoes. *GPN* **2003**, 78–85. Available online: http://gpnmag.com/wp-content/uploads/p78%20Morgan.pdf (accessed on 6 June 2021).
20. Treftz, C.H.; Zhang, F.; Omaye, S.T. Comparison between Hydroponic and Soil-Grown Strawberries: Sensory Attributes and Correlations with Nutrient Content. *Food Nutr. Sci.* **2015**, *6*, 1371–1380. [CrossRef]
21. Karakaya, D.; Ulucan, O.; Turkan, M. Electronic Nose and Its Applications: A Survey. *Int. J. Autom. Comput.* **2020**, *17*, 179–209. [CrossRef]
22. Park, S.Y.; Kim, Y.; Kim, T.; Eom, T.H.; Kim, S.Y.; Jang, H.W. Chemoresistive materials for electronic nose: Progress, perspectives, and challenges. *InfoMat* **2019**, *1*, 289–316. [CrossRef]

23. Marsili, R. Combining mass spectrometry and multivariate analysis to make a reliable and versatile electronic nose. In *Flavor, Fragance and Odor Analysis*; Marsili, R., Ed.; CRC Press: Boca Raton, FL, USA, 2002; pp. 349–374.
24. Berna, A.Z.; Buysens, S.; Natale, C.D.; Grün, I.U.; Lammertyn, J.; Nicolaï, B.M. Relating sensory analysis with electronic nose and headspace fingerprint MS for tomato aroma profiling. *Postharvest Biol. Technol.* **2005**, *36*, 143–155. [CrossRef]
25. Gliszczyńska-Świgło, A.; Chmielewski, J. Electronic Nose as a Tool for Monitoring the Authenticity of Food. A Review. *Food Anal. Methods* **2016**, *10*, 1800–1816. [CrossRef]
26. Hong, X.; Wang, J. Detection of adulteration in cherry tomato juices based on electronic nose and tongue: Comparison of different data fusion approaches. *J. Food Eng.* **2014**, *126*, 89–97. [CrossRef]
27. Pichersky, E.; Noel, J.P.; Dudareva, N. Biosynthesis of Plant Volatiles: Nature's Diversity and Ingenuity. *Science* **2006**, *311*, 808–811. [CrossRef]
28. Johanson, L.; Haglund, Å.; Berglund, L.; Lea, P.; Risvik, E. Preference for tomatoes, affected by sensory attributes and information about growth conditions. *Food Qual. Prefer.* **1999**, *10*, 289–298. [CrossRef]
29. Li, J.; Di, T.; Bai, J. Distribution of Volatile Compounds in Different Fruit Structures in Four Tomato Cultivars. *Molecules* **2019**, *24*, 2594. [CrossRef]
30. Oluk, A.C.; Ata, A.; Ünlü, M.; Yazici, E.; Karaşahin, Z.; Erogulu, E.Ç.; Canan, İ. Biochemical Characterisation and Sensory Evaluation of Differently Coloured and Shaped Tomato Cultivars. *Not. Bot. Horti Agrobot. Cluj-Napoca* **2019**, *47*, 599–607. [CrossRef]
31. Murphy, M.T.; Zhang, F.; Nakamura, Y.K.; Omaye, S.T. Comparison between Hydroponically and Conventionally and Organically Grown Lettuces for Taste, Odor, Visual Quality and Texture: A Pilot Study. *Food Nutr. Sci.* **2011**, *2*, 124–127. [CrossRef]
32. Yilmaz, E. The chemistry of fresh tomato flavor. *Turk. J. Agric. For.* **2001**, *25*, 149–155.

MDPI
St. Alban-Anlage 66
4052 Basel
Switzerland
Tel. +41 61 683 77 34
Fax +41 61 302 89 18
www.mdpi.com

Applied Sciences Editorial Office
E-mail: applsci@mdpi.com
www.mdpi.com/journal/applsci